About the Author

Steven Dolby grew up in a variety of places throughout North America and in Japan. He was drafted into the US Army during the Vietnam War era and served as an artillery officer. Stationed in Germany while in the service, he was a briefing officer to the NATO General Staff as well as an artillery line and staff officer. He is a graduate of California State University, Northridge, father of two, and grandfather of three. He lives in Phoenix, Arizona with his wife, Yvonne, and Labrador Retriever, Boo Bear.

BOOMER

Steven R. Dolby

BOOMER

Vanguard Press

A CIP catalogue record for this title is
available from the British Library.

ISBN 978 1 80016 713 1

*Vanguard Press is an imprint of
Pegasus Elliot Mackenzie Publishers Ltd.*
www.pegasuspublishers.com

This is a memoir. It follows the life and times of the Baby Boom Generation as
seen through the eyes of the author. The events are true to the best of the author's
recollection. Names have been changed to protect both the innocent and the guilty.

First Published in **2023**

**Vanguard Press
Sheraton House Castle Park
Cambridge England**

Printed & Bound in Great Britain

This book is dedicated to my wife, Yvonne, who has stood by me for more than 40 years. There has never been a better match since peanut butter and jelly. She fills the gaps in my life, plugs the holes, and makes the pieces fit. If it wasn't for her, I would still be looking for the power button to turn on my computer.

Acknowledgements

Most of the information in this book comes from my memories. As a result, I do not have a large research staff to thank for their contribution. However, I do give thanks for the good life I have experienced. It has been a great ride, and I would not trade it with anyone else on earth.

I have so much to be thankful for that I don't know where to begin. A fantastic wife and family are a good place to start; however, it goes far beyond that. I recognize and I am so grateful for our good health, nice house, food on the table, warm bed, reliable transportation, and good friends.

I have traveled the world and visited places beyond most people's imaginations. I was drafted into the military during the Vietnam War and made it through unscathed. And, I have managed to escape several near-death situations over the years. Looking back on these events, I often think about just how lucky I was; all along, picturing myself like Mr Magoo walking down the road oblivious to the dangers that surrounded me as I stayed one step ahead of the storm and grinning along the way.

Contents

PREFACE

Every generation in American history is unique, and labels with distinguishing titles separate them from others not only by age, but by their common experiences and social norms. This book is written in recognition of the generation known as the BABY BOOMERS, the generation following the World War II era, but for completeness of storytelling, also includes Boomer parents and offspring.

It follows the life and times of that generation as seen through my eyes and experiences along with my friends, acquaintances, and relatives. The names have been changed to protect both the innocent as well as the guilty.

No holds barred, it addresses the innocence of youth, the stupid things that kids do prior to their brains being developed enough to think like rational human beings — the happy times, sad times, tragedy, and all the unexpected turns in life that just show up.

Specific dates for generations are loosely defined. In other words, there are no "start dates" or "end dates" set in concrete, rather general dates that are used as guidelines to distinguish one generation from the next. The Baby Boomer generation, according to one source, states the years 1946 through 1964 are representative of that era. Another source says the Baby Boom years were 1943 to 1960. A common definition identifies this generation as all the little farts that were born as World War II came to an end, which was 1945, and subsequent years up to the mid-1960s.

During the most recent century (1901–2001), six generations have been identified. The first was called the GI Generation. They were born during the first quarter of the 20th century and appropriately named because they were the young Americans who donned uniforms or contributed to the war effort during World War II; be it man, woman, soldier, or civilian.

Next came the Silent Generation, those born between 1927 and 1945; followed by the Baby Boomers, born between 1945 and 1964. Generation X (1965—1980) followed the Boomers. And, Generation Y, also known as the Millennials (1981–2000), followed the Xs. This brings us up to the sixth and newest generation, Generation Z born after 2001, nicknamed the Boomets. The beat goes on, and it will be interesting to see what subsequent generations will be called in the years to come.

The GI Generation were the mothers and fathers of the Baby Boomers. Without them, the Boomers wouldn't be here. The GI generation went on to be known as the "Greatest Generation" when news anchor and journalist, Tom Brokaw, wrote and published his book in 1998 with the same title. *The Greatest Generation* was written to recognize and honor those Americans born in the early 1900s who survived the Great Depression and went on to fight in World War II or contributed greatly on the home front to support the war effort.

Men and women went off to war, stationed domestically and abroad. Husbands and wives, mothers and fathers, boyfriends and girlfriends, and parents and children were torn apart. Sometimes these separations lasted a couple months, and in many cases, several years. When the war ended and couples reunited, there was a lot of catching-up to do. The weapons manufacturing plants began to shut down; however, baby manufacturing plants sprang up in millions of households. During the Baby Boom years that followed, it is estimated that 76.4 million babies were born.

CHAPTER 1
GAME ON

BOOM! He came flying out of the chute, making his debut in the delivery room of St. Mary's Hospital. It was a hot, sultry summer day in the sleepy Texas town of Port Arthur, which lies just inland from the Gulf of Mexico and a couple miles west of the Louisiana state line. From the moment Steve entered this world, the excitement began. So, who is Steve? Well, that would be me, the author of this book. I was one of the first to arrive in this new generation known as the Baby Boomers.

The year was 1945. World War II had just ended, and US servicemen and women were returning home from Europe and the Pacific to re-build their lives and start families of their own. They were our mothers and fathers, and they were known as the GI generation.

August 1st was a pivotal day. I was lounging in my bed-womb minding my own business. It was dark, warm, and wonderful, so I decided to sleep in. After all, I had been laying there for nine months already so what was the hurry in getting up? However, my mother, and Mother Nature, had their own agenda. At 10 a.m. I had a rude awakening when all hell broke loose. Mom's water broke and she was in pain. I didn't know what was going on, but hands and cold metal instruments were pulling me through a tunnel with a diameter less than half my size. I felt like a watermelon trying to pass through a soda bottle. Once in the open, there was a lot of commotion with several people moving rapidly in various directions.

One of them, by the name of Doctor, grabbed me by the ankles, turned me upside down, and slapped me on the butt. I didn't even know this guy, and he was trying to pick a fight with me before I could take my first breath. I made a fist and tried to take a swing at him to get even but that was pretty hard to do when I was hanging upside down, and all

I could see were lights and shadows. Well, I guess it was all a big misunderstanding because they cleaned me up and handed me back to my mother before I hurt someone.

Actually, as it relates to my arrival, I jumped the gun by showing up a couple months ahead of other Baby Boomers so I could get a head start. So, sit back, buckle up, and enjoy the journey that encompasses travels through all 50 states and 77 countries and/or islands, and involves over three dozen moves to 13 states and several foreign countries. You are going to be entertained as you meet many of the Baby Boomers I met along the way through school, the military, my career in the airline industry, and my life as a family man.

As you may have guessed by now, this book, BOOMER, is about the generation of Americans born between the mid-1940s and the mid-1960s. There were 76 million of us. According to 2017 statistics, about 72 million were still kicking, and by 2019, 10,000 of us were turning 65 every day.

CHAPTER 2
WEST POINT CADET

Since this is a memoir, it seems appropriate to begin the story by introducing two members of the GI Generation that had the biggest impact on my life — my father and mother.

William F. Dolby

My dad, William Frederick Dolby, was born on July 19, 1917 in Oil City, Pennsylvania, a small town in the northwest section of the state and just about a two-hour drive north of Pittsburgh. William was the son of Maude Calkins Dolby and Frederick William Dolby.

Grandma Maude was a very sweet, mild mannered, quiet woman with two interesting physical features that stand out in my memory. One was that her face reminded me of a Persian cat. Secondly, her tits hung down to her waist. If those tits had drooped any closer to the ground, she would have needed to wrap them in spark arresters.

Grandma Maude in her intergalactic, anti-gravity sports bra

I always got excited when I learned that we were going on vacation to visit my grandparents. They lived in a very poor section of town about two blocks from the Allegany River in a small house that sat on top of a four-stall garage. The structure itself was made of sagging and rotting timber that somehow managed to withstand the test of time and harsh elements. The rest of the neighborhood wasn't any better. However, there were plenty of kids to play with, and they were happy when we came to town.

Nobody had any money, but we didn't need any. We had the riverbank, creeks, woods, and hills for our playground. There were plenty of mud ponds and oil seeping up from the ground to make sure we got extra dirty. One day I came home looking like I had just passed by the south end of a north-bound cow when it let loose. My dad took me into one of the garage stalls and threw me into a laundry tub along with a cup of laundry detergent and a bar of Lava soap. The chemicals were so harsh that by the time my dad got finished scrubbing me, my skin was as red as a baboon's ass. I laid awake all night scratching myself raw and praying that the irritation would pass. I tried to stay a little cleaner on future outings.

The stories of my dad's youth were similar to the stories of all the other dads born about that time. They all walked five miles every day in the snow to get to school. Their families were very poor, and in their youth, they had to shoot deer to put food on the table.

My dad had an older sister, Mary, who was 14 years his senior. She fell in love with a guy named Larry who was a real character. A bricklayer by trade, he was a hard-working, tobacco-chewing, fun-loving son-of-a-gun. Mary and Larry got married and drove from Pennsylvania to Florida for their honeymoon. One day, by chance, they walked into a pet store. Larry spotted a monkey he just had to have. So, he paid $25 for Jocko the monkey and put him in the car for the long drive back to Oil City. The monkey turned out to be a pain in the ass and after a month or two, Larry couldn't take it any longer. He devised a plan to dispose of the primate in the most humane way he could think of.

One evening, he put Jocko in the car and stopped at a grocery store to buy a bunch of bananas. Then he drove to the railroad switching yard and put the monkey and the bananas in an empty box car, shutting the door behind him. He then sat on a nearby hilltop and waited for the train that would hook up the box car and head for an unknown destination. So long Jocko. Have a nice life.

With Mary married, my dad was raised as if he was an only child. Grandma Dolby pampered him, and he pretty much became a "mommy's boy." I'm not sure if he played any sports in high school; however, he learned to play musical instruments, and with a couple buddies, formed a band that performed at various social events.

After graduating from high school, he joined the Army and was assigned to the Coastal Artillery. My grandmother, a member of the Daughters of the American Revolution (DAR), was determined to elevate his social status by sending him to college, but she had no money to pay for it. So, she leveraged her contacts with the DAR and found a congressman that would sponsor him for an appointment to the United States Military Academy at West Point. The strategy was successful. Dad entered the academy in 1939 and graduated with the class of January 1943. At that time, there was no Air Force as a stand-alone branch of the military. However, there was the Army Air Corps. While his classmates were being assigned to the various branches of the

Army, such as the infantry and artillery, Dad chose aviation. Several years later, the Air Force became a branch of its own, and this would be my dad's career for the next 28 years. He served in World War II and the Vietnam War, achieving the rank of Colonel.

My mom always taught her children that if you did not have anything nice to say about someone, don't say anything at all. My dad, on the other hand, felt that if you dug deep enough, you could always find a flaw in any person deserving of a full-blown character assassination. His spoiled upbringing led him to believe he was superior to everyone else. And, with him being the self-proclaimed superior human being, everyone else was either a stupid idiot, incompetent ninny, inferior dimwit, or an unpatriotic worthless pile of crap. Dad did not have many friends, and the ones he did have didn't last very long after he reminded them of just how inferior they were.

He did, however, have one friend that seemed to stand by him through the years. His name was Brinley Ross. I'm not sure how Brinley came into Dad's life, but I suspect that they befriended each other while in the Army Air Corps during World War II when they were stationed together on the island of Guam in the Pacific.

Brinley was a great guy, and our family sort of adopted him, referring to him as an uncle. From time-to-time, he would come for a short visit. He was always well dressed, often showing up in a nicely tailored new suit. Following his military service, Brinley worked in the automobile industry so when he pulled into our driveway, it was usually in a brand-new car like an MG or Mercedes Benz. He always had a big smile on his face and a joke or interesting story ready to tell. You just couldn't help but like this guy. My only negative impression of Brinley was that he and my dad shared a love for Limburger cheese and onion sandwiches. The combination of these ingredients created an odor so bad that their breath could knock a buzzard off a shit wagon.

Despite my dad's lack of social skills, he did have several qualities that I admired about him. One, he never said a cuss word around his kids. Two, we never saw him drink in excess. Three, he was extremely patriotic. And four, he was a very honest person almost to a fault. For example, one day he and I took a trip to the car dealership to purchase a new car. The dealer offered him $300 for the trade-in on his 1952 Ford

Rustmobile. My dad responded, "Three hundred dollars? This car is a lemon. It's not worth $300!" He settled on $200 for the trade-in and probably paid a premium for the new car. I thought to myself that I would leave my dad at home when it was my turn to go car shopping.

My dad could never admit that he was wrong or that he had made a mistake. Somehow, he always managed to shift blame to someone else. I always had the feeling that he didn't really care for me very much and could not figure out what I did to get on the wrong side of him at an early age. Decades later the lights came on, and I think I figured it out. It goes clear back to World War II.

My father got my mother pregnant with me just prior to shipping out to his extended wartime assignment as a B-29 pilot stationed on an island in the Pacific. The entire squadron lived primitively in a tent city, and the latrine was a trench dug out behind the tents.

During mail call one evening, he received a letter from my mother announcing that he was now the proud father of their second child, a six-pound baby boy. So, he grabbed a bottle of Jack Daniels and sat on his cot with a couple of his buddies to celebrate my arrival. Apparently, he had one too many, and when he went out back to relieve himself, he lost his balance and fell in the latrine. Since he could do no wrong, guess whose fault it was that he fell in? *That's right, me*! He already had a case of the ass against me, and we had not even met. Things went downhill from there.

From what I could tell, Dad was one hell-of-a good airplane driver, and he flew them all. The Martin B-26 was his first plane as a bomber pilot. His crew called that plane "The Prostitute" because parts kept falling off in flight and it had "no visible means of support." He graduated to the B-17 and eventually became a flight instructor stationed in Del Rio, Texas. Then it was on to the B-29. He became the aircraft commander, and the crew named their plane the "Caboose." Something tells me they were the last plane in the formation. He flew countless bombing missions over Japan and stayed with it until the end of the war. When the war ended, he graduated to the B-36 and finally retired from flying on the B-52.

CHAPTER 3
DYNAMITE

Martha Ann Evans, my mother, was born February 22, 1918 in Franklin, Pennsylvania. Franklin is located across the river from Oil City, Pennsylvania, the town where my father was born. Martha was the daughter of Leroy Evans and Beatrice Keener Evans.

Martha Evans Dolby (Dynamite)

The Evans clan were coal miners from Wales and immigrated to the United States in the early 1800s. Leroy's nickname was "Shorty," the name he answered to. Nobody knew him as Leroy. He earned his name by his physical stature. Despite his size, he was an outstanding athlete and an excellent football player. After graduating from high school, Shorty went on to become a surveyor for the State of Pennsylvania.

Afterwards, he became the director of human resources for the Atlantic Oil Company and was eventually transferred to Port Arthur, Texas where he finished out his career.

The Keeners came from Freiburg in the Black Forest region of Germany. They were butchers and managed a family grocery store in Franklin. This was especially difficult during the Great Depression. My mom's Grandpa Keener ran the business. He was a very kind and generous person. When customers came to buy food, they often would show up with no money. Rather than turn them away, he would give them the food and tell them to pay him back when they could. Of course, they never could, and the business suffered greatly.

My mom was the polar opposite of my dad. She had all the friends she could handle. Everyone loved her, and she was voted the most popular girl in high school. She never had an enemy and never knew a stranger. Although Shorty was short, my mom was even shorter, checking in at five foot nothing. As mild mannered as she was, she could hold her ground when crossed, an attribute that earned her the nickname "Dynamite."

My mom loved her high school years. Lawrence Welk performed at her senior prom. She loved the band and their music. From that point forward, she became a life-long Lawrence Welk fan. She watched his TV show for years and then all the re-runs until her death in 2005.

I was always considerate of my mother and tried to do thoughtful things to show her how much I appreciated her. However, like any other kid, I would do things to irritate her as well. When I made her mad or disobeyed, she would chase me around the house with a broom and threaten to beat the tar out of me if only she could catch me. She never could. I would look over my shoulder and see her coming, swinging that broom, and yelling, "Get back here you little imp," like that was going to happen.

When I was 12 years old, Mom was still chasing me with the broom. Her threat to beat me within an inch of my life had me a little concerned, but I was bigger and faster. One day I got cornered. She looked at me and suddenly realized that I was about a foot taller than her and there would be no loss of life at the business end of her broom.

We both laughed, and that was the end of the broom. She had to resort to diplomacy.

I don't know how my mom and dad met, but they started dating when he was a senior in high school, and she was a junior. In 1943, Dad graduated from West Point, and they were married the next day — a marriage that lasted 62 years. They had seven children. When the seventh one was born, my sister Cindy overheard my dad as he walked down the hallway shaking his head in disbelief and saying to himself, "How does this keep happening?"

My mom never went to college but did attend a business school for a brief period before she got married. She went to work for the Ford Motor Company in an administrative capacity once her mother and father were transferred to Port Arthur, Texas shortly after her graduation from high school.

Once married, Mom took over the household. With a husband, a constantly increasing number of kids, and a dog, it was like running a small business. She did it all from being a wife and mother to managing the family finances. Although my father was the college graduate, I think she was the smarter of the two. My dad would consult with her about what investments to make and when would be the best time to buy the next car. However, my dad always let it be known that he was king of the house, and my mother was his obedient servant. She was faithful, dedicated, and stood by him through thick and thin.

CHAPTER 4
HERE COME THE BOOMERS

When William and Martha Dolby got married in January 1943, they did not waste any time contributing to the growing population. The first one to arrive was my older brother Bill, born December 12, 1943. He was named after my father, so now there were two William F. Dolbys in the house, Bill, Sr. and Bill, Jr. They could not have been more different. Bill, Sr. was the stern military disciplinarian. Bill, Jr., on the other hand, was a free spirit. He was happy, goofy, lived for the moment, and dealt with life one hour at a time. He was going to do things his way and on his schedule.

Bill, Jr. never felt pressured to get things done. He was an intellectual genius with an IQ of 140+, and he was a member of the American MENSA Society. (The MENSA Society is an organization for extremely gifted people with IQs of 130 or better, placing them in the top 2% of the population. Those with an IQ of 140 and above are considered genius level.) Because he was highly intelligent, everything was easy for him. He immediately understood new concepts and was a whiz with math and physics. He "got it" the first time and then moved on. Bill never brought a textbook home from school, and he didn't do homework. He just listened to what the teacher said in class, either by earshot or through osmosis, and was always a straight "A" student and number one in his class.

Conversely, my father had to work much harder for his grades. When he graduated from West Point, he ranked 384 academically out of a class of 409 cadets. That's 25 from the bottom. However, four years at any of the military academies is brutal, and anyone who makes it through deserves respect. As the riddle goes, "What do you call the cadet that graduates at the very bottom of his class?" "Lieutenant!" Although Dad wasn't the brightest bulb on the tree, he made it through, and that was all that counted. However, I think he was quite envious of Bill Jr.'s natural intellect, and it showed from time-to-time as we were growing up.

Although Bill was almost two years older than me, I surpassed him in size and strength by the time I made it to high school. I was more involved in sports and had a passion for playing football. As a result, I bulked up and was accustomed to getting the crap knocked out of me. I could dish it out as well as take it. I would not back down from a fight, on the football field or off.

As for my scholastic aptitude, I inherited my dad's genes. I couldn't comprehend anything until it was drilled into me several times. My mind is like a steel trap; nothing gets in until about the third or fourth try, but once there, it stays forever.

Growing up, Bill and I always shared a bedroom. After dinner, we would go to our room, and I would start my homework. Meanwhile, Bill would lay on his bed reading *MAD* magazine, laughing his ass off, and cackling like a mother hen. He had little patience for slow learners. Often, I would ask him for help with my math assignments, but this cut into his quality time reading about Alfred E. Newman. Reluctantly he would walk over to my desk and impatiently ask, "What's the problem now?" I would say, "Can you please help me with these math questions?" He would explain it, I wouldn't get it, he would explain it again, I wouldn't get it, and then he would explode yelling, "How can you be so f****** stupid? This is so obviously simple I can't understand why you don't get it."

Fortunately for me, I had something Bill needed. One day he came home from school and said he had a problem that required my help. He said there was a guy at school that was constantly giving him a hard time and he wanted me to "take him out." I asked, "What exactly does that mean?" He replied, "It means, I want you to go up to him after school and beat the shit out of him and get him to leave me alone." I thought for a minute, then said, "Okay, I'll do it if you promise to help me with my math homework for the rest of the school year without bitching about it." He agreed. The next day I met his foe and physically convinced him to back off. We never saw the guy again. That evening I asked Bill to assist me with my homework. He did, but shortly into it, I could see that he was losing patience and about to explode with one of his tirades. I shook my finger at him before he could get a word out, reminding him of our deal.

My mother's family had relocated from Pennsylvania to Texas in the early 1940s. They built their new home in the coastal town of Port Arthur. When my father graduated from West Point and married my mother, he was being transferred around the country constantly in preparation for his military assignments in the Pacific Theater during World War II. By this time, my mother was pregnant with my older brother Bill. With so much uncertainty as to where my father would be stationed from one week to the next, my parents thought the safest thing to do was for Mom to move in with her parents until the dust settled. It didn't settle for a long time. Bill was born at St. Mary's hospital in Port Arthur, and my dad was assigned to be a flight instructor on the B-17 in Del Rio, Texas.

Sometime later, my dad received his new B-29 from the Boeing Company. He was a captain by then and would become the aircraft commander. At that time, female pilots would ferry the planes from the manufacturing plant in Seattle to wherever the flight crew was stationed. In my dad's case, that was Wright-Patterson Airfield in Dayton, Ohio. After taking delivery, the crew began their inspection of the ship. My dad was inspecting the nose gear when he stumbled across an envelope taped to the inside wall of the wheel well. It had been placed there by the female pilot that delivered the plane. It read, "To the crew of this B-29, may God be with you and protect you." I was very touched when my dad told me that story, and I always wanted to track that woman down to thank her for such a nice gesture.

For the next several months, the crew of the Caboose flew around the country doing practice bombing missions. They might be flying out of Grand Island, Nebraska one week, and Great Falls, Montana the next. Eventually they would ship out to their permanent combat base of operations, the island of Guam in the Pacific.

Before leaving the United States, my father was able to get home and spend a few days with my mother. She was pregnant with me when he flew off into the sunset. Nine months later my mother ended up back at St. Mary's Hospital in Port Arthur where my brother Bill was born two years earlier. Now it was my turn.

After a couple days in the hospital, we moved to Grandpa and Grandma Evans's house down on Los Alamos Street. This was like a training camp designed to learn all about life. Quickly I mastered the first challenge, how to fill a diaper. That was easy. I could do it with my eyes closed and one hand tied behind my back. Then, I had to learn how to eat. If I was going to fill the next diaper, I had to learn how to reload the cannon. This took a bit more coordination and assistance from those who had gone before me. Learning to walk and talk were even more challenging, but I was off and running by the time I was 18 months old.

World War II ended in the Pacific on August 15, 1945, when the Japanese surrendered to the US Armed Forces and ended in Europe on September 2, 1945, when the Axis Powers surrendered to the Allied Forces. Many of the GIs began to return to the States and resume their lives as civilians. However, others remained behind with the occupational forces to help restore and maintain an orderly transition back to normalcy as these war-torn countries began their rebuilding process.

My father was one of those who stayed behind. He left Guam and was sent directly to Japan as part of the occupational forces that would help rebuild that country. He and his colleagues set up shop at Tachikawa Airfield in the city of Tachikawa, west of Tokyo. He knew he would be there for quite some time, so he made arrangements for my mother, Bill, Jr., and me to join him as soon as it was safe. The "all clear" signal came in February 1947.

My mother took Bill and me in tow and boarded a train from Port Arthur, Texas to Los Angeles. By the time we got to California, we were met by my mother's Aunt Dorothy who was living in Pasadena. Dorothy and her husband took us in for a couple days, then drove us down to the ship that would take us to Japan.

CHAPTER 5
DINNER WITH THE DRAGON

Since I was too young to remember, I must rely on my mom's account of the events that took place during our voyage.

Don't think of this trip as a cruise by today's standards on luxury ocean liners. The journey took about 12 days, and the vessel we were on was a military troop ship with a cement hull. This was the true definition of a "barf barge." There were no stabilizers on the ship, so passengers had to learn to rock and roll with every wave. There was no place for fine dining, just one mess hall. We were served three meals a day, but with the rough seas, we would meet each meal at least twice, once going down and once coming back up.

Me, Bill Jr. (on the hood of the Jeep), and my mom
with the family car in Japan

My dad met our ship as we pulled into Tokyo Bay. By this time, we had been seasick for so long we looked like the walking dead. Once on dry land, we expected smooth sailing, but nothing could have been further from the truth. We did not have a family car, so Dad came to pick us up in a military Jeep. We piled in and headed for our new home, driving down a road that had been a major target for the bombs that were dropped by the B-29s toward the end of the war. We hit one pothole after another and bounced so high we wished we were back at sea.

Then, the rain hit and filled all the potholes with muddy water. The road became so saturated that it was impossible to distinguish the surface of the road from the potholes. Several times we hit holes that were so deep we thought we would be swallowed up, never to be seen again.

When we arrived in Japan, I was coming up on two years of age, and I met my father for the first time. It all seemed so strange to me. Who is this guy and what is a father? I learned that a father is a guy that shows up from time-to-time who keeps getting my mother pregnant. Shortly after we arrived in Japan, my mom was expecting a third child. My sister, Cindy, was born on December 5, 1947, Dolby Boomer #3.

All the houses in our neighborhood were alike. They were made of wood, constructed with the least possible amount of materials, and they all had basements that could be used for storage. Most families would go to the commissary and buy as many canned goods as they could get their hands on because they never knew when the next shipment of food would arrive. The excess of everything they purchased was stored down in the basement. The downstairs in just about everyone's house looked like a mini-market of canned goods.

One rainy day, when I was about three years old, a band of kids decided to duck into someone's house to play where it was dry. We went down the stairs into the basement and spotted all the canned goods. We thought it would be great fun if we tore off all the labels. When the parents discovered what we had done, it was too late. The poor lady of the house, trying to prepare a meal, would open a can of what she thought would be tomato soup only to find out that it was a can of dog food. Shortly thereafter, parents started putting locks on the basement doors.

I lived in Japan for two years, from the time I was one-and-a-half years old until I was three-and-a-half. Because I was so young, I don't remember too much about it. However, in addition to the canned goods incident, there was one other event I will never forget.

One evening my dad decided to take Bill, my mom, and me out to dinner. We went to a Japanese restaurant called the Golden Dragon. It had a big sign out front with a picture of a dragon shooting fire out of its mouth. I didn't think too much of it at the time until we went inside and sat down at a table for four. The restaurant was dimly lit and had a hallway that led from the dining room to the restrooms. It was curved so that you could only see a portion of the hallway. It had a recessed light that you could not see but cast a red shadow on the hallway walls. It looked like there might be a fire at the other end.

While we were waiting to be served, I announced that I had to go to the bathroom. My dad pointed me in the direction of the hallway and told me to watch out for the fire-breathing dragon along the way. The red shadow helped reinforce in my mind the fact that there really was a dragon at the end of the hall. I had a panic attack and said I was not going to the restroom by myself. My dad said, "Yes you are. Show me that you are a man and go it alone."

I thought to myself, "But I am not a man. I'm only three years old."

He insisted, "You gotta do it."

I thought, "I'd rather sit here and pinch a loaf in my britches at the dinner table. I'm not walking into the mouth of that dragon."

Eventually Dad persevered, and I cautiously walked the 30 steps to the bathroom by myself. To my good fortune, there was no dragon. I did my business and returned to the table unscathed. By this time, I had lost my appetite and my desire to ever go out to dinner with this guy again.

After two years in Japan, it was time to move on. The year was 1949. Between Guam and Japan, my dad had been out of the country for over four years. When he got his orders to return to the States, I'm sure he jumped at the chance. Prior to leaving Japan, he purchased and took delivery of a new Buick. He got rid of the Jeep, and now we had a real family car at our disposal. With Cindy's birth we needed the extra space.

The trip across the Pacific Ocean was uneventful, and we sailed into San Francisco Bay a couple weeks later. We loaded up the Buick and headed east to Shreveport, Louisiana. My father was on a temporary duty assignment, so we only lived there for three months. Before we could unpack too many boxes, new orders came in requiring us to move again, this time to Wright-Patterson Air Force Base in Dayton, Ohio.

CHAPTER 6
OUTRUNNING THE BREADMAN

My parents decided that a fantastic way to celebrate our new location in Ohio was to have another baby. My brother Chris, Dolby Boomer #4, was born in Dayton, Ohio on September 29, 1949.

With an ever-expanding family, the time had come for my parents to buy a house. They purchased a small but nice brick home on Tudor Street that had every convenience a family needed at that time.

Living in Dayton was great. All the kids in the neighborhood were military brats so we made friends quickly. There were a couple things about Dayton I especially liked. One was the milkman. I thought it was magic the way he came and went before we even woke up in the morning, leaving fresh milk waiting for us in a box sitting on the front porch. The other was the breadman. He showed up a little bit later in the day. He would park his truck in the driveway, load up some samples into a carry basket, knock on the side door to the kitchen, and try to convince my mom to purchase his products. I would be hiding in the bushes. While they were preoccupied with the sale, I would sneak into the truck, grab a package of cinnamon rolls, and take off running like a striped-ass ape. My mom and the breadman would spot me running down the street at lighting speed with the stolen goods, and Mom would casually say, "Well, you better put those on my bill as well."

Life was good. My mom organized a birthday party for me in a local park when I turned four years old in August. We got a new baby brother, Chris, born in September. In October, my dad put a sandbox in the backyard. In December, my brother Bill got a 20-inch bike with training wheels that I would inherit one day. In January, it snowed, and we built a snowman. All of this sounds rather common, but they were first-time events for us, and it was all very exciting.

Telephone lines were scarce, and if you were lucky enough to have a phone, you shared a party line with several other families. Each house had its own identifiable ring. The Smiths may be three short rings, and the Dolbys two short and one long ring. There were up to four households on the same line, and if we really wanted to have fun, we would eavesdrop on our neighbors' phone conversations.

Television was recently invented, but nobody had one. Television stations, broadcasting systems, and television shows had yet to be created and refined. Therefore, evening entertainment was limited. Families did, however, have radios. They were usually mounted in a big wooden console that was considered a piece of living room furniture. The evening radio shows were very creative and entertaining but left much to the listener's imagination to create the visuals. The radio announcers did a spectacular job with just their microphones and a few hand-held sound effect props to work with.

Other forms of evening entertainment consisted of families sitting together in the living room playing games such as "Button, Button, Who's Got the Button" or a variety of other interactive games. And of course, there were always board games at the kitchen table and bedtime stories.

My dad was a great bedtime storyteller. We had a 20-volume set of children's books. Each book contained about ten stories, such as *Goldilocks and the Three Bears, The Little Engine That Could, The Three Little Pigs,* and *Little Red Riding Hood.* Each story was enhanced by several pictures. When my dad announced which story he was going to read, my siblings and I would collectively thumb through the pages to look at all the illustrations associated with the story. Once we saw what the story was about and who the characters were, my dad sent us back to our beds. He instructed us to close our eyes and visualize in our minds the pictures we had just seen as he read the story. This was great psychology on his part because we would all fall fast asleep within five minutes, long before the story was finished. Then he would slip out of the bedroom and join my mother for a nice quiet evening. The next morning, we would wake up and wonder what the story was about.

Then, one day in the spring of 1950, a miracle occurred. Our neighbor across the street bought a television set and invited all the neighborhood kids over to watch it. The picture was of such poor quality we could hardly tell what it was we were watching. But that was okay. A new era had been born, and TV was here to stay.

Shortly thereafter, my father received a new set of orders. He was being transferred to the Pentagon in Washington, D.C. Time to pack our bags and head out of town. So long Ohio. Hello Virginia.

CHAPTER 7
PYROMANIA AND OTHER SINS

Mom and Dad purchased a home in Arlington, Virginia, just across the Potomac River from the Pentagon in the summer of 1950. Shortly thereafter, I had my fifth birthday. My parents celebrated the move the same way they celebrated every other move, getting Mom pregnant. My sister Sue would be Dolby Boomer #5, making her debut on November 25, 1951.

Arlington was fantastic. I don't know if it was Arlington so much as it was me growing older and becoming more aware of life in general, but we lived there four years, and many memorable events took place during that period.

This was the time in my life that I literally started playing with fire. When school started in the fall, the neighborhood cleared out, and I was left behind. I was only five years old, and there was no kindergarten, so I had no school to go to, and I had nothing to do. I would walk down to the school bus and watch all the grade school kids hop on, knowing that I would be left alone until they returned at 3:30 in the afternoon. With nobody to play with, I was bored and lonely. The hours passed like days.

My dad smoked Chesterfield cigarettes, and he had a big Zippo lighter. One day, before he left for work, I lifted the lighter off the dresser and stuck it in my pocket. I waited until everyone had cleared out of the neighborhood before implementing my plan. In the front yard, we had three Blue Spruce trees, and I decided to see if I could set them on fire. The needles on the trees were as dry as the Mojave Desert in July. Behind the trees and well hidden, I pulled out the lighter, ignited the flame, and held it under a branch. The tree lit up like an atomic bomb, and I stood there watching in amazement. My mother was sitting in the living room at the time wondering why it was getting so bright outside. She opened the front door looking for an explanation. When she saw the fire, she yelled out to the neighborhood for help, and then she ran back inside to call the fire department.

A quick-thinking neighbor heard my mom's scream, ran over to our house, grabbed a hose, and put out the fire just as the fire trucks pulled up. Meanwhile, as everyone was going crazy with excitement, I crept back in the house and placed the lighter back on the dresser like nothing happened. When questioned about the incident at dinner that night, I proclaimed my innocence, but I was found guilty and grounded for 30 days. As for the Spruce trees, we had two left. And in my way of thinking, two out of three wasn't bad. The first round of disaster and punishment did not diminish my obsession with pyromania.

The next year I turned six and entered the first grade. By this time, I had plenty of friends in the neighborhood. There were about five of us, and one of the kid's dads bought us all squirt guns. The next day after school, we took the guns and started playing in the woods nearby. Somebody got the bright idea to build a fire, and then put it out with the squirt guns. So, we started fire number one and let the squirt guns work their magic. The fire went out, but we still had water in our guns. We built fire number two for a repeat performance — another successful round! So, we decided we could do it again. We got fire number three going but ran out of water in our weapons. Somebody got the bright idea to pee on the flames. All five of us stood around in a circle peeing, but the flames went higher, and we ran out of pee.

Panic set in, and we all ran out of the woods. There was a row of houses across the street, so we banged on the front door of the closest one. We explained to the homeowner that we spotted a couple kids playing with matches, and now the woods were on fire. We felt it was our duty to tell him as an adult so that he could call the fire department. Then we all took off running, moving faster than a toupee in a hurricane. Eventually we were caught, and yours truly was grounded for another 30 days. Lesson still not learned though.

In second grade, I befriended a schoolmate that had a brother one year older than us. The oldest was named Chucky Long, and the youngest was George. The three of us would hang out together after school. A couple blocks from their house was a ballpark at the bottom of an embankment. At the top of the embankment was a road with an industrial-size road grader parked on the side. It was one of those big yellow pieces of construction equipment with the small wheels in front and the great big fat tires on the back. By this time of day, the construction crew had gone home for the day, so we decided to play on the road grader.

After a while we got bored, and Chucky pulled out a box of matches and said, "You know, rubber burns. Let's see if we can set this big fat tire on fire." We held a match close to the tire, but nothing happened. Then Chucky said we need a bigger flame. So, we gathered paper and twigs and piled them under the tire and lit another match. That did it. Our little bonfire eventually set the tire ablaze. After the fire trucks left and the construction company was notified, the Long family and the Dolby family agreed to pay $200 in restitution. I was grounded for 30 days.

When I was in third grade, another group of kids I hung out with got this wild idea to set a farmer's wheat field on fire just about harvest time. I decided I did not want any part of it, so I ran home and told my mother what was about to happen and convinced her that I had learned my lesson and had nothing to do with it. My pyromaniac days were behind me.

I spent my first three years of school at a Catholic grade school called St. Agnes, in Arlington, Virginia. Many of the Catholic school children complained or made fun of the nuns for being a very strict and stern group of ladies that ruled their classrooms with an iron fist. Discipline included rapping students' knuckles with a ruler every time they got out of line. As for me, I was a real class clown, and if anyone deserved to get whacked, it was me. But I endured the three years and came out unscathed. For some reason I got along with the nuns. All three of my teachers were sweet ladies that treated me well, and if anything, were protective of me. Somehow, I charmed them into thinking I was a sweet kid, or they just didn't catch me when I was up to mischief.

In the summers between school years, we would go on vacation. As a family with so many kids and so few dollars to budget for vacations, my parents had to be very frugal as to how they spent their money. Rather than hotels and amusement parks that cost a lot of money, my parents would rent a cottage down on the Chesapeake Bay for about a month — nothing fancy, but we had a ball.

One summer we rented a house that had a screened-in front porch which helped keep the mosquitos out that were such a nuisance. The days were hot and humid. After dinner, we would pull our mattresses and blankets off the beds and drag them to the porch where we played board games until it got dark. When bedtime rolled around, we would sleep on the porch and wake up to the cool morning air.

During the 1950s, smoking was prevalent everywhere. Newscasters were smoking cigarettes while presenting the evening news on television. Newspapers, magazines, billboards, and television ads all made it look glamorous. My mom and dad would always end their evening dinner with a cigarette and a cup of coffee. Even professional athletes were hired to promote smoking. It's no surprise that the Baby Boomers became addicted. We all wanted to be like Mom and Dad, and if you didn't smoke, you just were not cool.

When we got together with our friends during summer vacations at the shore, the conversation always came up about where we could get some cigarettes to smoke. In my case, it was easy. By the time I was six, my mom gave me money to go to the store and pick up a couple packs for her. I would hike down to this old, dilapidated country store and tell the clerk that I needed two packs of Chesterfields, and if he didn't have them, Old Golds would do. I would bring them home, and she would light up. When she wasn't looking, I would take two or three smokes out of the package, pushing the ones from the other side of the pack toward the opening to make it look like nothing was missing. I was a pro at this.

I would alert my friends that I had the goods, and if someone could come up with the matches, we were in business. We would mosey into our little fort in the woods and light up. We all agreed that these things tasted like shit. However, if we smoked enough of them, perhaps we would discover the pleasure our parents found in them. In the meantime, we would turn green until one guy had a revelation. He said that the trick to enjoying cigarettes was to inhale. So, we did that and got deathly sick, but decided to stick with it until we mastered the fine art of smoking. I'm not sure we ever did, but at least we were cool.

Just shy of my sixth birthday, we purchased our first television set. I often think back on those days and wonder how we did without it. Then again, you couldn't miss what you never had. Now I think about the kids of today and they can't even comprehend a day without TV, cell phones, and other electronic devices.

By this time, my sister Cindy was four years old, and it was obvious that she was "Daddy's little princess." In my dad's eyes, she could do no wrong. Undoubtedly, she was the favorite, and my brother Bill and I were more like the unwanted stepchildren it seemed to us. We got stuck with household work assignments while we watched Cindy get a piece of candy or a cookie. Over time, jealousy set in, and we were out for revenge. Whenever my dad wasn't watching, we would haul off and slug her or devise some other way to make her life miserable. And since she was born in Japan, we called her "The Jap" or "Tokyo Rose." Later in our adult life, she reminded me of all the slugs and bruises wondering when, or if, it would ever stop.

After three years in Arlington, we were overdue for a transfer — we seldom lived anywhere that long. But the transfer didn't come, and my parents were itching for the big event that came with moving. Childbirth! Since we weren't going anywhere soon, my mom got pregnant and gave birth to Dolby Boomer #6. My brother Mark was born on March 16th, 1953.

Shortly after Mark was born, I woke up one Sunday about 5 a.m. with an incredible pain on the right side of my abdomen. I was still a young child and walked into my parents' bedroom complaining about how much it hurt. Irritated by my intrusion, my dad insisted that I go back to bed, assuring me that everything would be fine. By 7 a.m., I could hardly make it to the breakfast table as I was doubled over in pain. Dad called me a wimp and a pansy and told me to run laps around the house to work out the soreness. I followed his instructions, and the pain got worse. So, he suggested that I make a fist and beat the sore spot as if it was a piece of meat that needed to be tenderized. I did as I was told and beat the shit out of myself. The pain got worse.

At 5 p.m. that evening, we were sitting at the dinner table, and I was in so much pain I could not eat my dinner. Dad threatened to ground me for a month if I didn't eat. At this point I told him, "Do what ya gotta do, but I can't eat." My mom intervened and said to my dad, "Bill, this isn't like Steve. I think he really has a problem." By this time, I am stretched out on the floor, so she took the initiative and called for an ambulance. The ambulance arrived, and the emergency crew took my blood pressure, checked a few vital signs, and rushed me off to a military hospital somewhere in Washington D.C.

Once in the hospital, the staff checked my vital signs again and diagnosed me with severe appendicitis. They said they had to get me to the children's hospital immediately, and they loaded me into another ambulance. We whisked across town with lights flashing and sirens blaring. Upon arrival, we were met by a team of doctors and nurses standing at the curb with a gurney. They pulled me out of the ambulance, slid me on to a gurney, and ran full speed to the emergency room.

I didn't understand what was happening but sensed that I was in good hands. I was pulled off the gurney and slid onto an operating table. Everything was happening so fast I did not have time to panic. The medical staff put a mask over my nose and mouth and began to administer ether. Wow, did that smell terrible. After the first whiff, I refused to take another breath. I held off as long as I could, then inhaled. Seconds later, I was out like a light.

The doctors and nurses performed magnificently. They cut open my abdomen and removed my appendix. They placed it on a tray, and within ten seconds it exploded. Had that happened inside my body, I would have been a dead duck. Two weeks and 20 penicillin shots later, I was released from the hospital. I had just dodged my first brush with death.

Meanwhile, the house was filling up with kids. And if that wasn't enough, my dad went down to the pound and picked up a large dog that resembled a mixture of breeds including a hint of pit bull. This was one junk yard dog. The dog's name was Rip. It was mean as hell and lived up to its name. After several incidents with neighbors nearly getting appendages torn from their bodies, it was time to return the dog to the pound before my parents got hit with a major lawsuit.

The family car was a 1951 Ford sedan. However, with a family of eight, we needed a bigger car, so Dad purchased a 1954 Ford Country Squire station wagon. That gave us a little more room, so he decided we had space for another dog. This time he brought home a boxer puppy that we named Taffy. She turned out to be a great dog, and we became the best of friends. The only problem with the dog was that after she ate her dinner, she would fart all night long. No ordinary farts, Taffy's smelled like burnt rubber, and the odor lingered forever.

About the time I finished third grade in June 1954, my dad received his next military assignment, Maxwell Air Force Base in Montgomery, Alabama.

So long Virginia. Hello Alabama`!

CHAPTER 8
ARE WE YANKEES OR REBELS?

We knew in advance that we would only be in Alabama for one year. Rather than buy, my parents decided to rent a house. The rental agreement was signed prior to our leaving Virginia, so when we arrived in Montgomery, all we had to do was pull into the driveway and start unpacking boxes. As we got out of the car, we were approached by a half-dozen boys about Bill's and my age asking, "Are you guys Yankees or Rebels?" That was a question I had never pondered so I looked at Bill and said, "Are we Yankees or Rebels?" Seeing that we were outnumbered and about to become residents of the South, my quick-thinking brother announced that we were "Rebels and proud of it." With that, we were immediately accepted into the neighborhood. When we were alone, I asked Bill, "What are Yankees and Rebels?"

I fell in love with Alabama immediately because most of the kids came from poor families, and in the warmer months, we were allowed to go to school barefoot in order to preserve shoes for the colder months.

I don't know when my school was built, but my guess would be sometime before the Civil War. Goode Street School was an old two-story red brick building in serious need of repair. My classroom was on the second floor, and many of the floorboards were cracked or missing. Walking down the hallway, we had to watch our steps to keep from falling through to the ceiling below. There was no cafeteria, so we had to pack our own lunches. However, there was a lunchroom with tables and benches. There was a recess area, but no playground equipment and very little grass. A lonely elm tree sat out front that provided shade. We drew a circle in the dirt and played marbles.

Saturday afternoons were exciting because usually one of our parents would take us downtown to the movie theater and drop us off.

The movie only cost a dime, so everyone could afford to go. Prior to the main feature, there would be two to three five-minute serial segments of cowboy movies like *The Lone Ranger* or *Roy Rogers*. You got to see enough to pique your interest, but if you wanted to see how the story played out, you had to come back at a later time. This was not only a smart marketing move on the theater's part from a revenue perspective, but it kept the kids in suspense wanting to come back for more.

If we weren't at the movies, we would be outside playing "Civil War" with our friends. At that time, there were people in the South that hadn't accepted the fact that the war was truly over. We learned to eat collard greens, grits, black-eyed peas, and cornbread. They became the staples of our diet.

One Sunday after church, Bill and I got into an argument with my dad. We decided we had put up with enough of his crap and it was time to run away from home. I was nine years old, and Bill was 11. It was a cold and rainy day as we slipped out the back to make our getaway. We started hitchhiking. We were sopping wet when some old geezer in a pick-up truck gave us a lift for a couple miles then dropped us off on the side of the road in front of an old rundown café. We went inside where there was a heater on the floor. So, we took off our shoes and socks and laid them on the grate to dry out while we ordered lunch. Fortunately, we remembered to empty our piggy banks before we took off, so we had enough cash to buy a meal.

With a full stomach and dry shoes, we hit the road again. Our destination was Birmingham. We had an aunt and uncle that lived there, and we decided we would go live with them for a while. We hitched a ride with a very nice man that took us all the way to our destination. How we found my aunt and uncle's house is beyond me. But we made it, and that's all that mattered to us.

What we didn't count on was the reception we received from my uncle. He gave us a hot shower while my aunt dried our clothes and fed us. Then they put us in their car and drove us all the way back to Montgomery. Upon our arrival, my dad was ticked off and said if we didn't want to live there, we had until the count of ten to get out of his house. We were out the front door before he got to six. By this time, it was late in the day, getting dark, and we were getting hungry. We decided that we'd had enough traveling for one day, so we would just hole up in the neighborhood for the evening and hit the trail the following day.

Fortunately, all the houses were single story. So, we went to one of our friend's houses and banged on his bedroom window. When he came, we explained our situation, so he agreed to sneak into his family's kitchen and steal some food for us. With our tummies full, it was time to figure out where we were going to spend the night. There was an easy fix. Our friend next door had a fort in his back yard that his dad made for him out of old wooden shipping boxes. It had three levels to it, and we chose the top as a place to sleep because it had a window that we could use to observe as the enemy approached.

Now my mom was very upset with my dad for kicking us out of the house and concerned for our safety. It was about 6 or 7 p.m. when she called the police to locate us. They drove up and down the street, shining their spotlight everywhere, including the fort where we were hiding. The light and the police car scared us, so we hunkered down low to stay out of sight. My mother started calling the neighbors looking for us at about 8 p.m., and the dad that built the fort came out to look around and found us. He walked us home, and reluctantly we went inside ending the saga. We were grounded for a month, an anticipated consequence of our domestic dispute with Dad. We knew we were right, but that screwball always won.

No sooner had I been released from my 30-day backyard detention center punishment when we got hit with a bad rainstorm. I had strict orders not to play on the bridge that went across the creek when the water was high because it was rotten and unsafe. The temptation was too great so my buddy, my dog, and I headed down to the bridge to observe the rushing water. When my dad found out that I disobeyed him, he took me into the bedroom for a little refresher course about disobedience. He had me drop my pants, drop my underwear, and lay face down on the bed. Out came the leather belt, and I knew this was going to be a serious meeting. I decided that no matter how bad the whooping was, I wasn't going to give him the satisfaction of letting him know how bad it hurt.

The first blow came, and my ass felt like I sat down on a hot waffle iron. Instead of crying or yelling, I conditioned myself to laugh instead. When my dad heard me laugh, it really irritated him, so the second whack was more powerful than the first. I laughed harder. The third strike was like someone shoved a cherry bomb up my ass. Once again, I laughed. The fourth blow was so bad I wondered how many more were headed my way and how much longer I could keep up the façade. About that time, a miracle happened. On the fifth lashing, the belt broke, and the spanking stopped. I looked around to assess the situation, and there was my dad holding a belt buckle with about two inches of leather attached to it. Upon seeing the expression on his face, I really did burst out into genuine uncontrollable laughter. My dad was so exasperated he threw the belt buckle against the wall and stormed out of the room. I was grounded for a month.

One of the unique things about the move to Alabama was the fact that my mother did not get pregnant. This was the first move where that didn't happen, but there was still one more Dolby Boomer to come in later years. I guess she figured that since she bagged two in Virginia, she could give herself a break for a while, or maybe she just didn't want to give birth to a rebel!

Me learning to ride a horse in Alabama in 1954

By 1954, the year we moved to Alabama, the Baby Boom era was in its ninth out of 18 years. As a point of reference and looking back to the

1930s through the mid-1940s, new births in the United States were averaging about 2.5 million per year. However, in 1946, the first year of the Baby Boom, an all-time, record-breaking high of 3.47 million births was recorded. New births continued to grow, peaking out to 4.3 million in 1957, then slowly dropping to 4 million by 1964, the final year of the Baby Boom. During that period (1946–1964) nearly 77 million babies were born in the US.

In 1955, my father received orders to report for duty at Travis Air Force Base in Central California. The plan was for my dad to drive the family car to California with Bill, Jr., me, and our dog Taffy. My mother, along with the other four siblings, would remain behind in Montgomery until the new home was ready to receive them.

Dad was eager to see Yellowstone National Park, so we headed to Wyoming. Bill and I were excited to visit this place we had heard so much about. When we arrived, it was colder than a witch's tit frozen to a crowbar. We had jackets, but they were so flimsy they couldn't keep a gnat's ass warm in a frying pan.

After seeing Old Faithful and the other sights, my dad checked into a motel for the evening. If it was him alone, it was one rate, but with two kids and a dog, the rate doubled. To save money, Dad elected to have Bill, me, and Taffy sleep in the car. The temperature dropped to 28 degrees that night. Bill and I, along with the family pet, were shivering and shaking like a dog shittin' peach seeds.

My dad was in the motel room watching the news on TV, and when he heard the weather report, he came to the car to fetch the dog because he felt she would get too cold. He rapped on the window for us to release the dog. We pleaded with him to let us come into the motel room as well. I offered to sleep on the floor and give up my allowance if he would just let us in. He did. The dog crawled in bed with my dad. Bill and I made our bed on the floor and were grateful. The next day we headed for California.

CHAPTER 9
WHOOPY AND THE BUMBLE BEE

My parents purchased a home in a small town called Vacaville (which is Spanish for cow town). The population was 4,800 people at the time. Located in the San Juaquin Valley, Vacaville was 35 miles west of Sacramento and 55 miles east of San Francisco. In other words, we were out in the middle of nowhere. In the summer, it got hotter than two rats screwing in a wool sock behind a water heater. Temperatures could easily get above 110 degrees.

I liked this town and settled in with ease. When we lived in Alabama, I learned to ride horses and wanted to continue the adventure in California. There was a horse stable at Travis Air Force Base. You could board your horse there if you owned one, or you could rent a horse for $1.25 an hour if you had the money. I received $1.25 per week in allowance, so that financed a one-hour ride. In time, I befriended a horse owner that needed someone to exercise his horse. He agreed to let me ride for free if I agreed to show up at least once a week to exercise his horse. This was a great set-up and it worked well for a while. The horse was named Whoopy and was easy to work with.

One day, as just the two of us were out riding the trail, we meandered past a beehive. A bee flew up and stung Whoopy on the ass. The horse took off like a wild goose in winter. At that speed, he could have won the Kentucky Derby. At ten years old, I did not have the strength to control this animal that had now turned into a beast. He started bucking and threw me off his back. I flew up in the air and managed to grab his neck on the way back down.

We were now traveling at lightning speed. I was upside down with my arms around his neck and my legs wrapped around the saddle. Whoopy wanted me off. He saw that I was still hanging on for dear life, but he had his own agenda. He turned his head to bite me which made things worse for both of us. Every time he tried to bite, I would slug him in the jaw. I had two choices. One was to let go and run the risk of getting trampled or hang on until he decided to stop. I chose the latter. He finally settled down. I grabbed him by the reigns and walked him back to his stall. Once I had him locked inside the corral, I wrote a note to the owner to inform him that I would not be returning, ending my career as a horse sitter.

My best friend in fifth grade was Mike Van Well. He had a good sense of humor and was always out for fun. He had a sister named Carol that was 13 years old. Carol was just starting to blossom, and she had two little titties that were beginning to pop out. He would say to me, "Watch this." Then he would run up to her, squeeze them, and take off running and laughing his ass off. Carol got mad and chased him, but to no avail. He could always outrun her.

Living out in the middle of nowhere as 10-year-old kids, we had to be very creative in finding ways to entertain ourselves. Mike called me up one day in springtime to let me know that our little town was sponsoring an Easter egg hunt, and he thought we should go. I agreed, and we met at the assembly area that morning. When the start bell went off, so did we, gathering as many eggs as we possibly could. When it was all over, we took our stash and headed for home when we noticed the long line of cars parked alongside the road. We examined our eggs and the tailpipes on the cars. Their diameters looked like a perfect match. We really did not want the eggs, and we thought it would be funny to stuff the eggs into the tailpipes. We envisioned the car owners starting their vehicles, and when the exhaust built up enough pressure, it would send the eggs flying out like artillery projectiles. We would lock and load the eggs but never waited to see the aftermath. The vision in our mind was sufficient satisfaction.

In the Fall of 1956, a new school opened in Vacaville called Alamo Elementary. Because of my residential address, I was required to change schools, and it was there that I entered sixth grade. That was okay because the people that transferred with me were already good friends from the previous school. I liked Alamo, but I was having a heck of a go at it. Either I was picking a fight with another student, or another student was picking a fight with me. I was sent to the principal's office 13 times for fighting. It was a record-breaking year.

Me in sixth grade

One time I picked a fight with someone I thought would be easy prey. He turned out to be tougher than I thought and got me in a death-defying headlock that was extremely painful. I couldn't work my way out of it and didn't know what to do. The only option I had was his ear, so I tried to bite it off. Luckily, someone came along and stopped the fight before my parents incurred a hefty lawsuit. (Incidentally, that was ten years before Mike Tyson was even born.)

My father was transferred to Elmendorf Air Force Base in Anchorage, Alaska in the spring of 1957. I still graduated from sixth grade even though I got out of school several months early to make the move. I'm certain the principal had something to do with it as I'm sure he was happy to see me go and wanted to make sure I didn't come back.

During this period (1955–1957), it seemed as though the world was accelerating in many new directions. In 1955, Ray Kroc opened his first McDonald's restaurant. Hamburgers were 15 cents, and cheeseburgers 19 cents. The opening of this store launched a major change in the fast-food business and turned it into a multi-billion-dollar industry.

In that same year, Walt Disney opened the doors to Disneyland, sparking another major change in the amusement park industry. Although Walt struggled for many years, once the doors to the kingdom were opened, he became a household legend. In addition to the opening of Disneyland, *Walt Disney Presents* introduced a five-part television mini-series on the life of Davy Crockett. Davy was a frontiersman and Indian fighter, and his legacy was the coonskin cap that he wore. Davy became the hero of boys my age, and we all went out to buy a replica of his hat. About 100 million dollars' worth of raccoon caps were sold in just one year. The raccoon population was drastically reduced, and the scariest thing on the planet was to be a raccoon in 1955.

In 1956, IBM invented and released the first computer with a hard drive, and mothers were able to purchase disposable diapers for the first time. Elvis Presley appeared on the *Ed Sullivan Show* with his song, "Heartbreak Hotel," and Rock'n'roll music was here to stay. The average cost of a new home was $11,700, a gallon of gas cost 22 cents, and the average cost of a new car was $2,050. The average yearly wage was $4,450.

In 1957, the Russians launched the first artificial satellite into space. The satellite was named "Sputnik," which, in English, means "fellow traveler of earth." This event kicked off the "space age" as well as the "space race" between the United States and the Soviet Union. Twelve years later, we would be landing men on the moon.

Meanwhile, back on Earth, I was packing my bags for Alaska.

CHAPTER 10
VANISHING DONUTS

Due to the fact that my dad's assignment in Alaska was only for six months, my parents decided not to sell the house in Vacaville because there was a very good chance that they would be returning to it. It was also decided not to uproot the entire family.

My parents had a niece that had recently moved to the area with her husband and three small children. They needed a place to stay, and my parents needed a babysitter/housesitter. It was agreed that the niece and her husband would move in and take over the house in exchange for caring for the four brothers and sisters we were about to leave behind.

My dad headed north to set up living arrangements with the idea that Bill, my mother, and I would soon follow. He purchased an old 1950 Hudson that served as the family car and found a comfortable apartment on "L" Street in Anchorage.

In April 1957, Mom, Bill, and I traveled to Seattle where we boarded a troop ship bound for Alaska. This was a military tub called the *USS Frederick Funston*, similar to the ship that we took to Japan years earlier. I refer to it as a "tub" because that is what it was. However, from the eyes of an 11-year-old boy, this was a luxury liner about to set sail on the greatest adventure ever.

We were at sea for three days, and I was about as happy as a pig in shit. Our stateroom was modest, but the beds were comfortable. The cafeteria food was acceptable. Entertainment consisted of bingo games and reel-to-reel movies. When the movies were not running, I would grab several pieces of bread and feed the albatrosses off the deck as they followed the ship. They were very aggressive birds, and I was lucky not to lose a finger when they snatched the bread from me.

On the third day, we sailed into the Kenai Fjord docking at the port of Seward, Alaska. It was about 7 a.m. as we entered the fjord. The water was sapphire blue and smooth as glass. The mountains shot straight out of the water and had a purple hue to them just like in the song "America the Beautiful." I had never seen beauty like this in my entire life and thought I had died and gone to heaven.

Alaskan glacier and icebergs

My father met the ship, and the four of us piled into the Hudson headed for our new home. I will never forget the smell of that car. Although I was only seven years old, it smelled like Hogan's goat. I'm sure the Alaskan winters had a lot to do with it. As we drove to Anchorage, I remember the sky being overcast and the temperature quite cool. Along the way, we passed a body of water that was full of icebergs, and I asked if we could stop. The icebergs were bumper-to-bumper in the water, lined up like a five o'clock traffic jam at the end of the workday. Bill and I jumped up on one and played hopscotch from one to the other. The colors were striking. I had always expected icebergs would be white, but these were a brilliant array of white, turquoise, pink, and black. The first three colors made sense, but black? I could only imagine that it was a result of ash from a volcano some years past.

Downtwon Anchorage in 1957
(family car in the foreground)

At Elmendorf Air Force Base, there was a summer camp set up for boys and girls. On their way to work, the dads would drop their kids off in the morning and pick them up on the way back home in the evening. Every morning my dad and I would ride together listening to the traffic report on the car radio as we negotiated our way through Anchorage. Some of the streets were paved while many were still just gravel roads. Alaska was still quite primitive in 1957.

Unlike most people reporting the traffic conditions in metropolitan areas in the lower 48, the Alaska traffic report went something like, "Well folks, there is a bear blocking the northbound lane on Husky Street. Please try to avoid 14th Street near the downtown area as there are a bunch of mountain goats blocking traffic. And there is a moose on Juniper Avenue that will not let anyone pass." Trying to get to the Air Force base each morning was an adventure in itself.

Our summer camp was named, "The Artic Adventure Club." It was very well organized, and the staff kept us busy with arts and crafts, swim meets, other sporting events such as soccer and baseball, and long day hikes. We had a great time, and I was never bored.

One day we went on a hike through the woods. As we walked along the trail, we came upon a pool of mud that blocked our path. The good news was that a huge tree trunk had fallen over the pool providing us with a natural bridge that allowed us to continue the march. I was in the lead, and as we navigated the tree trunk, I looked down and saw what looked like moose tracks in the mud. I pointed them out to my fellow hikers and one of them said, "Those tracks look pretty fresh." I thought to myself, "How would you know if they were fresh or not? Who do you think you are, Daniel Boone? You wouldn't know a fresh track if it came up and bit you in the ass." By now, we were off the trunk and back on the path which made a sharp turn to the right. As soon as I made the turn, there in the middle of the path stood a giant bull moose. "Holy shit," I thought. "I'm a dead man`!" I took off running in one direction. And the moose did the same in the opposite direction. I thought for sure he would do me in; however, I apparently startled him as much as he did me. Thank God I was safe and unscathed. However, at the first opportunity, I had to check my underwear for skid marks.

On the weekends, our family of four would usually take off on two-day fishing trips. Within an hour's drive, we could be in the wilderness. We would park at the trailhead, load up our fishing and camping gear, and take off down the path to nowhere. Within a mile or so, we would be deep into the forest where we would set up camp next to a stream. Naturally, the streams were full of salmon and trout, so we never came back empty-handed. There was never a bad day fishing.

One day, as we were hiking along the river, we spotted a king salmon that another fisherman had caught but left behind on the bank of the river. Amazed at its size, which was bigger than Bill or me, we went to have a closer look. Neither of us had ever been that close to a fish so big, and we didn't realize that they had fairly good-size teeth.

Shortly thereafter, my mom, dad, and I were fishing from the side of the stream, but Bill slipped on a pair of waders and meandered out into the water. Within a few minutes, he hooked into another king salmon, and it took off downstream taking Bill with it. For some reason, and only the salmon would know for sure, the fish turned around and made a beeline charge for my brother. He saw it coming, recognized its size, and imagined the teeth we had recently observed. It only took a fraction of a second for Bill to assess the situation and determine that he wanted nothing to do with it. He threw the pole up in the air and made a mad dash for dry land. We never saw the fish again as it and the pole headed back upstream to wherever fish go.

In the summertime, the sun didn't set in Alaska until about 10 p.m. or later. However, if you were in the forest, things got dark a bit earlier. After an exhausting day of fishing and hiking, we would head back to our camp in the late afternoon and settle in for the evening. We would clean the fish while my mother prepared the rest of the dinner. Then Bill and I would gather firewood and build a nice campfire for cooking.

I loved the smell of the forest. The air was so crisp, clean, and fresh — I couldn't get enough of it. As the sun slowly began to sink, I would watch the mountains systematically change colors from purple, to deep blue, and then to black as the light of day was overtaken by nightfall. Then a whole new show would begin. The stars would come out and sparkle like diamonds, and because there was neither air nor light pollution, it looked as though you could reach up and scoop a handful right out of the sky. And, if there was a full moon, you could watch the moonlight dance on the water as the stream slowly pushed the water, the fish, and my brother's fishing pole to an unknown destination.

With dinner done, we would sit around the campfire talking and roasting marshmallows. I always enjoyed the smell of the smoke as the fire slowly burned down, signaling that it was time to call it quits for the day. We had two tents. Mom and Dad in one. Bill and me in the other. Bill and I would crawl into our fartsacks and talk until we slowly fell asleep. This would give me about eight hours to lay there and dream about a big-ass Kodiak bear that would come in the middle of the night and drag me up to his den for a little midnight snack. In the morning, I would wake up and realize that the bear never came, and I would live another day.

The smell of bacon cooking in the frying pan would wake me up. My parents would get up first. Dad got the fire going, and Mom got the breakfast started. I found it very difficult to get out of bed, not because I was tired, but because the mornings were quite cool, and the sleeping bag was warm and cozy. However, by this time, nature was calling so I got dressed and headed into the woods to drain the dragon.

On one fishing weekend, we drove to Lake Louise, Alaska. There was a large lake and recreational area set up strictly as a vacation spot for military personnel and their families. It wasn't anything fancy; however, it had amenities that were upscale from sleeping in tents in the woods. There were motorboats available for lake fishing. There also were trailers with beds in them, and those would be our accommodations, kind of like a motel room on wheels. There were communal bathrooms, one for men and one for women, equipped with toilets, sinks, and showers. A Quonset hut made of sheet metal served as the dining hall with a kitchen and an eating area.

Mom, me and Bill fishing in Alaska

One morning, I woke up at about 4 a.m. and had to go to the bathroom. So, I hiked over to the communal bathroom in the dark. On my way back to our trailer, I smelled something outrageously inviting. I followed my nose which led me to the Quonset hut. The cooks were in the kitchen preparing for breakfast. And as I walked by, I could see they were making donuts. As they pulled them out of the fryer, they sat them on a plate and parked the plate on the windowsill for the donuts to cool.

Wilderness cabin in Alaska

I got back to our trailer and woke Bill up. I whispered to him so as not to wake my parents and told him to follow me as I had just made a great discovery. It was still dark outside, and we snuck under the window where the donuts were. When the cooks weren't looking, we swiped a couple, sat under the window, and ate them. As the staff continued their work, we would bag a couple more. One of the chefs brought out a new batch to cool and discovered the first batch had all but disappeared. He yelled out to the rest of the kitchen staff to quit stealing the donuts as they were intended for the guests of the facility. The kitchen staff defended themselves by saying that none of them had touched a single donut. The chef responded by saying "If you guys aren't eating the donuts, then they must just be flying out the window." He had no idea how right he was. At the crack of dawn, Bill and I were stuffed so we tiptoed back to the trailer before it got too light and went back to sleep. We caught a lot of fish, ate a lot of donuts, and made some lasting memories on that trip. However, summer was coming to an end, and it was time to return to the lower 48 and get back in school.

CHAPTER 11
FORWARD COMBED BOOGIE

The return trip to California was uneventful. However, it was great to see all my old friends again. The year was 1957, and I had recently turned 12 years of age. I entered yet another new school, Monte Vista Junior High, and settled into 7th grade. But I needed a haircut to start the year off right.

Up until this time, my father had always cut my hair to save money. However, I discovered a new hairstyle called the "forward combed boogie," and it certainly was not within Dad's skill set to deliver the desired outcome. I thought it was the coolest thing I had ever seen, so I took a dollar from my allowance and marched myself down to the barber shop, pointed to the picture on the wall, and said, "Give me one of those." Now the forward-combed boogie is difficult to describe. It starts out with a flat top, the sides are swept back, then up, over, and forward to form a "V" on top of the flat top. It is then finished off with a ducktail in the back. A Google search provides some great images of what this looks like. I came home as proud as a peacock and sat down at the table for the evening meal. My dad didn't say a word all through dinner. However, at the end of the meal, he looked at me and told me to meet him in the garage. When I arrived, he was holding a pair of clippers and a stool. He held out his hand, gesturing for me to have a seat. Ten seconds later I looked like a newly-hatched bird. I didn't have a hair on my head. Dad then said to me, "Don't ever do that again." I didn't. What a waste of a dollar!

The Baby Boomers were filling up the classrooms faster than they could build them. To put things in perspective, new births in the United States during the 1930s through the mid-1940s averaged between 2.3 to 2.8 million per year. The year I was born, 1945, there were in fact, 2.8

million of us to pop out of the chute. Some historians like to use 1946 as the official first year of the Baby Boom. However, for those of us that arrived in the latter part of 1945, we were considered Boomers as well; it's just that we jumped the gun by a few months. In that first year, 1946, the birth rate exploded to 3.47 million. New births continued to increase each year, hitting a peak of .3 million in 1957, the year I entered 7th grade, and again in 1961. In the final year of the Baby Boom, 1964, 4 million babies were born in the United States. And in 1965, there was a substantial drop to 3.76 million, a good indication that the trend was declining. During the 19-year Baby Boom stretch, approximately 76.4 million babies were born.

Nineteen fifty-seven was a momentous year. Technological advancement in television was enhancing the entertainment industry. Three major broadcasting companies were on the air, and the quality of the shows just kept improving.

Saturday mornings were especially good. There was nothing better than sitting in front of the TV with a bowl of Sugar Crisp watching cartoons. The Road Runner, Wile E. Coyote, and *Looney Tunes* with Bugs Bunny, Daffy Duck, and Elmer Fudd kept us entertained for hours.

To me, this was the golden age of television. Cowboys and cowgirls were our heroes. There were so many of them. Gene Autry, Hop-a-long Cassidy, the Lone Ranger, the Cisco Kid, Roy Rogers, Dale Evans, and Annie Oakley to name a few. All these shows had a similar theme — teaching kids the difference between right and wrong and the good guys from the bad guys. If they weren't on horseback wearing white hats, our heroes were in their living rooms establishing family values. TV shows like *Leave It to Beaver*, *The Danny Thomas Show*, *The Real McCoys*, and *Father Knows Best* all reinforced morality. These were followed by more shows with western themes designed to appeal to a more mature audience (our parents), and once again, aimed at promoting human kindness and high ethical standards. Television series such as *Bonanza, Gunsmoke, Maverick, Paladin, The Rebel,* and *Wagon Train* come to mind, but these were just a handful of a list of high-quality shows. Although we only had three channels to choose from, it was hard to decide what to watch because everything seemed so good, entertaining, relatable, and wholesome. We now have over 300 channels, and I seldom find anything worth watching. Instead, I flip though channels for 30 minutes, turn off the TV, go to bed, and read a good book.

In addition to television, other good things were happening. People had the utmost respect for the President of the United States, who happened to be Dwight D. Eisenhower at the time. People respected firemen, policemen, and military personnel. Our youth respected our flag, our country, their parents, and their teachers. Our parents respected each other and their neighbors. Becoming a Boy Scout or Girl Scout was all about respect, and that included having respect for ourselves. All in all, the Boomers were taught to recognize high moral values, ambition, and a code of ethics in the workplace. During this era, we had plenty of things to be proud of that set the stage for the years to come.

I started a lawn-mowing service, sold magazines, and sold all-occasion greeting cards to earn a little extra cash. At school, I signed up to play a musical instrument, but our family couldn't afford it, so I had to drop out. I joined the Boy Scouts, and I really enjoyed being a Scout. This allowed me to go on camping trips in the summer in addition to weekend campouts during the rest of the year. My family couldn't afford this activity either so I agreed to finance it myself if they would agree to let me join. They did. I paid.

That summer, we took a vacation to Yosemite National Park in California. My parents rented cabins to accommodate the family. The problem was that the family was too big. In addition to my parents and six kids, we had my grandparents with us. They managed to get beds for everyone except for Bill and me. We were stuck out in the station wagon again, and we thought that was okay. At least the temperature was warm enough to keep us from freezing to death like the experience we had in Yellowstone several years earlier.

There were communal bathrooms to provide showers and toilets for everyone. You had to hike a little way to get to them, and at night it was very dark. If you had to use the bathroom in the middle of the night, you'd better have a flashlight with you to find your way.

The first night the family retired into their cabins and snuggled down in their beds. Bill and I set up housekeeping in the car. In the car with us was an ice chest and a couple boxes of food. Just about the time we fell asleep, a big-ass bear came strolling into camp and smelled the food in the car. He stood up on his hind legs, put his front paws on the window, and started rocking the car to find a way to get to the food. At first, I thought it was Bill playing games, and I told him to knock it off. Then I opened my eyes and saw 900 pounds of fur outside. I screamed, "Holy shit, Bill, wake up, we have a visitor."

Eventually, the bear got frustrated and left. However, I got so scared I had to go pee, but I wasn't crazy enough to hike to the bathroom in the dark with a bear on the loose. I opened the ice chest and found a jar of pickles with only one left. I ate the pickle, peed in the jar, and set the jar on the ground outside. It was a long and sleepless night. The next morning, Bill woke up and said, "What kind of stupid vacation is this?" I agreed. We were both ready to go home. "Thanks, Dad. This is another fine mess you got us into!" There were no more bear incidents. We finished out the week and went home praying that Dad would never think about taking us on an African safari.

In the Fall of 1958, shortly after I turned 13, I entered 8th grade. I tried out for the junior varsity football team and made it. I always wanted to be a halfback and was able to play that position. I loved this sport and took it very seriously. One day at football practice, we were having a scrimmage, and a play was called requiring me to go out for a pass. I was running down the field like a bat out of hell, looked over my shoulder and saw an image of two footballs coming at me. I was confused and had to make a choice which one to catch. I reached for one, coming up empty-handed, while getting hit in the head with the real one. It was at this time I realized I had a vision problem, and perhaps it would be a good idea if I went to see the eye doctor. He determined that I had a condition called amblyopia or lazy eye. This disorder is characterized by an inability of the eyes to work together which in turn can cause double vision to occur. The doctor suggested that I wear a patch over the good eye making the lazy eye work harder, and in time, this might correct the problem.

My dad decided that we could not afford $5 for an eye patch; however, he would make one for me that would not cost a dime. He pulled out an elastic waist band from a pair of my mother's old underwear. Then he found a rag made of brown polyester. He cut out a pattern, folded it over the elastic, and with a piece of black thread, hand-sewed it all together.

"Here," he said, "try this on for size." I thought, "You have got to be out of your mind'! Do you honestly expect me to wear something like that?" I went to school the next day with the patch over my eye, looking like a 13-year-old version of the one-eyed Israeli Defense Minister, Moshe Dayan.

The patch lasted about two days, giving the entire student body an opportunity to laugh me off campus. I didn't give a rat's ass if I saw 15 footballs coming at me, I was not wearing that stupid thing again.

One day before my first football game of the season, my father announced at the dinner table that we were moving to Omaha, Nebraska, and the move would be immediate.

I thought, "Time out! What do you mean we are moving to Omaha? Do you mean to tell me that I must give up all my friends and leave a state that has 800 miles of coastline, palm trees, mountains, National Parks, and Redwood forests for a state that has 500 miles of nothing but corn? What have you been drinking, Dad? Sewer water?"

The Dolby kids had no say in the matter. Two parents, six kids, and a dog squeezed into our station wagon, and we headed east. We sat in that car for three days, traveled 1,500 miles, and were packed in like sardines.

My parents bought a house prior to the move. Unfortunately, it was under construction and would not be completed for another six months. As we settled into the booming metropolis of Omaha, we were able to find a rental that would barely accommodate our needs. It had three bedrooms that took care of most of the family, except for Bill and me. We got stuck down in the basement. Fortunately, we saved enough packing boxes to build a make-shift bedroom for the two of us, and when we got done, I must admit it was quite cozy. The only problem was the cold winters. Of the 50 coldest cities in the continental United

States, Nebraska has six of them. I managed to scare up five blankets to keep me warm throughout the night as the basement got colder than a penguin's pecker.

CHAPTER 12
CORN, COWS, AND THE SHIT BOX

Nebraska is approximately 500 miles long and 200 miles wide with plenty of corn and cows. It is the 15th largest in land mass of all the states, encompassing over 77 thousand square miles most of which are covered with cornfields. It is appropriately nicknamed the Cornhusker State, and although it has hundreds of little towns, it is ranked 38th out of 50 in population with less than two million people residing there.

Nebraska has made an impressive contribution to the pool of famous people. A partial list includes Johnny Carson, Larry the Cable Guy, Fred Astaire, Marlon Brando, Ward Bond, Montgomery Clift, James Coburn, Henry Fonda, Dick Cavett, Gerald Ford, Dick Cheney, Max Baer, Warren Buffett, and Crazy Horse. In addition to the celebrities, Nebraska is famous for its friendly, hospitable residents. Having lived in so many places by the time my family moved to Nebraska, it was immediately obvious just how great these people were. Although I only lived there five years, I still call it home.

As we got settled in Omaha, I entered the 8th grade at Westside Junior High/High School in 1958. The movie star, Nick Nolte, was there as a senior at the time. I never met him in school but did years later when I spotted him at a football game in Los Angeles. We sat down and had a friendly halftime conversation. He actually encouraged me to attend my 50th high school reunion, which I did upon his advice.

I loved my school and bonded well with the other kids immediately. The school year was well underway by the time I arrived in October 1958, so it was too late in the season to join the football team. I did, however, meet our paperboy and asked him how much money he was making and how could I get a job like his. He replied, "You can have my job. I am getting ready to quit." I jumped all over it like a mad dog with rabies and became the replacement paperboy. By the time I took it over, the paper route was already the largest in Omaha. And since we were living in a newly developed housing tract, it was easy for me to grow it even bigger as new residents moved into the neighborhood. At 13 years of age, I was already making $125 per month, and that was a lot of money in those days.

Back in school, I was always bored, and always looking for ways to entertain myself. One day, it was pouring down rain, and I took a squirt gun to school with me. I sat in the back row of the class, and when nobody was looking, I would shoot a stream of water up onto the ceiling in such a manner that it would drip down and hit the kid in front of me landing on his head. He thought the roof was leaking because of the rain and slid his desk a couple inches to the right to keep from getting wet. Then, I would readjust my aim a couple inches to the right and deliver another assault. Once again, the water would drip down on his head, and he would reposition his desk. This went on all morning, and that poor kid could not figure out how to resolve his predicament. By lunch time, he was sopping wet. I finally ran out of ammo, and miraculously the roof stopped "leaking."

Meanwhile, the babies of the Baby Boom generation kept coming. Nineteen fifty-eight marked the 13th year of the boom, and 4.2 million more were added to the growing list, for a running total of 50.3 million by the end of that year. And there were still six more years to go before the boom ended. Those that were new arrivals were just getting started. But for those of us that came with the first wave, we were now getting ready to enter high school. I was starting to get interested in girls, and my class had quite a few cute ones that caught my attention. I was doing my best to get to know them, however, unbeknownst to me, my parents had other plans.

In March 1959, construction on our home was completed, so we moved out of the rental and up the hill to the new house. Four blocks away from our home was an all-boys Jesuit Catholic high school. At dinner one evening my parents informed Bill and me that they were pulling us out of public school and sending us to the Catholic school, Creighton Prep.

"WAIT A MINUTE!" I protested. "What about all my friends?"

"You will make new ones."

"What about the girls?"

"You don't need them."

"This is a private school. Who is going to pay for this?"

"You are."

"But there is tuition and books to buy."

"You have plenty of money saved from your paper route to pay for it."

"But I had other plans for that money."

"Argument over. Case closed. You are going."

Well, I'll be dipped in dog shit`! Just what I didn't want to happen, happened. I would start my freshman year of high school at Creighton Prep.

When we moved into the new house, I started to do the math on my life up to that point. I was 13 years old, and this was my 11th move. And when I started the ninth grade at Creighton Prep in the fall, this would be my seventh school. "Are we shootin' for a spot in the Guinness Book of Records? Why can't we just unpack and be done with it?"

Because it was a private school, there was no school bus, not that we really needed it with just a four-block hike. But in the wintertime, Omaha was the coldest and windiest place on the planet, and the windchill factor literally took your breath away. Sometimes that four-block walk seemed like four miles. We needed to figure out a way to beat the cold. Then a miracle happed. Bill turned 16 years old in December, and he got his driver's license. In addition to the family station wagon, we had an old 1952 Ford clunker, and my dad gave it to Bill. We could now drive to school instead of walk. No more freezing hikes, we were traveling in style. That was the good news. Now, for the bad news. Within a month, Bill got in a wreck and totaled the car. We were now back to the shoe leather express as our primary means of transportation.

One evening shortly thereafter, Bill and I held a staff meeting in our bedroom. Bill suggested that we buy our own car. I thought that was a splendid idea. I thought we could each kick in 50% and have our car. "No, you don't understand. I don't have any money. You have to buy the car," Bill said. So, we worked a deal. I would buy the car and give it to him, with the understanding that he would make improvements as finances allowed. In addition, he would have to haul me around to my various commitments. Then, when I turned 16, he would have to give the car back to me with no strings attached. He agreed.

At 14 years of age, I bought my first car! It was a 1950 Plymouth Deluxe two-door coupe. As we went car shopping, we only had two prerequisites to cement the deal. We had to have a radio, and we had to have a heater. This shit box had both!

1950 Plymouth Deluxe
(my shitbox did not look quite this good)

The car was a piece of work with a personality all its own. The rocker panels were rusted out on both sides, but a gallon of Bond-O, a putty knife, and some sandpaper would take care of that. The floor on the driver's side was rusted through, leaving a hole about six inches in diameter. We could pull back the rubber mat and see the ground pass underneath the car as we drove down the road. So, instead of a moon-roof, we had a view of the pavement. This was a great source of entertainment for anyone that was a first-time passenger.

We wanted white walls but didn't want to spend the money for new tires. So, for eight bucks we went out and bought a set of port-o-walls and bingo, these slap-ons gave us the appearance of new white-wall tires! The car needed a paint job. We drove it down to Earl Scheib, and for $29.95 we had a shiny, brand-new, metallic blue Plymouth the very next day. The upholstery was in bad shape. Bill found a discount tuck-and-roll shop, and a couple days later we had new seats, front and back. Things were looking pretty spiffy, and this car was now dressed to impress. Then, Bill found a bowling pin. He brought it home, drilled a hole in the bottom and screwed it into the gear shift lever. I said, "Bill, what on earth are you doing? You can't shift gears with a 25-pound bowling pin for a gear shift knob." I won that argument, and it was replaced with something more reasonable.

One Friday evening, Bill announced that we were out of gas. I said, "Okay, let's go to the Texaco station and fill up." Gas was only about 30 cents a gallon at the time.

He said, "No, no, no. We are not going to Texaco. That costs money. We are going to the 'midnight acquisition fuel station' where the gas is free." I thought, "What in the hell is he talking about?" He opened the trunk of the car and showed me a syphon hose and said, "Let's go." I had no idea what he had in mind.

We drove into a residential neighborhood and found some cars parked out on the curb. Bill pulled up to one, got out the hose and connected our tank with the tank of the parked car. Somehow, he mastered the laws of physics and fluid dynamics, and soon the fuel was being transferred from one car to the other. About that time, the homeowner woke up, opened the window of the second story dormer, and yelled out, "What in the hell are you kids doing?"

Bill looked up at him and yelled back, "We're stealin' your gas you stupid son-of-a-bitch. What's it look like we're doin'?"

I'm thinking, "Oh Bill, can't you be just a little bit more tactful than that? Not only were we stealing his gas, but we were also adding insult to injury by calling him a stupid son-of-a-bitch."

I yelled to Bill, "Let's get out of here."

He replied, "Relax. It will take at least 30 seconds for him to get down here. Take your time and put the hose back into the trunk of our car." I did and jumped into the shotgun side. Calmly, Bill slowly meandered back to the driver's seat, and we took off. I looked out the rear window and saw a mad man in pajamas standing in the middle of the street, flailing his arms in a manner that said, "If I ever catch you, I will kill you." Sorry Pop, next time we will be moving to another neighborhood, so get over it.

That summer the entire family took a driving vacation to Yellowstone National Park. Bill and I had been there with just my dad five years earlier and told him we were not going on this vacation unless he promised not to make us sleep in the car again. He agreed. My youngest sister was not born yet, so there were eight of us in the car as we embarked on the vacation from hell. My dad had just put new tires on our station wagon prior to the vacation, but they were all recaps. We didn't so much as make it to the edge of town when the tread unraveled from all four tires. Once again, we bought new tires, but we were several hours late getting started. This created a problem because we had reservations at the Yellowstone Lodge, and if we didn't check in on time, we were apt to lose our rooms. We stopped in Grand Island, Nebraska for gas and headed on down the road. We were about 20 miles out of town when my dad noticed flashing red lights in his rear-view mirror. His first thought was that he was being stopped for speeding, but that wasn't the case. He pulled over, and the highway patrolman approached the car. "Are you Mr Dolby?" he asked.

"Yes, I am," my dad replied. "And just how many children do you have?"

"Six," said my father.

"Take a headcount," said the cop. Dad could only come up with five. Obviously, we forgot someone during out last stop. This guy was very nice and gave us a police escort back to the gas station where my little brother Chris was sitting on the curb, patiently waiting to be rescued. We were now about three hours behind schedule.

There were no interstates at the time, just two-lane highways. Underway once again, we were passing a cattle truck when one of the cows let loose with a recycled bale of hay, spraying our car with about five pounds of wet cow shit. It went everywhere on the car, and the windshield got it the worst. My dad turned on the wipers but all that did was smear things around so that visibility was down to nothing. He spotted a gas station, pulled in, and undiplomatically barked out orders for the attendant to clean his window. The attendant looked at my dad as if to say, "One, don't talk to me in that tone of voice. Two, this is your problem not mine. And three, this is a gas station, not a car wash." Despite my dad's nasty attitude, the guy managed to get the windshield clean. However, if he'd had a gun, I think he might have shot my dad just for being such a jerk.

"Hey Dad, would you please quit pissing people off, especially the ones that are helping you," we all thought.

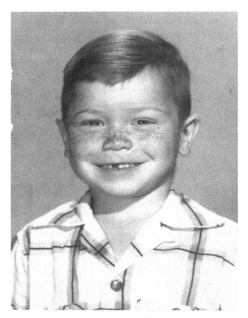

My brother Chris

We were now three-and-a-half hours behind schedule. My mom called the lodge from a pay phone to explain our dilemma. They were very understanding and held our room for us. As we were driving across the state, it was one of those hot and humid Midwest days. The car had an after-market air conditioner mounted under the dashboard, and that made things comfortable for those in the first two rows of seats, but Bill and I were in the back row next to the tailgate. It was so hot it felt like the devil was farting in our face, and with the cow shit, it smelled that way too. Once we checked into the lodge, Bill and I found a garden hose and washed the car. The rest of the vacation went okay, and we made it back to Omaha just in time to start school.

With school underway, the freshmen were experiencing mild shock. None of us had ever been in an all-boys school before, so the initial reaction was confusion. And, 35 boys in one room turned all of us into a band of renegades, and it was total chaos. The faculty was expecting this, and they had their plan for discipline well in place. The first week they confiscated over a dozen peashooters, but we kept replenishing them with new ones. One day, as the pea-shooter wars were taking place, I fired one off at just the wrong time, hitting the teacher in the back of the head as he was writing something on the blackboard.

Unbeknownst to me, one of the Jesuits was standing in the hallway staring through a tiny window in the door and saw me do it. This priest was named Father Albert Krendaline, and he was meaner than two wildcats with their tails tied together. He opened the door, and with his finger, motioned for me to come out and join him. Once in the hallway, he picked me up and slammed me against the lockers saying, "How would you like it if I shoved you right through this wall?"

Like the smartass that I was, I said, "Well, I'm already halfway there, so you might as well finish the job."

"That's it," he screams, "Report to Jug Hall after school today."

Jug Hall was held in the large school library and was designed to be a detention center for all the malcontents, dingbats, misfits, ne'er-do-wells, and knuckleheads. I venture to say at least 90% of the student body spent at least one day in Jug Hall during their academic career at Creighton Prep. And, 75 percent made multiple visits. Sometimes I would go in there, and it was so packed that it was difficult to find a seat. We were assigned unrealistic math problems that were impossible to complete, such as multiply two times two. Then take the resulting product and multiply that by itself. Then repeat the exercise 26 more times. By the time we got done, the number was so astronomical that there was not enough lead left in the pencil to record the answer.

I tried to avoid Jug Hall because I had football practice after school, plus I had a paper route. Except for my early Sunday morning deliveries, my route required me to deliver the evening edition of the paper during the rest of the week. At Creighton Prep, I developed a friendship with a guy by the name of Mark O'Rilley. Mark wanted to earn some extra money, and I needed help, so I invited him to assist me. We made a great team, and he was a very reliable guy.

One day, Mark and I were delivering papers on 78th Street when we spotted a black cat meandering through the neighborhood. We decided this was a prime opportunity to have some fun. Mailboxes were mounted on posts at the side of the street. They were the kind that were rounded on the top, the door folded down in front, and there was a red flag on the side to notify the mailman that there was outgoing mail to pick up. I knew the mailman would show up momentarily, so we grabbed the cat and stuffed it into the mailbox and raised the red flag. Within seconds, we spotted the mailman coming down the street, so my buddy and I took a seat on the curb a couple houses away to observe the excitement that was about to unfold.

The mailman opened the mailbox door, and the cat flew out, landing on the mailman's face. The mailman was in such shock that he must have shit his pants every color of the rainbow. The cat took off one way, and the mailman took off running in the opposite direction.

The next day, without the cat, we raised the red flag on the same mailbox. The mailman came by, still nervous from the previous day, and cautiously opened the door, one-eighth inch at a time until he was convinced that there were no more angry felines ready to pounce. That day it was equally as funny just to see the expression of trepidation on his face. We never saw that poor guy again. He must have quit the post office and gotten a job in the grocery store or something safer.

During my second year at Creighton Prep as a sophomore, I made the football team along with my buddy Mark O'Rilley, and our team was undefeated. Although I was making a lot of friends, I was not able to spend much time with them during non-school hours because this was a private school, and my classmates were scattered in a 20-mile radius throughout the city as opposed to all of us living in one unified school district. Mark lived within walking distance (about a mile from my house) so we spent a considerable amount of time together.

At the completion of my sophomore year, I decided to give up my paper route of three years. Mark and I got a summer job working for a landscaping company. Their primary product was sod. At about 5 a.m., we got into flatbed semi-trucks in Omaha and drove about an hour to the sod field located just outside Red Oak, Iowa. The sod field was more like a cow pasture with grass for the most part. There was a machine that cut the sod on the ground, and we came behind, rolling it up like strips of carpet that were about two feet wide, six feet long, and three or four inches thick. Then we would have to stack it on the flatbed and haul it back to Omaha. If we were lucky, our day would end about 5 p.m.

It was back-breaking work. We worked in the sun all day with heat, high humidity, and no shade. The sod balls weighed about 30 pounds each, but when they were wet after it rained, they would swell up to about 40 pounds. In addition to 12-hour days, five to six days a week, we had a few other issues. Since cows were grazing in the field, many of the sod balls were covered with wet, smelly cow shit. We just rolled it up with the rest of the grass, but the smell would knock us for a loop. In addition, when we rolled up the freshly cut sod, we would frequently discover a huge colony of red ants underneath, and before we could react, they were all over our hands biting the hell out of us.

At noon we would break for lunch. Next to the field we were working in was a railroad track, and at precisely 12:05 p.m., a commuter train would come through with about ten passenger cars. We could hear it coming and had just enough time to line up, drop our britches, bend over, and moon the passengers. I imagine we looked like a row of honey cured hams as they went flying by. You can bet those passengers had some stories to tell their families at the dinner table in the evening. "Gertrude, you won't believe what I saw today on the train coming from Omaha to Clarkdale."

By the end of the summer, my forearms looked like Popeye's, and I had built up muscle in places I didn't even know muscles existed. I was in great physical shape and ready for football season to begin. Mark's father was transferred to Missouri, so I lost one of my best friends. Meanwhile, since I no longer had my paper route, my parents decided to send me back to Westside High School to avoid having to pay tuition for me to attend a private school.

As for my brother Bill, he was up to his old tricks of creating excitement. There wasn't much to do in the form of entertainment in Omaha, so you had to create your own. Like most American cities in the 1960s, entertainment for teenage boys consisted of getting three or four of your buddies together, everyone pitching in a dollar for gas, and cruising up and down the main street of town on Saturday night. One evening, Bill and three of his buddies were cruising Omaha's main drag, Dodge Street. One of the guys had purchased a World War II German Luger handgun from a military surplus store. Half of the parts were missing including the bolt, the trigger, the magazine, and the firing pin. Although it was rendered useless, it still looked rather intimidating to the unsuspecting eye.

My brother Bill

Bill and his friends spotted a hitchhiker on the side of the road and stopped to pick him up. Or, so he thought. This guy was excited to receive a lift and came running up to the car. One of Bill's friends rolled down the window and pointed the gun at the hitchhiker. In a deep authoritative voice, he said, "Get in." The hitchhiker froze in his tracks and threw up his arms. Trembling, he said, "That's okay, I think I will walk." Once again, a voice from the car sternly said, "Get in!" The poor guy took off running like a scalded dog, just a-shittin'-and-a-gettin' into the night. As he disappeared into the darkness, the guys in the car had a good laugh, then drove off, looking for their next victim. Another successful evening in Omaha! (At the time, it all seemed like good old harmless fun. However, in today's day and age, they would have all been arrested and punished for their mayhem.)

On another occasion, Bill invited me to tag along with him. It was St. Patrick's Day, and we drove out to the small farming community of Elkhorn, Nebraska about 30 miles west of Omaha. We pulled into the parking lot of an old ramshackle tavern and walked in. Bill was only 17 years old at the time, and I was 15. Bill slammed the door open and yelled, "I want all of you farmers and hicks out of here." I'm thinking, "Holy shit, Bill, all the guys in here are between 200 and 300 pounds of solid muscle aching for a fight, and we are about 140 pounds soaking wet. Are you trying to get us killed?" Fortunately, nobody paid any attention to my brother except for a 300-pound drunk in bib overalls. He walked up to Bill and got right into his face. On the suspenders of his overalls was pinned a shamrock made of a green pipe cleaner. He grabbed Bill and pointed to the shamrock. "Do you see this shamrock?"

Calmly, Bill says, "Yes, what about it?"

The farmer says, "Well, I cultivated it."

Authoritatively, Bill says, "Okay. Then you can stay."

I'm getting really uncomfortable about this whole mess and said to Bill, "You might think that you are the presiding judge as to who can stay and who can go, but I'm leaving while the gettin' is good. See you at the car. Bill followed. Our lives were spared.

My dad, true to form, had his own agenda. For some reason, he seemed to take immense pleasure in sending Bill and me to our room without dinner. We would sit down at the dinner table, and out of nowhere, Dad would blow up. "Bill, Steve, off to your room. There will be no dinner for you tonight`!" It wasn't just me, and it wasn't just Bill, it was usually the two of us. We would leave the table, walk upstairs to our room, shaking our heads wondering what on earth we did to piss him off this time. Bottom line was that it didn't matter. That's just the way it was. Personally, I think the guy was trying to save money on the grocery bill.

Bill and I developed a strategic plan that would help us overcome these periods of food deprivation. In our bedroom was a small cubbyhole built into the wall. It was more like a half door that led into a small attic that would normally be used for storage. Inside, it consisted of a roof, rafters, and insulation. In the winter, it was like a refrigerator in there with a temperature just above the freezing point. It was ideal for food storage. We went to the store and bought cookies, potato chips, Coke, 7-Up, Slim Jims, beef jerky, Hostess cupcakes, and Twinkies. Before my dad got home from work, we hauled in our stash and neatly tucked it away in the attic. We were so well provisioned that we could go a month without dinner.

One evening when we were ordered to our room without dinner, my mother was feeling sorry for us. When my dad wasn't looking, she brought some food to our room. We thanked her for her efforts, told her it wasn't necessary, then showed her our mini-market in the attic. She was amazed and said, "I always wondered why you boys never complained about being hungry."

The summer of 1961 was a banner year. I turned 16 years old in August and got my driver's license. Bill had not totaled the car during the previous two years, so he honored our agreement and turned the car over to me in one piece.

About that same time, my mother announced that we were going to have another member join the family. The seventh Dolby sibling, Mary Katherine (Kit), made her debut in January of the following year. Everyone was excited about the new arrival. However, Bill and I were wondering how much longer this was going to continue. After all, Mom had been pumping out babies since 1943. That's a span of 18 years.

In the fall of 1961, I entered Westside High School for my junior year. Shortly after the semester started, a new student came strolling into class, obviously a transfer from another school. I was sitting near the back of the room when "Cool Hand Luke" showed up. He plopped down in the back row and threw his feet up onto the desk in front of him like he owned the place. I thought to myself, "This guy must have balls the size of grapefruit. Nobody does that — my kinda guy." I felt a sense of urgency to get to know him, so I walked up to him and said, "Howdy, I'm Steve Dolby, and I just transferred here from a local high school." He said, "My name is Pete James, and I just moved down from Sioux City, Iowa." That got the ball rolling, and we became the best of friends. Pete's parents bought a house about ten houses away from where I lived, and that made it geographically convenient for both of us.

Together, Pete and I were renegades in a sense — not that we did things that were bad or harmful to others, but because we did things that pushed the envelope when it came to following rules and regulations. We were both so creative in our mischief that it was difficult to determine which one of us was the "bad influence." Regardless, we managed to drag each other into situations that got us in trouble.

Our principal's name was Mr LaCarr, and his name and title were etched on a plastic nameplate that was attached to his office door. The standard joke among our school buddies was that the sign should have read "The office of Dolby & James" because it seemed as though we spent more time in there than Mr LaCarr did.

CHAPTER 13
HUMP DAYS

In today's world, we refer to Wednesday as "hump day" because it's halfway through the week and sliding down the backside toward the weekend. Pete and I created our own version of hump day back in 1961. We didn't have a name for it, we just celebrated it by skipping school. We decided that Wednesday was set aside for us to enjoy a break away from school and get recharged to make it through the rest of the week.

Pete was the brains of the outfit. He thought he had an IQ of around 120, and guessed mine to be about 100, but we didn't know for sure because we were never tested. However, when we were together, his IQ dropped to about two, and mine bottomed out at about one.

On our first day of playing hooky, Pete came to pick me up. He asked, "Where do you think we should go?" I replied, "I haven't thought it through, so what do you think?" He came back with, "Let's drive up to Sioux City and visit my old school." We did. Pete explained to the teacher that our school district had the day off, so we drove up to see his old classmates. We were well received, and the teacher offered us seats in the classroom. When the final bell rang for the day, Pete and I got in his car and drove back to Omaha. It was 100 miles each way.

On the way back, I suggested to Pete that we recap our accomplishments for the day. He was in total agreement and let me go first. I said, "Pete, I realize that you are the smarter of the two of us, but I am trying to connect the dots, and there are no straight lines. Here is my problem. First, we skip school, only to drive 100 miles to another school. We spend the entire day in the other school, and then drive 100 miles back to where we started. Please explain to me what we accomplished." Pete took a deep breath and pondered the question but drew a blank and suggested we put a little more thought into the next hooky plan.

The following Wednesday, we headed west from Omaha and stumbled into a small town called Freemont. Driving down Main Street, we spotted a small café and decided to stop for breakfast. As we were eating the "Blue Plate Special," the waitress asked if we were on our way to the Freemont sand pits. We had never heard of them and wanted to learn more. She explained that it was a rock quarry that had a body of water in it with a small sandy beach. She said that teenagers often went there to go swimming. Pete and I thought this was worth checking out, so we finished breakfast, got directions, and off we went.

When we spotted the pond and beach, we thought we had discovered paradise and decided that it would be our destination of choice on warm days. Next trip, we would be sure to bring our bathing suits.

One day, Pete and I were approached by one of our classmates. He mentioned that it was well-known among our peers that we managed to disappear on Wednesdays, and he was curious to know just what it was we were doing. We told him about hump day and the sand pits and asked if he would like to join us. His eyes lit up like a Christmas tree, and he jumped at the invitation. We told him to meet us at the Crossroads Shopping Center the following Wednesday morning at 7:30 a.m. and to bring a bathing suit and a sack lunch.

We all jumped into my car and now it was Pete, Mike, and me driving down the highway toward Freemont. The sun was out, and it was a glorious day. Mike must have spread the word because a week later we were approached by others who wanted to come. When Ted and Ward joined the group, my car was at capacity. Then Tim and Dave showed up at the shopping center the following week, so we had to start taking two cars.

When we first arrived in Freemont, we always stopped at the Bluebird Café for breakfast before we went to the pits. On the warm days, we would swim and sunbathe. On the cooler days, we would play football or volleyball, followed by a sack lunch break. We had our summit meetings to discuss whether-or-not we should go to war with Russia. Or, we might conduct character assassinations on certain members of our school faculty. If it was the latter, the conversation usually gravitated toward a certain science teacher that became a legend for accidentally setting himself on fire while performing a chemistry experiment.

In the interest of sparing him embarrassment, we will call him Mr Crispy. Crispy was standing in front of the chemistry lab one day trying to demonstrate the properties of mist and vapor. He put some gasoline in his mouth and forced out a fine mist toward the Bunsen burner. The window happened to be open at the time, and as the mist was about to hit the flame, a gust of wind came through the window, forcing the ball of fire back toward Crispy's head. He went up in flames. Fortunately, we got the fire out before he sustained any permanent injury.

One hump day, it was particularly warm and sunny. Our classmate, Tim Green, was with us. Tim had red hair and a very light complexion. He got so sunburned that he glowed from top to bottom. There was no hiding it. We dropped him off at his house on our way home, and when his mother saw him, she was in shock. "What in the world happened to you?" she asked. His reply was a classic. He told her that his PE class was held outside that day and that is what caused the sunburn. When he came to school the next day, he was so sunburned he didn't look any better than Mr Crispy.

Meanwhile, the school staff was beginning to realize that the absentee rate was on the rise. Pete and I were in the same advanced Algebra class. Our teacher, Mr Shore, came up to us one day after his class was over and said, "Boys, I've got to give a mid-term exam next week, and I want to make sure you are there to take it." Pete's response was, "Well then, make it for Tuesday or Thursday because Wednesday we'll be gone." We settled on Thursday, and we were grateful that he saw things our way.

One morning, Pete was walking by Mr LaCarr's office, minding his own business when he heard a loud voice yell out, "Peter James, get your ass in here." "Why weren't you in school yesterday?" Pete told him he was sick and spent the day in bed. "Okay then. Bring a note from your mother and meet me here at 8 a.m. tomorrow."

Pete really had been sick, so his mother was willing to write the note. When Pete went to school the next day and presented it to Mr

LaCarr; he got mad and said, "Your mother didn't write this note, you did." Pete fired back insisting that his mother had in fact written it. LaCarr then opened his desk drawer and pulled out a stack of notes that had previously been submitted by Pete. He said to Pete, "Then explain to me why the handwriting on this note does not match the handwriting on all these others." Pete says, "Because I wrote all the notes in that stack, but this one came from my mother`!" Pete was ordered to report back to school on Saturday to perform community service.

Interestingly enough, yet not related to hump day, another incident occurred that involved skipping school. Our football team, of which I was a part, was having a rough season. We lost the first four games and tied the fifth. At a pep rally one Friday afternoon, Mr LaCarr was invited to speak. He announced to the student body that if we won the game that weekend, he would declare Monday a school holiday. Of all the schools you could play in Nebraska, coincidentally, we ended up playing against Freemont High. Furthermore, we won the game 30-14. LaCarr, who thought we didn't have a snowball's chance in hell of winning the game was now faced with the dilemma of how he would get out of his commitment to the student body. The student body, on the other hand, wanted to hold his feet to the fire.

Although we all went to school on Monday, we expected an announcement that would say, "school dismissed." That announcement never came, and by 10 a.m., we decided to storm the doors and leave. Mr LaCarr anticipated this and ordered the teachers to guard the exits and not let any of us escape. By the time we got organized, the doors were blocked, so four of us went into the boy's restroom thinking we would escape through the window. Paul got out, Ken got out, Pete got out, and I got halfway out when two teachers came running and grabbed me. It was a tug of war between the teachers trying to drag me in, and the other three guys trying to pull me out. I felt like Stretch Armstrong.

The teachers won, and I remained behind in confinement. Meanwhile, other teachers rounded up the guys on the outside, and the rebellion was over. Once again, Pete was ordered to perform community service the following weekend. Poor Pete!

CHAPTER 14
DRIVE-IN MOVIES

The drive-in movie theater provided three benefits. The first benefit: it was a good source of family entertainment. The second benefit: it was a great place to take a girl on a date. As teenagers, with hormones running wild, a car parked in a drive-in theater was like a library and a laboratory all rolled into one, allowing you to conduct research and perform experiments related to carnal knowledge. And, the third benefit: it was a convenient place for a bunch of teenage boys to gather when they were not lucky enough to participate in the second benefit.

By 16 years of age, I had heard so many stories about the various ways guys got lucky, I decided it was my turn to give it a shot. After all, I was young, stupid, strong, and handsome (so I thought). And, I had the keys to a 1950 Plymouth shit box. What more could I possibly need to be successful in this endeavor? The only things I lacked were knowledge and experience, but I figured a little on-the-job training would take care of that.

The first girl I took out was very nice, however, I think she was a little short on patience. Before I could figure out how to get her bra off, she was already dating someone else. I wasn't counting on this and didn't think it would be that difficult. Furthermore, I figured out that I needed to do some homework so that I could learn from my mistakes.

I went down to Brandies Department Store and into the ladies' undergarment area to conduct a little research on bras. I immediately discovered the problem. There was no standardization. Every one of them had options. Some fastened in the back, while others fastened in the front. Some had hooks, while others had snaps. Some had straps, while others were strapless. No wonder I was having problems.

The second girl I took out was very nice as well, and most cooperative. I got the bra off but there was nothing there. She was flatter than a squashed frog laying in the middle of the road after getting run over by a semi-truck. I wondered why she would wear a bra if there was nothing to put into it. I thought, "Perhaps I should give her a call back in a couple years."

The third attempt was the most interesting of all. This girl was cute as a button, very nice, and the bra came off like I really knew what I was doing. However, just like a box of Cracker Jacks, there was a surprise waiting inside. Although she was rather developed, she had hair growing out of her nipples. Not just a little hair, but long, black, stringy hair. Holy smokes, what was I supposed to do with these things, braid them? I decided to package those little puppies back up and put them away for the evening. The date and the relationship ended.

After round three, I thought I needed a little break from all this and decided the following weekend I would just hang out with the guys. I contacted Pete, Rob, and Tim and suggested going to the drive-in the following Friday night to watch a war movie. They agreed.

I picked them up one-by-one. Once in the car, Rob produced a brown paper bag. Rob's dad was a liquor distributor, and he pinched a bottle of Johnny Reb bourbon to enhance the evening. Once we secured our spot at the drive-in, Rob opened the bottle and passed it around. I took a swig and passed the bottle to Pete. Round and round it went. I passed on subsequent offerings because I was driving, and because I did not like the taste of bourbon. Good thing Pete was there. He drank his share, and my share as well.

During intermission, Pete decided that he had to go to the bathroom and excused himself to hike down to the concession stand. On the way back, the bourbon took over and hit Pete's brain and body like the kick of a mule. Suddenly, he went from "stone sober" to "knee-crawlin', commode-huggin', slip-slidin', snot-flingin', rat-faced, ass-kissin' drunk."

The shortest distance between two points is a straight line. However, it looked like Pete was trying to navigate through a plate of spaghetti to get back to where we were parked. First, he bounced off the left rear fender of a Ford Fairlane. Then he ricocheted off the front bumper of a Chevy Impala. Eventually he saw us and made a beeline toward our location. As he approached, his eyes grew wide and began to cross. It looked like his right eye was pointed toward Boston while his left eye was focused on Miami Beach.

He embraced the hood of my car like it was a long-lost lover. He got violently ill and barfed up everything that was not nailed down. With the entire parking lot at his disposal, why did he choose to let loose on my car? It remains a mystery we discuss to this day.

With a pile of what looked like corn beef hash sitting on my hood, I thought it was an appropriate time to call it an evening, take everybody home, and get the car cleaned up. The plan was to drop Pete off first. By the time we got him home at about 11 p.m., he was passed out, and we could not wake him up. He was dead weight, so it took all three of us to get him out of the car. The other two guys helping me asked, "What do we do with him now?" I was so pissed with what he had done to my car, I ordered them, "Just dump him out on the front lawn." They agreed. When we took off, I was thinking, "Sleep tight, Pete. Nighty night night`!'"

By the time I got the other two home on that hot August evening and then myself, the barf was so fried on the hood I couldn't wash it off. I was tired, hot, and angry, so I decided I would take care of it in the morning. But I would have to get up early and get out of the house before my parents woke up. I went to one of those self-service car washes, grabbed a power hose, and started feeding quarters into the machine. Twenty-five cents got about five minutes of hose time, and I think I went through at least six quarters before I got everything cleaned up. On the way home, I drove by Pete's house. He was no longer on the lawn, so I figured he woke up some time in the middle of the night and got himself to bed.

He called me about midday and was upset that we dumped him out on the lawn. I said, "Wait just a minute and hear me out. You have no idea what you did last night. You have no idea of what you put the others through last night. You have no idea about what you did to my car. And by the way, you owe me $1.50 for the car wash." Once he heard the complete story, he became a little more contrite.

I loved being back in a co-ed school, and the timing could not have been more perfect. I managed to get up enough nerve to start dating several girls at the same time. There was one girl I really liked. Her name was Nancy. She was a transfer student like me, and we seemed to hit it off quickly. Her father worked for IBM and was transferred to Omaha from Armonk, New York about the same time I re-entered Westside.

After Pete arrived from Sioux City, Iowa and found a girlfriend for himself, the four of us started double dating, and we ended up back at the drive-in movie theater again. Nancy had a great personality and was fun to be with, but she had a large lower unit. Pete didn't like her much and nicknamed her "Gobble-Ass."

After several double dates, Pete came to my house one day and gave me an ultimatum. He knocked on the front door and I invited him in. He said, "No, no, you come out here." I guess he didn't want my mother to hear what he was about to say.

We sat on the front porch, and he said, "Dolb," (he always called me Dolb), "this is it. It's me or Gobble Ass. I can't take it any more, so you've got to choose between the two of us. What's it going to be?"

I said, "Well, if I have to make a decision right now, Gobble Ass has two tits, and you don't have any, so I guess I'll have to choose her." Pete wasn't expecting that answer and got very frustrated that I called his bluff. He started to back-peddle, and said, "I'll still be your friend, but we won't be doing any more double dates." I told him that was fair, and that on future double dates I would find another girl. He was pleased with that. We compromised, and everyone went away happy.

CHAPTER 15
MY FIRST AND LAST YACHT

For my birthday one summer, my dad went out and bought me a boat with an outboard motor and a trailer. Seems like a nice enough gesture, but it was done for the wrong reasons. First, I didn't even want a boat, but he did. He disguised it to make it look like it was for me when all along it really was for him. This three-piece ensemble was not new equipment. One of his colleagues got transferred out of state and didn't want to haul the boat with him, so he sold it to my dad. It looked like someone salvaged a lifeboat from the *Titanic* after sitting at the bottom of the ocean for the past 50 years. My dad backed this dilapidated stack of kindling wood into the garage and said, "Let's get to work and refinish it." We turned the boat upside down, and with fiberglass and epoxy, we resurfaced the bottom of the boat hoping that would plug up enough holes to make it seaworthy. While Dad went to work each day, I was in the garage sanding six hours a day for the following week.

My 16th birthday present looked a lot like this

Pete showed up one day and asked, "Where have you been? I haven't seen you for the past eight days." I invited him into the garage to show him my birthday present. He laughed uncontrollably and then asked, "What on earth is this pile of shit?" Sheepishly, I explained to him what it was, ordered him to quit laughing, grab a sheet of sandpaper, and get to work. An hour later he was gone — he didn't want any part of it. I didn't either. Days turned into weeks, and weeks turned into months. It ruined my summer vacation, and I hated that boat from the get-go.

Finally, the day came when we would launch that tub of crap into Carter Lake for a test run. Dad told me to take it for a spin. However, he had installed the steering wheel backwards. When the boat was supposed to go left, it would go right, and vice versa. I took the boat out to the middle of the lake, then headed back to the dock. The boat responded to the way it was hooked up but did not respond to the way the driver would intuitively steer. I ended up smashing the bow into the dock, causing some minor damage. I thought my dad would lose his mind, but surprisingly he remained very calm, and did not say a word to me. That was a first! He recognized there was no denying it was his fault for rigging the steering column incorrectly. I was off the hook.

There were other problems. My dad intended for this to be a boat for water skiing. To pull a skier, it needed at least a 35-50 HP engine. All we had was 25 HP. That was about enough power to open a can of soup. You couldn't pull a turd out of the water let alone a 160-pound man.

For some reason, my father took great pleasure in grounding me for extended periods of time. I honestly think he would lay in bed at night and think up ways to impose a new punishment just about the time I was to get released from the prior incarceration.

One day, the two of us were working together restoring that stupid boat. We had just completed refinishing the deck. Dad said, "What do you think?"

I said, "Gee, that sure looks pretty."

He exploded and yelled, "You're grounded for the next two weeks. Come straight home from school. Stay in your room. No friends allowed, and no phone privileges. Do you understand me?"

"Yes sir," I said, "But what did I do wrong that got you so upset?"

He replied, "You said 'Gee,' and that is short for Jesus, and that is taking The Lord's name in vain. That is why you are grounded."

I just shook my head and said, "Okay. Have it your way." But I was really thinking, "Dad, I think you are running out of reasons for grounding me, and now you are just making up shit."

At any rate, I was grounded again for the umpty-umpth time. One Sunday afternoon, my father decided to take the whole family out for some entertainment to an outdoor event. I wasn't invited because I was grounded. After they all left, I thought this would be a fantastic opportunity to make some phone calls and get caught up with all my friends. I poured myself a coke, lit up one of my dad's cigarettes, threw my feet up on the kitchen table, and started dialing. Meanwhile, my dad had forgotten his wallet and doubled back to the house to get it. When he walked in and saw me sitting in the "executive position," I thought he was going to have a heart attack. I'm sure his blood pressure spiked, so I waited until it dropped low enough for him to be able to speak.

The first words out of his mouth were, "Your punishment has been extended from two weeks to four weeks." No big deal. I was expecting that.

What I wanted to say was, "Hey Dad, it is obvious that you are upset. Why don't you sit down and have a cigarette with me and relax? After all, I have your favorite brand sitting right here, and this will give us the opportunity to have one of those loving father/son conversations that is way overdue."

Meanwhile, Pete was getting rather irritated. He wanted to do things with his old buddy Dolb, but his old buddy Dolb was never available because he was always grounded. Since I was not allowed visitors, Pete would sneak up to my house at night and crawl into my bedroom through the window. We would visit for a while, and then he would leave the same way he came in. One evening my mother came in my room. She told me Pete's mother was on the phone and was looking for him. Pete was halfway out the window when he waved to my mother and said, "Oh hello, Mrs Dolby. Tell her I'm on the way and will be there in five minutes." For years, my mom joked that she only knew Pete from his back side.

Pete's dad had a Lincoln Continental about the size of an aircraft carrier, and Pete asked him if he could borrow it for the senior prom. Surprisingly, his dad said, "Yes." Even more surprising, I wasn't grounded at the time, and that meant I could go as well. We decided to double date.

Having secured decent transportation, our next step was to get the tuxedos. Pete was an impeccable dresser, probably the best dressed man on campus. So, when it came time for tuxedo shopping, we agreed to let Pete be in charge. We were on a budget, and Pete found the cheapest rental shop in town. The selection was slim, but that was okay because in his mind, he found the best-looking tuxes on the planet. He chose a plaid metallic blue one for himself and a paisley metallic blue one for me.

I looked at them and gasped, "You have got to be kidding. These are so ugly they won't let us on the dance floor." We went around and around, and finally I caved in, reluctantly agreeing that he was the fashion expert, and I should trust his judgement. As it turned out, I was right, and Pete was wrong. We went to pick up our girlfriends, and they were mortified, so much so, they both wanted to cancel the date. We convinced them to go, but they let us know that they were never so embarrassed in all their lives. By the way, neither of us got lucky that night.

I was graduating from high school in June of 1963. We had lived in Omaha for nearly five years, and that was a long time by military standards. I sensed that a move was forthcoming.

That time arrived sooner than expected. At dinner one evening, my father announced that we would be moving back to California the day school let out. Even though I knew it was coming, I was greatly saddened by the thought of having to say goodbye to all my friends. However, this was the life I was accustomed to, and I accepted the new challenge without question. You don't have to like it. You just do it!

So, our family of nine started to pack suitcases as we prepared to leave Omaha and head west. We had a Ford station wagon that would pull the stupid boat, and we had a Chevrolet Corvair. My dad told me to sell my car as he needed me to drive the Corvair while he drove the Ford. I wasn't happy about that, but I sold the car in a day for more than I paid for it. And, for some reason I don't recall, Bill would be staying behind in Omaha for the time being.

We stayed in the Bachelor Officers Quarters at Offutt Air Force Base our last night. Five of my buddies drove out to say their good-byes to me, and we sat in the car talking until the wee hours of the morning. It was a sad evening.

My parents' contribution to the Baby Boom generation:

Front (left to right): Cindy, Mark, Kit, Chris
Back (left to right): me, Sue and Bill

CHAPTER 16
MOUNT VESUVIUS

The next day the caravan moved out on dawn patrol heading west. I had the pleasure of seeing 500 miles of corn out my windshield and 500 miles of corn through my rear-view mirror. That was ten hours of pure excitement. We went through Colorado, New Mexico, Arizona, and into Southern California, arriving at our destination on June 20, 1963. My dad would be stationed at March Air Force Base, and our new home was in Riverside, just ten miles away.

About a month later, my brother Bill showed up. He had purchased a 1954 Pontiac Chieftain convertible and drove out on his own. The next day, we decided to check out our new campus. I would be entering college in the fall along with the first wave of Baby Boomers.

Originally, I pictured myself entering the University of Nebraska with all my friends from high school. This was a big sprawling campus with one of the most powerful college football teams in the nation.

Unfortunately, with my dad's transfer and no money for college, my dreams would have to be modified to whatever Riverside, California had to offer. When I saw the campus, it was like someone hit me in the gut. It was not a big university, but a small junior college, not that there was anything wrong with that. It just wasn't what I was expecting. At the time, the campus consisted of a courtyard surrounded by one building on each side, and it occupied perhaps a city block or less. They had a football team, but no football field and no stadium. However, the local high school was across the street, and the college used their facilities. I decided to suck it up and give it my best shot.

So, I went out for football and made the team. The problem was that I only weighed 165 pounds. You can get away with that in high school, but if you are a lineman in college, you better come up with an extra 100 pounds if you want to survive. At practice, I was getting thrown around like a rag doll and realized that perhaps I bit off more than I could chew. One day we held a scrimmage that was quite demanding. A play was called, and someone accidentally kicked me in the side of the face. That didn't bother me much since that is what football is all about. Those things happen. But what did bother me was spitting blood and pieces of a tooth. The impact of the blow shattered one of my molars. That night I had to do some real soul searching and evaluate if playing football was a wise thing to continue doing. Sadly, with a heavy heart, I turned in my gear the next day. The coach tried to convince me to stay, but I was committed to my decision.

Once football was behind me, I got a job after school at a local grocery store working about 20 hours a week. I tried to bank every penny I made since I desperately needed a car. At school, I met an Air Force veteran that had the most beautiful 1958 Chevy Impala convertible. He was willing to sell it for $500, and I had plenty of money saved to buy it. I considered it to be the deal of the century.

About the time I was ready to make the purchase, my brother Bill pulled another one of his "Good-news, bad-news, shenanigans." He went out on a date. He and the girl had both been drinking, and he rolled his car. Nobody was hurt, but the car was totaled. That was the bad news. The good news was his date just so happened to be the daughter of the chief of police. They could have gotten arrested for drinking and driving; however, the chief didn't want the publicity, and swept everything under the rug. Case was closed.

Then there was more bad news. I approached my father and told him about the car I wanted to purchase. He was so upset with Bill he said, "No more cars. Request denied."

I said, "Dad, let me get this straight. First, you make me sell my car in Omaha so that I would be available to drive your car to California. Second, Bill wrecks his car, and now I have to suffer the consequences?"

"Yes," he said, "There will be no more cars in this household." — another conversation that defied the laws of logic!

On my 18th birthday in August 1963, I was required to register with the Selective Service Board (military draft board). There were three possible classifications. The first was I-A (available for military service). The second was II-S (student deferment) for those going to college. And, the third was IV-F (those not qualified for military service usually due to a physical disability). I bounced back and forth between I-A and II-S until I finally got nailed. The Vietnam War, which began in November 1955, was really starting to heat up by 1963 so I figured it was only a matter of time before I was called in.

Then in November, President John F. Kennedy was assassinated, and Vice President Lyndon B. Johnson was sworn into office as the 36th President of the United States. So, 1963 was turning out to be a significant year of change, including my move to Riverside.

Things got off to a bad start on the move. I wasn't playing sports. I had no car. I wasn't making friends the way I was accustomed to doing, and I missed Nebraska. My relationship with my father was going downhill like an elevator with a snapped cable. Our home in Riverside was like the city of Pompeii, Italy. The volcano, Mt. Vesuvius, that overshadowed the ancient city laid dormant for centuries, suggesting tranquility on the surface. However, seismic activity below told a different story. It was only a matter of time before the lid blew. Then, one Sunday morning in March 1964, the explosion took place.

As a family, we had just come home from church. My father was standing in the kitchen cooking a breakfast of fried mush with maple syrup. "Are you kidding me? Where in the hell did he come up with this recipe?" I thought to myself. This stuff tasted like supreme allied cosmic hammered dog shit.

I voiced my opinion in a very undiplomatic manner. This led to a screaming match between my dad and me. Vesuvius blew, and I was ordered to move out of the house by sundown. I marched to my room and started packing. In the meantime, my mother must have had a serious talk with my dad because an hour later, he came into my room and said that I didn't have to move after all, and I was welcome to stay.

In a calm voice, as I was packing, I looked up at him and said, "Thank you, but I think the time has come for us to split the sheets. If I stay, it is only a matter of time before I kill you, or you kill me."

The next day, Monday, I went to the bank and withdrew all my money. I went to Riverside Junior College and withdrew from school. Then I went to the train station and purchased a ticket on the Union Pacific railroad for the 12:05 to Omaha, the only home I really ever knew.

CHAPTER 17
WEDDING BELLS BUT NO FRONT TEETH

The train trip took three days, and I arrived in Omaha about 8 p.m. Wednesday evening. I knew Pete was away at school in Lincoln, Nebraska so I called his parents in Omaha. Fortunately, they were home, and Pete's dad drove down to the station to pick me up.

I explained to them about the mishaps in California. They invited me to spend the night with them but made it clear that they wanted me out as soon as possible. When Pete heard I was in town, he came back to Omaha to spend the weekend with me.

Pete's dad had recently purchased a case of beer and stored it in the basement. After his parents went to bed, Pete and I went downstairs and enjoyed the inventory. We drank the beer and pissed in the floor drain in the laundry room. This went on until the beer was gone. The next morning Pete's dad made the discovery and lost his mind. He ordered Pete to get his ass back to Lincoln and ordered me to get the hell out as well. I had just been kicked out of two houses in less than a week.

Fortunately, I found a place the very next day. It was in an old three-story Victorian house downtown at the corner of 36th and Douglas Streets. Actually, it was the third-floor attic that had been converted into a small apartment. It was furnished, cost only $60 per month, and served my needs for the time being.

I got a job driving a delivery truck, but it only paid minimum wage. So, I started looking for something that would be a little more lucrative. Shortly thereafter, I ran into Becky, one of my old classmates from high school and told her about my situation. She talked to her dad, and between the two of them, they got me a job in the overhaul yard for the Union Pacific Railroad rebuilding diesel engines.

In the Spring of 1964, Pete came home for a week-end get-together and told me that he had fallen in love with a girl at school. He announced they would get married shortly, and I was to be his best man. I was wondering if we should go back and rent the same tuxedos we wore to the senior prom the previous year?

I decided to throw Pete a bachelor party in my attic apartment and invited several of our old high school buddies over for some fun and games. Legal drinking age was 21, and all of us were only 18. We pooled our money together and found someone to buy beer for us in exchange for a six-pack for himself. Someone in the group discovered I had a set of steak knives in the kitchen and suggested that we use them for a game of darts. The knives would be the darts, and the living room wall would be the target. So, we drank beer and played darts until we ran out of beer. It was time to call it an evening. We looked over at Pete and noticed that he was drunker than a three-legged billy goat. We called for a taxi. Tim Green grabbed one arm, I grabbed the other, and we walked him down to the street. Just as we were about to put him in the cab, he got a sudden burst of energy and literally threw Tim and me off simultaneously. Pete then walked up to the cab driver and yelled, "Slide over, I'm driving."

The cab driver was in shock as total fear electrified his body. Tim and I picked ourselves up off the ground and ran over to save the cabby. We grabbed Pete and threw him in the back seat, paid the driver, gave him the address, and wished him good luck.

(One detail I need to add about Pete — when he was about 11 years old, he lost his two front teeth when another player accidentally hit him in the mouth with a bat during a baseball game. From then on, he had two false teeth.)

The taxi driver dropped Pete off. His mother was waiting for him at the front door. She marched him into the living room where they sat down for a little fireside chat. Pete's mom reminded him he was getting married the next day, and he would be held accountable for his actions. Pete patiently listened to her as she explained the virtues of responsibility associated with marriage. Pete said, "Hold that thought, Mom. I think I'm going to be sick. I will be right back." Then he made a beeline for the bathroom.

He hugged the porcelain throne much like he had hugged the hood of my car at the drive-in movies the year before. He barfed like it was a contest at the state fair, and he was bound and determined to win the blue ribbon. When it was all over, and he had cleaned himself up, he rejoined his mother in the living room. As they continued their discussion, Pete's mom asked, "Pete, where are your front teeth?" Pete replied, "Right here," as he went to touch his teeth. Unfortunately, the only thing that remained was a hole where the teeth had been. At that point, he realized he had just flushed his teeth down the toilet, and he was supposed to get married the next day. Uh-oh. I feel a red neck wedding comin' on!

Fortunately, Pete had a spare set of uncomfortable and ill-fitting teeth, but the wedding was beautiful, and everyone was able to deliver a full mouth smile for the photo shoot. Leave it to Pete to land on his feet.

With the wedding over, Pete and his new wife disappeared. The taxi driver disappeared. My friends disappeared, and I was all alone, but not for long! All-of-a-sudden, who showed up at my door? My dad! He had to return to Offutt Air Force Base for a meeting and decided to pay me a visit. I invited him into my apartment, forgetting that I had eight steak knives in the wall, 24 empty beer cans spilling out of the trash, and me, an under-age drinker. He never said a word. And, he actually spent the night at my apartment. I can't remember what we talked about, but the meeting was pleasant, and he must have made me feel that I was welcome to come home. I committed to nothing, and we said our good-byes.

CHAPTER 18
SWIMMING FASTER THAN A ROCK

A week later, Omaha got hit with a rainstorm that made the Biblical flood Noah and his Ark endured look like a wading pool. It washed the rails out south of town, and Union Pacific was forced to lay off hundreds of workers. I was low man on the totem pole, so I was the first to be let go.

I did a lot of soul searching and decided it would be wise to return to Riverside Junior College, knuckle down, get my grades up, and use that as a springboard to get out of there. Since I was unemployed with no prospects left in Omaha, I headed west.

With my attitude adjustment, the second time around in Riverside turned out to be fantastic. I signed up for 15 units at school and made the dean's list, placing me in the top four percent of the student body population academically. I joined a local fraternity and had more friends than I knew what to do with. These great guys turned out to be lifelong friends that I keep in touch with to this day. I was genuinely happy, and for some reason, my dad and I were getting along in a non-combative way. I was out of the hot seat for a change.

Front (left to right): four of my best friends and me
Tad Thaber, Phil Von Rems, Mark Duff, me and Mick Rose

Unfortunately, the hot seat was now occupied by my brother, Bill. He met a girl that moved to Southern California from Australia. They fell in love and decided to get married. My father was opposed to the marriage for reasons only he would know. At any rate, he gave an order stating that anyone of our family members that went to the wedding would not be allowed back in the house ever again.

Even my mother, who was always submissive to my father's demands, scoffed at this one. Except for my dad, the entire family attended the wedding. "Hey Dad," I thought, "Enjoy living in an empty house all by yourself." Of course, that never happened, but he did mope around the house for several days knowing that his authority had been compromised.

It was at this time I began to see and understand one of my dad's character flaws. Whenever anyone was about to experience a joyous event in their life (and Dad was not the center of attention), he was bound and determined to spoil it for them with the most dramatic strategy his mind could conceive. He did it with my mother, his children, and his grandkids. That gave him three generations of lives to emotionally upset at one time or another, and he never missed a cue. Each time it was very hurtful to the one that was about to take center stage. This sort of behavior continued until the day he died at age 95. Just prior to his death, he indicated that he was aware of these wrongful acts and was afraid to die for fear of the retribution that was waiting on the other side.

Bill purchased a 1960 Mercury Comet, and he and his new bride moved to their apartment in Pomona, California. He enrolled at Cal Poly University and got a part-time job. Marriage seemed to make Bill more responsible and helped him set goals for the future. He and his new wife were very compatible, and Bill's siblings were happy to welcome her into the family.

With Bill gone, I had the bedroom all to myself, but this came with a high price. I was back in the hot seat, and I had to deal with the brunt of the storms all by myself.

When I was back in Omaha the second time, I befriended a guy named J.P. Kirkpatrick. He mentioned that he would be moving to Los

Angeles soon, and I told him I would be returning to Riverside. We agreed to get together once our moves were complete.

With both of us now in Southern California, J.P. called and suggested that we get together and take an overnight trip up into the San Bernardino mountains. The plan was for him to drive to my house and pick me up on Saturday at 10 a.m. My father agreed to let me go as long as I got all my week-end chores done first.

I was working in the back yard desperately trying to wrap everything up before J.P. showed up. Ten o'clock came and went, but no J.P. I thought, "Okay, he is running a little late, so I will keep working until he gets here." Eleven o'clock came and went. Then, twelve o'clock. No J.P. Now I was getting tired, hungry, and angry. I took a break and walked around to the front of the house to get a drink of water and saw J.P. in the front yard with a shovel in his hand and my dad giving him orders on a landscaping project. Finally, my father released the two of us to go on our trip. As we drove off, J.P. said, "Who the hell is that guy?" I replied, "That is my dad." J.P. said, "I've been standing in your front yard for the past two hours doing yardwork with your dad. He didn't even introduce himself. He just handed me a shovel and put me to work."

The only thing I could think of saying was, "Welcome to my world."

We had been driving for about an hour when J.P. said, "My father died when I was ten years old, and I always wondered what it would be like to have a dad. However, after meeting yours, I DON'T WANT ONE!" Believe me. I understood.

With the fall semester well underway at Riverside Junior College, one of my fraternity brothers, Mick Rose, suggested we join the college swim team. Mick had been swimming competitively for several years and was a very good athlete. I said I didn't think that was a very good idea because I was 19 years old, and most kids start their swimming career at about 12-14 years of age.

Mick said, "You will do fine. The coach will recognize that you are new at this, so he will probably only stick you with the 50-meter freestyle." Mick was also a very good salesman and convinced me that this was the right thing to do. I drank the Kool-Aid and joined the team.

Riverside Junior College Swim Team
me in front and center and Mick Rose back, second from right

During the first swim meet, the coach was giving assignments to the swimmers. "Murphy, 100-meter backstroke. Reynolds, 50-meter freestyle. Rose, 200-meter butterfly. Dolby, 500-meter freestyle."

"What? 500-meter freestyle? Nobody wants that event. That's 20 lengths of the pool. I don't know if I can swim that far, let alone, do it competitively." Believe me, I was no Mark Spitz or Michael Phelps, but I stuck with it the whole season and even placed in a couple events. It was great to be part of a sports team again, and we had a lot of fun.

As 1964 came to an end, so did the Baby Boom Era. On December 31, 1964, the last Boomer took its first breath at 11:59 p.m., and the United States had 76 million young human beings that would collectively carry the nation into the future.

It was during that time that I met a great friend named Mark Duff. Mark wanted out of Riverside as much as I did. Together, we systematically scouted out colleges and got jobs to finance our next phase of education.

After researching colleges for a year, I decided that I wanted to go to Arizona State University in Tempe. Mark agreed, saying, "Count me in." We applied and were accepted. In August, Mark's father drove us the ASU campus, and we were off on a new adventure.

CHAPTER 19
MISS AMERICA

Shortly after my arrival in Tempe, I was also faced with a new challenge. When I applied to Arizona State University, I misinterpreted the cost and later discovered that I would be on the hook for an additional $1,000 per semester for out-of-state tuition since I was not a resident of Arizona. I was already strapped for cash, and this really set me back on my keister.

Mark chose to pledge Sigma Chi fraternity, and I chose Phi Delta Theta. So, once we arrived at the campus, we moved in different circles, but kept in touch as best we could.

Phi Delta Theta house at Arizona State
with me on the right

Phi Delta Theta was a wonderful fraternity that attracted a high-quality group of guys. We lived in the fraternity house, and I was lucky to get a roommate that was one of the funniest and most enjoyable guys I have ever met. Cliff Rifkin and I became friends instantly. Arizona State required every male student to take two semesters of Reserve Officer Training Corp (ROTC). We had two choices: Army or Air Force. Since both of our dads were in the Air Force, that is what Cliff and I chose. Every Monday morning, we would dress in our uniforms and head down to the parade field for close order drill. I am glad we did it, and it made us feel very patriotic which, in fact, we were. Pledging a fraternity had its challenges. Hazing and harassment were a way of life.

Me and Cliff Rifkin

But that was part of the game, and we were okay with it. The roughest spot was during hell week, the final week of being a pledge.

Each fraternity had a house mother. Usually, she was a widow about 70 years old. The fraternity provided her with an apartment, and her job was to provide law and order in the fraternity house and teach us manners and etiquette. Our house mother was Mrs Safford, and she was about as sweet as she could be — a real mother figure. If you were feeling lonely or homesick, you could knock on her door, and she would invite you in for a mother/son conversation. You would always leave feeling more confident about life in general.

We always dressed for dinner in a suit, dress shirt, and tie. We sat at a big rectangular table. Each night, two pledges were required to escort Mrs Safford to the head table. We said grace, and table manners were strictly enforced. At the end of the meal, the two pledges would escort Mrs Safford back to her apartment, and the evening would go downhill from there with fraternal bullshit that made no sense, but always ended up being the best part of the evening. We performed skits and did things that probably should have been against the law, but our antics were all in good fun. When I went home to visit my mom, she could not believe what a polite gentleman I had become, and I was grateful for the training I received. Too often, fraternities get bad publicity that they justifiably deserve. However, they seldom get recognition for the community services they perform and the character building they instill within their brotherhood.

As a fraternity, we also got to participate in some very memorable events. During the 1965—66 school year, our fraternity was asked to provide escorts for the Miss Arizona Pageant held at the Phoenix Country Club. The current Miss America at the time, Vonda Kay Van Dyke, was from Arizona, so she was in attendance as well. We had an opportunity to meet one another, and she was a charming and gracious person.

Miss America 1965, Vonda Kay Van Dyke, and me

In the spring of 1966, I was be-boppin' my way to class, minding my own business, when I walked by the Navy recruiters that had a booth set up on campus. They motioned me over to their table, and I had every reason to listen to what they had to say. The Selective Service Board had reclassified my status from II-S to I-A again for the umpty-umpth time. As the war in Vietnam was escalating, it seemed as though it did not make any difference if you were in school or not. As long as you could fog up a mirror, that was good enough for them. A lot of my buddies were getting drafted, and I figured it was only a matter of time before they got me.

What the Navy was offering me was an opportunity to join their Aviation Reserve Officer Candidate (AVROC) program. It sounded very interesting and the idea of becoming a Navy pilot was intriguing. The next thing I knew, I was reporting to Los Alamitos Naval Air Station in Southern California for testing and a physical examination. It seemed like I took eight hours of written exams, one after another. When it was all over, the staff said I passed and asked if I would like to sign up for the program. I said, "Yes," and they marched me down to the flight surgeon's office for a physical. Everything was going fine until we got to the eye examination. As we were going through the eye exam, the doctor was getting very frustrated with me. Finally, he said, "Hey kid, do you ever see double?"

I said, "Oh yeah, all the time."

He lost his mind, and yelled, "You are out of here. You can't take a million-dollar airplane and expect to land it on two aircraft carriers. Now go home."

I was walking down the hallway with my tail between my legs when two recruiters came running after me. When I told them about the dismissal, they immediately went into action. They were on a different agenda. Their job was to get bodies, and they got mine. The flight surgeon is now their enemy. The recruiters grabbed me, one by each arm, and marched me back to the flight surgeon's office. We all convened in the doctor's office, and the negotiations started. Actually, it was more like a full-blown screaming match between the doc and the recruiters. When it was all over, the flight surgeon won, and out the door I went for a second time. So much for a career with the Navy.

Shortly thereafter, the school year ended, and I returned to Riverside for the summer. By this time, I realized that going to Arizona State was a mistake. I loved it there, and I really enjoyed my fraternity brothers, but financially, I just could not afford it. So, I decided to transfer to UCLA and avoid having to pay any further out-of-state tuition. My application was accepted, and I was planning to enter school there in the fall.

CHAPTER 20
SAILING WITH JOE

My buddy, Mark Duff, returned to Riverside with me. He would not be returning to Arizona State for the same reason as me. We got summer jobs back at March Air Force Base, working construction on the flight line. Riverside was hot. It would get between 100 and 110 degrees every day. But on the flight line, it would get between 120 and 140. Therefore, we would report to work in the dark at 4 a.m. to beat the heat, and end our day about 2 p.m.

As I returned to Riverside for the summer of 1966, my father returned from Vietnam. This was a reunion worth mentioning. He brought presents for everyone. My brother Chris was the big winner. Dad bought him a Honda Trail 90 motorbike, so now he had transportation. Dad had custom-made rings with birthstones for my mom and all the girls — very nice as well. Bill got nothing because my dad was still pissed off about the wedding the previous year. He presented me with a wallet made of elephant hide. This hide was stiffer than King Kong's dick. I could not bend it, and therefore, I could not stick it in my pocket. I tried saddle soap, Lexsol, and everything else short of Crisco, but this thing would not fold. Finally, I threw it in the trash.

By now, I was dating a girl that lived 50 miles away. We had been seeing each other off and on for about a year, and we frequently got together on the weekends. Her father, Joe, and I got along well, and we would go sailing in Joe's boat from the Balboa Bay Club on the Pacific Coast. Sometimes, I would travel down to see her and end up spending the entire weekend with him on a sailing trip to Catalina Island. He owned a 27-foot Islander Bahama sailboat that was equipped with everything we needed including kitchen, bath, and bunks to accommodate up to four people. Joe was a real father figure. He gave me good advice and taught me how to sail and appreciate Budweiser beer.

Me on Joe's sailboat

Meanwhile, shortly after my dad's return from Vietnam, he received orders to report for duty at Vandenburg Air Force Base just outside Santa Maria, California. Vandenberg was located on the coast about 150 miles north of Los Angeles. I stayed behind to work my construction job and prepare for my fall entry into UCLA.

As the war continued to escalate, my college buddies from Riverside Junior College were getting picked up by the military right and left. To the best of my knowledge, the Marines always relied on volunteers. However, during the Vietnam War, so many troops were needed that young men were being drafted into both the Army and the Marines. As the summer came to an end, John joined the Army, Bob the Marines, Mark was recently notified to report for his physical examination, and I drove to Los Angeles to begin my new life. Since I was already a member of Phi Delta Theta, I asked if they had a room available for me. They did, and I moved into the fraternity house located on the UCLA campus.

CHAPTER 21
DRAFT BOARD CLOSING IN

The fraternity house at UCLA was a turn-of-the-century three-level home designed to accommodate four guys to a room. It was impossible to ignore the posted signs saying, "Keep your door closed to avoid a DRAFT." Obviously, everyone was beginning to feel the pressure that was brewing in Southeast Asia. My bedroom had two sets of bunk beds, and I shared the room with Curt, Gene, and Tom. One day, I came home after school and noticed that the mattress on one of the beds had been stripped down and rolled up. I asked Gene what happened to Curt. "He got drafted," came the reply. Two weeks later, I came home and noticed that a second mattress was rolled up. "Hey Gene, what happened to Tom?"

Gene replied, "He got drafted. We've got the room all to ourselves." We didn't realize it at the time, but that room would soon be empty. I guess we should have kept the door closed. Truly, at that time, all of us felt we were standing in the "lobby of life" and never really checked in. The future of college-age males was unknown.

Meanwhile, my fraternity brother and close friend from Riverside Junior College, Phil Von Rems, got married and moved to Beverly Hills, not too far from the UCLA campus where I lived. He took a job with Yellow Freight Lines. We reconnected at a time when I was really hurting for cash. Phil got me a job working the swing shift loading freight into semi-trucks. I did not have a car, so he drove over and picked me up and took me to work with him. I loaded trucks on Friday nights, and that gave me enough spending money to make it from one week to the next. I will be eternally grateful for Phil's help.

About that time, I received notification to report to the Selective Service Board (the draft board). They wanted to get to know me a little better. Specifically, they wanted to gather information on two parts of my anatomy: my brain and my asshole. My initial thought was, "The difference in the two may be imperceptible."

I arrived at a military facility in downtown Los Angeles along with about 50 other guys. First, they gave us a series of written examinations, the brain part. Then they marched us into a gymnasium where we lined up against all four walls. The command was given to do an about-face. So, all of us were now facing the walls. The next order was to drop our britches, bend over, and with both hands, spread our cheeks. Obviously, this was the asshole part of the screening. After the medical doctor examined us for what I thought was either hemorrhoids or brain tumors, he let us go. Back I went to campus.

UCLA was on the quarter system, and that meant 12 weeks of classes followed by a break. I had just finished my first quarter, and I had about a three-week recess, so I went up to Santa Maria where my parents lived to pay them a visit. As usual, I was broke. However, I quickly found a job with a construction company that paid top dollar. They were willing to take me on as a delivery driver during that three-week period, giving me some financial relief. After the three weeks were up, I picked up my final paycheck, thanked them for the opportunity, and left. They said they really needed me and asked if I would consider staying on. I told them I could not because I had to get back to school. They understood. We shook hands and we said our good-byes.

When I got back to my parents' house that Friday evening, my mom told me that I had received a piece of mail. My initial reaction was, "Who would send me mail at their address since I didn't live there?" The letter was from the Selective Service Board, and it read, "Congratulations, you have just been inducted into the United States Army. Report to the Riverside Induction Station, January 3, 1967. Have a Merry Christmas." I thought to myself, "Well, I'll be dipped in dog shit."

The following Monday I drove down to UCLA and announced that I had been drafted and needed to cancel the next semester's classes I had registered for. The school was very understanding and honored my request. I drove back to Santa Maria and got ready to enter the Army. The next day I received another letter from the Selective Service Board saying, "Due to the fact you are in college, your draft has been postponed until further notice."

I jumped into my car and drove back to UCLA. I explained that my draft status had been reversed and begged them to give me my classes back. Sympathetically, they told me they had given all my positions away, and all my classes were full. I was put on a waiting list to get back into my classes. However, each class had a waiting list so long I didn't have a snowball's chance in hell of getting in. I was screwed!

I drove back to Santa Maria and told my folks what had just happened. Trying to maintain a good attitude, I went back to the construction company and asked for my old job back. I figured I could work for the next few months, save some cash, and return to school in style. The construction company crew was happy to see me, but they had just hired my replacement as they needed to fill that position right away. There were no other job openings available. Screwed again.

Obviously Plan A to get my classes back at UCLA did not work. Plan B to get my job back did not work either. So, I went back to the drawing board to map out Plan C which consisted of me getting more information from the draft board to find out what their intentions were with regard to me and my future. During a phone conversation, they told me that because I was in college, they were going to let me finish this quarter. Then, they would draft me in the spring. I told them it was too late to get back in school because I dropped all my classes when they sent me my first draft notice. Since I was no longer in school, and they were going to re-draft me in about three months anyway, I said I would honor their first draft notice and go in right away. My thought was, "Let's just get this over with."

The draft board responded by saying that I could not go in right away because the draft quota was now full. I thought, "Are you guys shittin' me? First, because of you, I can't get back in school. Second, because of you, I can't get my old job back. And third, you won't let me in the Army because the draft had reached its quota. What am I supposed to do now, stand on the street corner scratching my ass?" I was screwed three times over.

During my phone conversation, the lady at the draft board said, "You could just volunteer for the draft, and they will pick you up on the next wave. Do you want to do that?" I said, "Yes. As of this moment, I am officially volunteering for the draft." She said, "It's done."

I waited for four weeks. Finally, I received a letter with instructions to report to the Riverside Selective Service Board on February 7, 1967 at 9 a.m. My dad drove me down to the Greyhound station about 5 a.m. to catch the bus from Santa Maria to Riverside. It was cold, dark, and windy. The bus station wasn't open yet, so my dad dropped me off at the curb and told me to wait for the bus. The bus ride was uneventful, and we arrived in Riverside about 8 a.m. I was greeted by about 50 other scared guys wandering aimlessly in the parking lot waiting for instructions on what to do next. We were loaded up on a couple Greyhounds, and I think one of them was the same bus I had just arrived on. We headed north on the same freeway and stopped in Santa Maria for lunch at Denny's. By now it was about 12:30 p.m., and I was right back where I started from earlier in the day. From there, we continued north to our Army induction station at Fort Ord, just outside of Monterey, California.

CHAPTER 22
WELCOME TO THE ARMY… WE'VE BEEN EXPECTING YOU

Now the fun began. As we stepped off the bus, we were greeted by a half-dozen drill sergeants in their Smokey the Bear hats. They were in our faces screaming and hollering hard and loud enough to break their own blood vessels.

First, they marched us into the barber and cut off all our hair. There would be no forward combed boogies coming out of that shop. The next thing they wanted was to inspect our assholes as if much had changed since they did that two months earlier. I wondered if they were checking to see if we grew hemorrhoids in the meantime, or if they just liked looking at assholes. Perhaps they just wanted to make sure we brought our assholes with us, or if we left them at home for safe keeping.

They gave us all new uniforms including socks and underwear. We bundled up the clothing we arrived in and sent it back to our mothers. We wouldn't be needing that stuff for a long time.

I was assigned to B-1-1, (Bravo Company, 1st Battalion, 1st Brigade). There were 184 of us. That makes four platoons of 46 troops each and four rooms in the barracks to house one platoon per room. By the time we got to bed, we were exhausted, but trying to sleep with 46 strangers in the same room, snoring, burping, farting, and crying made things a bit testy among the crowd. By the second night, we were exhausted and considered this to be our new home, and we all slept like babies.

Within our newly formed group of happy campers, five of us would be chosen to fulfill key positions within our ranks — kind of like a student council in high school. Jethro Pugh of the Dallas Cowboys was in our group. He was the biggest man I had ever seen. He looked like the Empire State Building in combat boots. The cadre immediately chose him as our internal platoon leader. It didn't take much to figure that one out. Then we needed four squad leaders. One would be A.D. Whitfield, Jr. and another was Brigman Owens, both from the Washington Redskins. The final positions were filled by two guys from the National Guard that were called into active duty.

First row (center to right): Jethro Pugh, A. D. Whitfield, and Brigman Owens
Fourth row, second from right: me

When the bugle blew at 4 a.m., we didn't have one second to think about it. The old Army expression, "Grab your cocks, and put on your socks," told the story. You had less than five minutes to go from a deep sleep, to fully dressed and standing outside in formation. You only had to show up late one time, and you never did it again. After formation, we did calisthenics followed by a one-mile run. By this time, the sun was beginning to break over the foothills, and we marched into the mess hall for breakfast. The food was okay, except on the days they served SOS (shit on a shingle). SOS is a military delicacy consisting of chipped beef on toast with country gravy and green peas. There were always a lot of leftovers on the days SOS was on the menu. One day, I decided to skip breakfast and wait for noon chow. Unfortunately, by lunchtime, I was so hungry I was farting fresh air. I would never skip another meal.

After breakfast, we returned to clean the barracks. Everyone had a job — dusting, mopping, cleaning toilets, etc. I don't do toilets. Period! So, I immediately volunteered to run the electric floor buffer. That became my permanent job in basic training, and I never cleaned a toilet once the entire time I was in the Army.

However, I did perform KP (kitchen police). Every one of us had to do it at least once during boot camp. Instead of getting up at 4 a.m., we had to get up at 2 a.m. and report to the mess hall for food service duty. It was a long day of assisting in the preparation of three meals, to include cooking, serving, washing dishes, and cleaning up after 250 troops.

If the breakfast menu called for eggs, that meant scrambled eggs. At two eggs per person, 500 eggs were needed. I was put in charge of the eggs. I started cracking eggs and did the math as I went along. I figured I could crack an egg once every five seconds. That is 12 eggs a minute. Five hundred eggs divided by 12 eggs per minute suggested that it would take me 42 minutes to crack all those eggs.

I started cracking eggs, and the cooks kept coming up to me saying, "Faster, faster." I went as fast as I could, and it was never good enough, so I came up with a new strategy. I grabbed one egg in each hand, crushed them, and threw the entire egg and shell in the pot. Now I was doing about 50 eggs a minute. Within the next ten minutes, that chore was done.

Later, I was in the serving line, dishing up eggs to the troops as they marched through the chow line. I watched them as they took a seat in the mess hall. Here were all these guys trying to eat scrambled eggs full of eggshells. Anyone who has ever bitten into an eggshell can imagine the sensation. I stood behind the counter enjoying the show.

The military had the ability to find the most god-awful places to establish their bases. As far as Fort Ord went, it had its drawbacks, but it sure beat the hell out of other places for basic training like Fort Bliss in Texas, Fort Polk in Louisiana, and Fort Leonard Wood in Missouri.

However, there were some problems at Fort Ord. We were faced with a spinal meningitis epidemic, and many troops were dying or getting very ill. Another problem was the rain. When it came down, it poured buckets on us. One day at the firing range, noon chow was being served outdoors when we got hit with a real gully washer. As we went through the chow line with our mess kits in one hand and our rifles in the other, the cooks were dishing out globs of crap and throwing them on our meal trays. First came a slab of beef, then a blob of instant mashed potatoes, followed by a scoop of peas. By the time I got to the end of the line, the mashed potatoes had completely dissolved, and the compartment that held the peas filled up with rainwater so fast that the peas all floated off the plate before I could get to them.

Besides health and weather issues, there were emotional issues. Many of the new troops had never been away from home, and when they entered the Army, they brought with them feelings of fear, panic, insecurity, and loneliness. One day, when we were on the rifle range, there were two troops missing. At the end of the day when we returned to the barracks, they were found hanging from a rafter with a note that read, "If I'm going to die, I would rather die here in the United States than in Vietnam." Another day, when we were on the rifle range doing target practice exercises, one troop stood up from his fox hole and placed the butt of his M-14 semi-automatic rifle on the ground and the muzzle in his mouth. A drill sergeant spotted this and went running toward him yelling, "Don't do it." BANG! Too late. He blew his head off. Thankfully, I did not actually see this; however, the cadre immediately held an emergency meeting telling all of us that if we witnessed any unusual behavior within our ranks, to report it immediately.

Prior to going into the military, I drove to the westside of Los Angeles to visit my buddy, J.P. Kirkpatrick, at his sister Barbara's house. Barbara was married to Greg, a Green Beret officer that had just returned from a one-year tour of duty in Vietnam. We sat in the backyard sipping on a beer. I explained that it was only a matter of time before I got called into the military, and when I did go, I hoped to be stationed in Germany. Greg told me that if that was what I wanted, it would be smart to go to Artillery Officer Candidate School (OCS), and that would enhance my chances of being sent to Germany. While I was stationed at Fort Ord, I applied for OCS, but didn't hear a word.

Basic training was exactly what I was expecting. We spent many days at the rifle range, followed by physical training, bayonet practice, forced marches, gas chambers, hand-to-hand combat, and the beat went on. Finally, the big day came. After ten weeks of basic training, we were transformed from civilian, low-life maggots into the finest soldiers America had to offer.

My mother, Aunt Mary, and my girlfriend of two years drove up to Monterey to see me graduate. My father never came, as he was unwilling to acknowledge the fact that I was in the Army. There was to be only one military hero in the household, and that would be him.

We only had an afternoon and early evening together, so we went out to dinner at a restaurant in Monterey. That was the first civilian meal I had eaten in two and a half months. As a private in the Army, my pay grade was E-1 (enlisted soldier of the lowest rank). That amounted to $91 per month. It was enough money to buy toothpaste, shaving cream, and cigarettes. I could not afford to buy dinner that night, but my mother picked up the tab.

I did not get to see my mom, aunt, and girlfriend again the next morning. They went their way, and I went mine. I reported to the airfield tarmac at 0-dark-30 with my duffle bag along with several hundred troops getting ready to ship out to our next assignments. My group was destined for Ft. Lewis, Washington for ten more weeks of Advanced Infantry Training (AIT), and then on to Vietnam as light weapons infantrymen.

I was standing in line getting ready to board an olive-drab DC-3 when a sergeant major walked up to me and said, "Are you Private Dolby?"

"Yes sir," I answered.

He said, "Grab your duffle bag and come with me. You are not going on that plane. You are going on this one over here."

As he pointed to another aircraft parked on the other side of the runway, I said, "Where is that plane going?"

He said, "Fort Sill, Oklahoma. You just got accepted to Artillery, Officer Candidate School." Holy cow. I made it. Not only did I make it, I had just avoided going to Vietnam as a grunt.

CHAPTER 23
OKLAHOMA OR VIETNAM

Fort Sill is home to the United States Army Artillery. It is located next to the city of Lawton, Oklahoma. Lawton is conveniently located 100 miles in the middle of absolutely nowhere. It is hot and humid in the summer and cold in the winter. Regardless of the season, the wind blows relentlessly, non-stop. The saying among the locals is, "If the wind ever stopped blowing, everyone would fall over." As I watched people walking into the wind at a 45-degree angle, it was easy to put a visual on that one.

Instead of infantry AIT, I would spend my next ten weeks in Officer Candidate Prep School. Officer Candidate Prep School was designed to weed out the weak-at-heart. It was actually harder than Officer Candidate School (OCS) that followed, and OCS was an unimaginable bitch.

Me at OCS Prep School

We stepped off the airplane, and the cadre was all over us like stink on shit. It was three times worse than basic training. They rode our asses into the sunset and back again. We did not know whether we were coming or going. This was ten weeks I will never forget. Assuming we made it through OCS Prep School, we were then faced with another half-year of OCS. What was I thinking?

Prep School was filled with a lot of classroom work. We were being trained to work in the Fire Direction Center (FDC) to do mathematical calculations to be sent to the firing batteries instructing them how to adjust their howitzer cannons to meet their targets.

The physical exercise demanded of us coupled with the classroom activity left us exhausted by the end of the day. We ran everywhere we went. Walking was not permitted.

So much happened during that time, it is hard to remember all that we did. One thing I do remember was Wednesday evening beer when we were allowed one beer. Somehow a beer run was made. Nobody had any money, so we got the cheapest beer money could buy. It was called Elkhorn, and I think it was brewed in Texas. A six-pack cost 99 cents. This stuff was probably made from skunk piss, but it tasted like champagne to us. We sat out on the step of the back porch and savored every drop.

Josh Boudron and me clowning around at Prep School

One morning about 3 a.m., we were all sound asleep when the lights came on and a team of cadre marched in, screaming at the top of their lungs. "All you assholes hit the deck. You've got 30 minutes to pack your gear and get on the bus." The tone of their voices told us this was not a social event. Ready to go and on the bus, we were informed that all of us were needed to work in fire direction centers in Vietnam immediately. Officer Candidate School for us was cancelled.

The airport in Lawton was a lonely runway sitting in a field. A nasty olive drab DC-3 was cranking up its two engines eager to take us to destinations unknown. We taxied down the runway, and just about the time we were to take off, the plane came to a screeching halt and the engines shut down. The cadre came to the front of the plane and announced that our orders had been rescinded, and we were to return to the barracks. The second time I was to go to Vietnam had just been cancelled. I thought, "Thank you very much."

By the time I completed Officer Candidate Prep School, I had been in the Army five full months. We were granted one week of leave and told to report back to Fort Sill to begin OCS.

Time went by fast, and it seemed in the blink of an eye, I was on my way back to Fort Sill. After Prep School, I was a bit apprehensive about what I was going to encounter next. I was nervous and wanted to back out, but I reminded myself that OCS was what I signed up for; march on soldier, let's get this done!

A good thing that happened right off the bat was that I got an immediate pay raise. I went from E-1 pay of $91 per month to E-5 pay of $250 per month. That was a pleasant surprise. The other surprises I was about to receive weren't as enjoyable.

OCS was a six-month ordeal. My class had about 400 candidates to begin. Only 198 would graduate. That meant about 50 % would not make the grade. It was my understanding that academically Artillery was the toughest of all the OCSs, probably because of the math that was involved. Of the 202 candidates that did not make it, some flunked out due to grades, some quit, and a few tried to commit suicide.

However, for those of us that hung in there, we had to endure 180 days of challenges. We counted them down one day at a time. And, each day seemed like an eternity. The bugle would blow at precisely 4 a.m. We had exactly five minutes to rise, get dressed, make our beds, and get outside in formation. There was no other option. After command reveille, we would take off on our morning run. I was so tired that I closed my eyes and learned to run in my sleep. The exercise uniform consisted of a t-shirt, red shorts, and combat boots. There would not be any Nikes or Reeboks in this formation. Why would we want to run in tennis shoes when we could be jogging in combat boots? It was a two-mile run, and by the time we made it back to the barracks, it was still pitch dark outside.

Now, we had 30 minutes to shine, shit, shave, and shower plus clean the barracks spotlessly to pass inspection. Mirrors were shined, floors were mopped, toilets were scrubbed, and even the toilet paper had to be folded a certain way. Our fatigue uniforms were laundered, starched, and pressed. Boots were spit-shined as well as our brass belt buckles. When the inspecting officer, known as our TAC officer, showed up, we could not have so much as a hair on our asses out of place. If we did, all hell would break loose. And, all hell did break loose every morning. We could never get it right 100 percent because it was designed that way. If they could not find anything wrong, they would make something up, and we would have to start all over again. In a rage, the TAC officer would rip blankets off the beds, knock uniforms off their racks, toss books and furniture around, screaming and hollering as he went. Just prior to him having a seizure, he would yell for us to get this mess cleaned up. Then he would leave.

After this affectionate interlude, we went back into formation as we marched toward the mess hall for morning chow. The food was incredible — steak, eggs, French toast, pancakes, and more. You could eat as much as you wanted, as long as you ate it all. Each meal was that way. We were burning calories faster than we could take them in, and the Army didn't want us to become emaciated, which was exactly what was happening. When I went into the Army, I weighed 182 pounds and had a 34-inch waist. When I graduated from OCS, I weighed 157 pounds and had a 28-inch waist. During the time my fellow classmates and I were there, we were eating 12 pounds of food per day and losing weight. A bale of hay would have been considered a snack.

Our days were filled with classes or trips to the firing range. Our ultimate goal was to learn how to become forward observers and direct artillery fire to the intended target. But before we did that, we needed to learn how to become cannoneers (nicknamed cannon cockers). So, we practiced being cannon cockers and learned to fire the 105mm and the 155mm howitzer as well as the big 8-inch gun. I never realized how heavy an artillery projectile was until I started loading them into the cannons. That was work, and I gained a whole lot of respect for the crews that manned the guns.

Cannon cockers on a 155mm howitzer, with me front and center

We were exposed to many facets of the Army and learned skills related to logistics, transportation, first aid and medical procedures, communication, weaponry, land survey, map reading, military justice system, leadership, escape and evasion tactics, and more. It was quite a thorough and valuable education. It was my understanding that it cost the Army about $10,000 to produce each Lieutenant. That seemed rather expensive to me back in 1967. Also, it was necessary for each of us to get a top-secret security clearance. From time-to-time, I would receive a letter from a friend or relative saying that the FBI had stopped by their house as they conducted their background check on each one of us. I hate to think what that must have cost.

Our training included escape and evasion tactics. The military was trying to teach us strategies on how to escape should we ever get captured by the enemy and end up in a POW camp. They built a mock POW camp out in the boondocks of Fort Sill. They loaded us into trucks and dropped us off at a checkpoint showing us on a map where the rendezvous point would be at the end of the day.

We heard all sorts of wild stories about this place, and the last thing any of us wanted was to get captured. The worst scenario was that the mock POW camp had three underground escape tunnels. If you chose the correct one, you were home-free. However, the other two were dead-ends and had rattlesnakes in them with their mouths wired shut. Whether that was true or not, I was determined not to get captured and learn about the snakes the hard way.

Within 30 seconds after being dropped off, we were surrounded by soldiers disguised as the enemy. They had guns that shot blanks, and each time they got a bead on one of us, they yelled out that we were captured and to freeze.

One of them jumped out from behind a tree to inform me that I had been caught. But I kept thinking of those tunnels with the snakes. He yelled at me to halt. I yelled back at him, "In a pig's ass," and somersaulted over a barbed-wire fence, running as fast as I could, never looking back. Soon I met up with others that avoided capture. Not sure if we would be ambushed again, we got out our topographical map and tried to plot a course that would get us to the rendezvous point with the least chance of getting caught. The course we chose was the most physically challenging yet gave us the safest opportunity to reach our destination. We made it; thirsty and exhausted, BUT NO RATTLESNAKES. I was glad that day was behind us.

OCS was divided into three segments — green, blue, and red. We attached a different color ribbon to our uniforms depending on what stage of completion we were in. We started with green, and we were referred to as Green Birds for the next two months. Needless to say, we were regarded as being lower than pre-historic frog shit at the bottom of the swamp at the bottom of the pile. For the second two months, we became Blue Birds. We were still lower than frog shit, but no longer on the bottom of the pile. And when we became upperclassmen, we were Red Birds with only two more months to go until graduation. But for now, we were Green Birds, and Red was a long way into the future.

As Green Birds, we were as vulnerable to attack as a goat chained to a post surrounded by a pack of wolves. Our TAC officers were trained to be disciplinarians, and they were ferocious. They were always yelling, screaming, and frothing at the mouth. They reminded me of rabid Rottweilers in a yogurt factory.

We got demerits for everything, and when we got enough demerits, we paid a stiff price. The price was called a JARK and required a jogging trip up a hill named MB-4. We had to run from the barracks to the top of MB-4 and back to the barracks in less than 45 minutes. If you didn't make it in time, you had to do it again. If you got 100 demerits, you were required to do a JARK on Saturday evening. If you got 200 demerits, you had to do a second JARK on Sunday as well. We all managed to get at least 200 demerits every week.

The JARK was brutal, and since we started OCS in the summer, it was hotter than hell, and we were running in combat boots. We always had two ambulances follow the herd as some of the guys would simply pass out due to heat exhaustion. I paced myself and always made it back to the barracks safely, but when I took my tee-shirt off, I rung it out and sweat poured from it like I just pulled it out of a tub of water. We would get extremely dehydrated. The JARKS went on for the entire six months; however, by the time we became Red Birds, the JARKS were down to about once a week.

I was being trained as a forward observer (F/O). It sounds funny, but the primary weapon for an F/O was a pair of binoculars. We were the eyes and ears for the artillery. The best way to describe our function is to imagine point "A" as the location of the firing battery also known as the "gun line." (A firing battery is an artillery unit that usually consists of six howitzers.) Point "C" is the enemy's location, and the F/O is point "B" located somewhere between "A" and "C."

The F/O, along with a reconnaissance sergeant and a radio operator, would jump in a jeep and head out to an observation post which was usually a lonely hilltop way ahead of our own troops. The idea was to look for enemy troop movement, identify their location, and call back to the guns to start firing. Two howitzers would fire one round each. Depending on where the first round of shells hit, the F/O would use his binoculars to determine what adjustments were needed and send back instructions to the fire direction center so they could make the necessary corrections for the next volley. The same two guns fired once more and hopefully that round came closer to the target than the first one. Through a series of adjustments, the F/O would use a strategy called "bracketing the target." Usually by the third volley, all necessary adjustments were made, and now the guns were prepared to hit the target in a manner that would create as much havoc as possible. The radio communication and sequence of events went like this:

F/O to the fire direction center, "Right 20, add 50, fire for effect." When the F/O said, "Fire for effect," that meant all hell was about to break loose. The fire direction center quickly calculated the final adjustments that told the cannon cockers on the gun line what to do. Once the guns were set, the battery executive officer would give the command to "Fire."

All six cannons were going ape shit, firing volley after volley. This would continue until the F/O radioed back to the guns that the mission was completed. The first job of every second lieutenant in the artillery was to be a forward observer.

As Paul Harvey would say, "Now for the rest of the story."

There was a substantial conflict of interest between US forces and our enemy, the Viet Cong. The mission of the Viet Cong was to die fighting for their country and spend eternity in heaven with Buddha, while the mission of the American soldier was to help them get there as fast as possible.

Once the enemy was engaged and the American artillery was drenching them with a hailstorm of artillery shells, the Viet Cong got really pissed off. They understood our system and realized that there was an American F/O sitting out on a hilltop somewhere directing a devastating blow that would eventually kill them all. In retaliation, the Viet Cong would send out squads of scouts looking for the F/O. Once found, they would kill him.

The life span of a forward observer in Vietnam in 1968 was not very long making it an undesirable position. From my understanding, F/Os lasted about three months and were returned to the States in a body bag. I remember in OCS, we were repeatedly told not to make friends, because more likely than not, the guy standing next to you on the left and the guy standing next to you on the right will not be coming home alive. Sadly, that was true.

Firing range at Fort Sill

Despite the fact that our job would put us in imminent danger, learning to become an F/O at Fort Sill was a memorable experience. Between the battery location and the impact area were a series of heavily reinforced concrete bunkers. A ceasefire was called while the busses dropped us off at the bunkers. Once we were safely inside, the range officer would give the command to commence firing, and the firing range was no longer safe. As officer candidates, we hunkered down in our bunkers with our binoculars and topographical relief maps. Our instructor would point to a hilltop and say, "Okay candidate, that is your target. Now blow it up." I took out my relief map and found the position of the bunker I was in, and then found the target. I radioed the Fire Direction Center (FDC) announcing, "Fire mission, over." They responded, "What are the co-ordinates of your target?" I sent the longitude and latitude back to them. Boom! Two shots went whistling over my head. About a mile or so in front of me two clouds of smoke appeared as the shells hit the impact area. I made the necessary adjustments and called for a second volley. We got closer. My third command was, "Add 100, left 50, fire for effect." Six guns responded and blew the target into never-never land. I was a very happy camper.

Finally, the big day came. Graduation. We assembled in a big room, and the cadre bestowed their congratulations on us for making it through OCS and becoming officers. Then one-by-one, they read our new orders, "Second Lieutenant Adams, short tour, Fort Carson, Colorado; Second Lieutenant Jenkins, short tour, Fort Lewis, Washington, Second Lieutenant Clark, short tour, Fort Knox, Kentucky," and one of my best buddies from OCS, "Second Lieutenant Josh Boudron, short tour, Fort Hood, Texas." And so, it went for the 198 of us that graduated.

"Short tour" meant a four-month assignment to a stateside Army post, then on to Vietnam as a forward observer with a three-month life expectancy. Many of the guys sat in despair and fought back tears as they learned their fate.

Of the 198 graduates, 186 received short tour duty assignments. Twelve received assignments to Germany. I was one of the 12. God was definitely looking after me. This was the third time that I would not be going to Vietnam. Thank you. Thank you. Thank you.

After the assignments were read, it was time to march up to the podium to receive our gold second lieutenant bars. It was Army tradition that, as a new officer, we were obligated to give a buck to the first enlisted man that saluted us.

In the room, proudly stood our sergeant major, handing out second lieutenant bars. He had the gold bar in his left hand and a snappy salute in his right. He was smiling like a possum eating shit as he said, "Congratulations, lieutenant," and collected $198 that night, one dollar at a time. Back then, that was a fair amount of money. The next day, a graduation ceremony was held for us. Neither Josh Boudron's or my parents attended the ceremony, so Josh pinned my gold lieutenant bars on for me, and I did the same for him. We were now free to go. Fifty years would pass before Josh and I reconnected.

Josh Boudron pinning on my gold second lieutenant bars

After graduation, I was given three weeks leave before I had to report for duty in Germany. By this time, Alice and I were engaged and planning a wedding. I used my leave time to go shopping for a ring, do what I could to help with the wedding plans, visit friends around Southern California, and then I drove north to Santa Maria to visit my family.

My in-laws did an excellent job putting together a fantastic wedding ceremony. Unfortunately, I was running out of time, and we were unable to go on a honeymoon. We did, however, escape to a mountain retreat for a couple days before I had to report for duty. On December 30, 1967, I hopped on a flight from Los Angeles to Omaha and spent the night with my high school buddy, Pete James. The next day I flew to Newark, New Jersey and hooked up with my OCS buddies that were also on their way to Germany.

2nd Lt. Steve Dolby – at last!

CHAPTER 24
DEUTSCHLAND

The 12 of us landed in the country in the early morning of January 3, 1968. It was a cold, windy, and overcast day but also very exciting to be starting a new adventure. Military personnel met us at the airport and helped to process us through. Originally, I was to be sent to a place called Baumholder along with four of my classmates. I was excited that we would all be together. However, the sergeant that was helping me find my way said, "Lieutenant Dolby, sir, your orders have been changed. You are not going to Baumholder, you are now being transferred to a town called Mainz." I rebelled, and said, "You can't be serious. I was looking forward to going to Baumholder with my friends."

The sergeant looked at me as though I was crazy beyond repair. He said, "Listen to me. You do not want to go to Baumholder. Trust me on this one. You are one of the luckiest guys to step off that airplane." Later, by the grace of God, I learned just how right he was, and how lucky I was.

Baumholder, I would learn, was a hellhole, and nobody wanted to be there. It was a very small town situated on a mountaintop where the wind blew, and the snow flew. Every GI that was stationed there was miserable and counted the days until they could rotate back to the States.

Mainz, on the other hand, was clean and pristine — a beautiful city in which to spend a military assignment. It is located in central Germany, nestled on the west bank of the Rhine River about 20 miles from Frankfurt. Today, it is considered the wine capital of Germany and has a population of approximately 209,000 people. Historically, the most famous resident of Mainz was Johannes Gutenberg. In 1439, he invented the modern movable printing press that allowed for the mass production of books and revolutionized the world. His name is memorialized on streets, hotels, restaurants, and parks throughout the city.

When the 12 of us second lieutenants arrived in Germany in unison, the Army did not have sufficient housing to accommodate us, so they put us up in the Gutenberg Hotel temporarily. This was a very nice hotel with a beautiful restaurant on the main floor. Six of us met there for dinner one evening, and we were wearing our class-A (dress green) uniforms. We looked rather impressive if I do say so myself. We sat together at one table, and the Germans had the remainder of the restaurant. It was obvious that we were not part of the local crowd. The waiter took our order, and when he asked me what I wanted to drink, I told him, "A glass of milk."

Mainz, Germany

I loved milk and had always drunk it at dinner since I was a little kid. But now I was a 22-year-old man and an officer in the military to boot. When the waiter brought me the milk, all the Germans stopped what they were doing and began to stare beyond belief. In their culture, real men didn't drink milk. They drank wine or beer. Babies drank milk, and when they were ten years of age or older, if they wanted a beer, that's what they got. From that point forward, I don't think I ever asked for another glass of milk in Germany. That was an embarrassing lesson to learn.

Of the 12 of us sent to Germany, five were sent to Baumholder, two went to Giessen, and five remained in Mainz. The five of us that stayed in Mainz were all assigned to the 1st Battalion, 28th Artillery. The 1st/28th was an Honest John Rocket Battalion. At Fort Sill, we learned to fire howitzers, but we didn't know anything about rockets. Soon, some of us would learn.

My first job with this outfit was the assistant supply officer, and my department had the responsibility of making sure the battalion had everything it needed to operate efficiently. This included guns, rifles, rockets, and ammunition; food, fuel, vehicles, and equipment; furniture, bunk beds, sheets, and blankets; tents, tools, and sleeping bags — in other words, anything and everything necessary for war and everyday living.

Within one week of my arrival, I was told that the Army was conducting a two-week logistics course in the town of Oberammergau, and it would be a good idea if I went there on a temporary duty assignment (TDY) to learn how to become a supply officer. I was scared to death. I didn't have a car yet. I knew nothing about the German language. I did not understand all the goofy road signs. I didn't have a place to live yet, and I was required to make a six-hour drive by myself to Oberammergau, a name I couldn't even pronounce.

I purchased a car the next day. It was a brand new 1968 Volkswagen Beetle, and I bought it for $1,650. I read the drivers' guide to Europe and got my driver's license. Then I bought a book of gas coupons and learned how to buy gasoline on the German economy. Talk about "baptism by fire," this was it. I converted my American dollars into Deutsche Marks, purchased a map of Germany, and I was all set to go. All I needed was confidence in myself to make the six-hour drive without getting lost. I still don't know how I did it, but I pulled into the driveway of my destination without one wrong turn.

Upon my arrival, I was in awe as I had never seen a town as beautiful as this. Oberammergau is nestled high in the German Alps in Bavaria and very close to the Austrian border. This quaint village had charm in every direction. A mountain stream meandered through town, and all the houses and shops had murals painted on their exterior walls depicting fairytale characters such as Goldilocks, the Big Bad Wolf, and Hansel and Gretel. The shops were spotlessly clean, and the window dressings were so inviting that you couldn't wait to go inside and check out the merchandise. Cuckoo clocks, dolls, and Bavarian trinkets were everywhere.

The aroma of coffee and pastries made it difficult to figure out which bakery to try first. At lunch or dinner time, the food smelled so good I would walk back and forth between restaurants several times before I could decide where to dine. The people were charming and colorful. The men wore bibbed shorts called lederhosen and felt hats with a feather sticking out the side. And the female store clerks and waitresses wore their dirndl dresses designed to create attractive cleavage even on the flattest of girls. Needless to say, tips from the men were usually more than generous.

My two weeks in Oberammergau went by quickly. I loved it and could have spent the rest of my life there. However, the time had come to return to my permanent duty station in Mainz.

Prior to my move to Germany, our plan was to have Alice stay behind in California to finish up a medical assisting course. I would find us a home in Germany. However, Alice got pregnant on our wedding night. She wrote me a letter saying she could not finish her schooling because she was pregnant, and the course she was taking required x-rays that may be harmful to a fetus. So, she dropped out of school and announced through a letter that she would be flying into Frankfurt at the beginning of March 1968.

I was living with a bunch of guys at the time, and the arrival of her letter suggested I find an apartment immediately. There was no military housing available, so I was forced to find an apartment on the German economy. I went to a German real estate agency that had an apartment that had just become available ten seconds prior to my arrival. It was located on the second floor of a private home in a suburb of Mainz. It was a lovely home, and the landlady, Frau Heidenreich, was as sweet as she could be. When she heard that we were expecting a baby, I think she became more excited than we were. I signed the lease papers immediately.

By now, I had been with the 1st/28th Artillery for two months. The Army Table of Organization and Equipment (TO&E) called for a staff of 29 officers. By the time we arrived, the staff was over budget by three. We now had 32 officers. That would change drastically very soon as the war in Vietnam continued to escalate.

The battalion's team of officers were a great group of guys. They all had that sarcastic military sense of humor that I loved. The supply officer, designated as the S-4 officer, was also the property book officer (PBO). He signed for every piece of equipment the battalion had, and he was also held accountable for it. His name was Lt. Jamie Buckler. His tour of duty and military obligation would end soon, and he would be rotating back to the States to return to civilian life. A request was submitted for a new PBO to replace Jamie.

The new PBO showed up at the battalion headquarters about the same time I did. His name was Gary Lewitts, and he was a career military officer whose specialty was supply officer. Whereas the lieutenants were all about my age (21-24), Gary was a generation ahead of us. He had a son my age serving on active duty in Vietnam. Gary and I worked together and became great friends. He was like a father figure to me, and I often relied on his wisdom and advice. He had a German wife and three daughters that my wife and I regarded as family.

Jamie and Gary began the task of inventorying all the property so that Jamie could sign everything over to Gary. In doing so, they discovered that the battalion was short about 35 bed sheets. Before Jamie could leave the Army, he was going to have to pay for them, and this got him very upset. After so many years in the Army, Gary knew every trick in the book and developed a plan to get Jamie off the hook.

There were about 150 soldiers that lived in the barracks. Every Wednesday was laundry day, so the GIs stripped the dirty sheets off their beds and turned them into the S-4 supply room in exchange for clean ones. The S-4 clerk would bundle up all the dirty sheets, load them on a truck, and drive them to the central military laundry exchange. Here, he would trade in the dirty sheets for clean ones and deliver them to the S-4 supply room.

On the next laundry day, Gary told the supply clerk to take 35 of the worst sheets, cut them in half, and mix them among the whole sheets. So, the clerk received 300 dirty sheets, cutting 35 of them in half to produce a pile of laundry made up of 265 whole sheets and 70 half sheets. He drove the load down to the military laundry exchange. The receiving clerk counted 335 pieces of dirty laundry and gave our clerk 335 crispy clean sheets. Gary had now made up the 35-sheet deficit. He was happy, Jamie was off the hook, 150 soldiers had clean sheets, and the workers at the laundry exchange were standing there scratching their asses wondering where all the half sheets came from as they pulled them out of the dryers.

At this point in time, my lifestyle was changing exponentially, and I was having trouble keeping up with it. Just 12 months earlier, I was a single civilian going to college and minding my own business. My wardrobe, and entire net worth for that matter, consisted of blue jeans, tee-shirts, and a couple pairs of tennis shoes. Now, I was in the Army, I was an officer, and I was married, an expectant father, and living in a foreign country. That was quite a transition!

My wife flew into Frankfurt the day after I returned from a three-day field exercise. I picked her up and drove her to our new home. We were expecting our first child in September. I had Alice join the officers' wives club hoping she would make friends quickly. She befriended other wives that were pregnant as well. I showed her where to shop for food and how to navigate her way through Mainz in our new car. I was glad this all happened quickly because I was about to be called away for five weeks, and I did not want her to be left all alone in a foreign country.

CHAPTER 25
WILD BOAR AND TOILET PAPER

In addition to the unscheduled alerts, we were required to go on field training exercises twice a year. These exercises would last anywhere from two to five weeks and would take place at a North Atlantic Treaty Organization (NATO) firing range two to three hundred miles away from our permanent base of operations.

There were two NATO maneuver areas established in Germany. One was located several hundred miles to the east of Frankfurt next to the Czechoslovakian border near a town called Grafenworh, pronounced Graf-en- veer. The other was located an equal distance north of Frankfurt between Hanover and Hamburg close to the town of Munster. This was always referred to as "Munsterlager" which means the military camp just outside the town of Munster. Traditionally, Americans and Germans conducted their military exercises at Grafenworh, while Great Britain, Belgium, Germany, and The Netherlands used Munsterlager.

When it was our turn to go, Grafenworh was completely full, so we were notified that we had to go to Munsterlager. The problem was that no American units had ever been there before, so we did not know what to expect. Our battalion commander suggested that Jamie and I along with another lieutenant drive up to Munsterlager on a reconnaissance mission. There were no American facilities up there and no American support systems. We had to rely on our NATO allies for everything.

We drove into a British compound, and to our surprise, they had an Honest John rocket outfit on post. We went into the battalion headquarters and requested to speak to the commanding officer. He was happy to meet us and was most accommodating, insisting that we be their guests. They put us up in their bachelor officer quarters (BOQ) for the next three nights. During our stay, we got everything we needed, and Munsterlager was "move-in ready" for the US 1st Battalion, 28th Artillery.

Our host explained that his Army was a little bit different from ours. Unlike the Americans, the British assigned what they called a "bat-boy" to every officer. A batboy is like an attendant or an aide. We were told that before we went to bed to be sure to leave our boots out in the hallway. We did. And when we woke up the next morning and opened the door to pick up our boots, they had been spit-shined to look like new. Wow was I impressed. Obviously, British officers got treated like royalty.

The batboy knocked on my door to inform me that breakfast would be served in the officers' mess hall in 15 minutes. In the American mess hall, it was metal trays, plastic chairs, wooden tables, and the service was cafeteria style. When I walked into the British officer's mess hall, the tables were covered with linen, the eating utensils were sterling silver, and the waiters were wearing dinner jackets and handing out menus. I thought, "Holy smoke, are you kidding me? Was this the Army or did we just walk into Europe's finest hotel restaurant?"

I read the menu and noticed that one of my options was porridge. I had never tried porridge, and I didn't even know what it was. I just thought it was some fictitious food that the three bears ate. I thought I better have some of it. The waiter took my order. Ten minutes later he returned with a big silver dome covering a silver tray of food. He sat it down in front of me, removed the dome, and there sat a bowl of oatmeal. I said, "This is oatmeal, and I ordered porridge." He politely explained that in England they call it porridge. Another lesson learned. After breakfast, we tied up the loose ends, thanked our gracious hosts, and headed south toward Mainz.

We gave our report to our commanding officer, Lt. Col. Carl Rucksler. He was extremely pleased with our accomplishments and felt that our unit could go on this mission with complete confidence. He told us that while we were up north the past few days, he received notification that we would be moving out in two weeks to conduct our semi-annual field exercise in Munsterlager. He then said, "Lieutenant Dolby, you are now appointed as the convoy commander." My heart came to a sudden stop. First, there is nothing more frightening in the

Army than a second lieutenant with a map. Second, I was so new to this country I had trouble finding my own way, let alone trying to lead 35 military vehicles 300 miles to the north. And third, these vehicles were so old it was highly unlikely that that they could make the trip without breaking down.

Me on the left with my convoy ready for Munsterlager

But the problems ran far deeper than that. The Army had a pecking order based on perceived priorities related to the mission of every battalion, brigade, and division. The units with the highest priority would get every piece of equipment they needed. Those units in the second echelon would be next in line, and the units designated as the lowest priority wouldn't get jack-shit. The 1st Battalion, 28th Artillery (my unit) was in the latter group, and as a result, we would always be sucking hind tit. If a piece of equipment broke down, we could not get replacement parts to save our souls, and we would often have to fabricate parts out of anything we could get our hands on. We could take a broom handle and fashion it into a pump handle to make a wind set work. We could take a coffee can and morph it into a cowling for a generator. And, we could use duct tape to hold things together when a specific type of screw was needed but not available. I often thought that if an original equipment manufacturer could visit our equipment and compare it to what it looked like when they first sold it to the Army, they probably wouldn't recognize it. Well, the big day came, and I got this rag-tag team of vehicles lined up and ready to move out. As we entered the autobahn, we looked like the circus leaving town. I prayed and prayed that nothing would go wrong, and it didn't. The entire convoy made it to Munsterlager without a single incident. My prayers were answered, at least for the time being.

We were in Munsterlager for five weeks. The main objective was to prove our ability as an efficient Honest John rocket battalion capable of fulfilling our mission. We ran fire missions, both "wet and dry." When we ran "wet," we were firing live rockets; however, we were using dummy warheads that released only smoke upon impact designed to measure performance related to hitting the target. It sounds funny, but by the nature of our weapon, if we came within 1,000 meters of the target, it was considered a "direct hit." Obviously, the Honest John had a wide-spread effect upon the intended area.

This weapon system was the first nuclear-capable surface-to-surface rocket in the United States' arsenal and was in service from 1953–1991. In addition to the US Army, it was also used by NATO forces throughout the Cold War. The Army started to take delivery of these rockets in late 1953, and in 1954, Honest John battalions were being deployed to Europe. It was an unguided rocket aimed in much the same way as a cannon. It was 27 feet long and weighed 5,820 pounds. With a 20-kiloton nuclear warhead, it had a range of 15 miles, and with a 1,500-pound conventional warhead, it had a maximum range of 30 miles.

The rockets were transported in three parts. Some of the parts were loaded into Army cargo trucks, and some of the parts were pulled by trailers. Once the battalion reached its destination, the rockets were assembled in the field, and with the help of a five-ton wrecker, were hoisted up and mounted onto the rail of another vehicle known as a rocket launcher. From there, the Fire Direction Center and the launcher platoon took over, and through a collaborative effort, made the final adjustments to fire the rocket. Finally, the launcher platoon crew, under the direction of the platoon leader (either a 1st or 2nd lieutenant), would sound the alarm to clear the area. Then they hit the red button, and off she went. It made one hell of a noise. The ground shook, and even the insides of your belly shook. It was very impressive.

All the equipment needed for this weapon system was massive in size. The bigger vehicles ran on gas and only got 1.2 miles to the gallon. If you were looking for an economy vehicle, this was not it. The five-ton wrecker is worth mentioning because it had a dual purpose — lifting rockets up to the launcher and towing broken-down Army vehicles. This was not your average tow truck sent out to help a stranded motorist. This was the large industrial-size capable of towing big stuff like semi-trucks and RVs. There were two firing batteries in the battalion, and each had its own wrecker. Thus, the battalion had a complement of two wreckers at its disposal.

March and April were cold and snowy in Munsterlager. We lived in tents in the woods with about five to ten men per tent. There were no bathrooms, so we used our helmets and canteens as a sink for shaving and washing our faces. When nature called, we would grab a roll of mountain money (toilet paper) and head for the woods.

Lieutenants Lewen Rengle, me, and Allen Covall
minutes before the wild boar scare

As was customary and part of our mission, a team of lieutenants would load up a jeep with survey equipment and head out to find suitable locations to launch our rockets. Ideal locations were wide open fields surrounded by forest. When we found what we were looking for, we would park the jeep in the middle of the field and begin our work. My team consisted of 2nd Lt. Allen Covall, 2nd Lt. Lewen Rengle, and me. Just as we were getting started, Lewen announced that he had not gone to the bathroom in three days, and perhaps it was time to commune with nature. He grabbed a roll of mountain money, said he would be right back, and took off for the woods to lay down a deuce.

Two minutes later, we heard this blood-curdling scream telling us to bring the jeep. Allen and I knew this was a dire emergency just by the inflection in Lewen's voice. So, we jumped in the jeep. I was driving, and Allen was kneeling in the back seat trying to assess the situation. Meanwhile, I'm driving like a bat out of hell and headed in the direction of where the voice was coming from. About that time, we saw Lewen running out of the woods with his pants wrapped around his ankles being chased by a wild boar. When boars attack, there is little chance for survival. As we pulled up to Lewen, Allen grabbed him by the arm and shoulder and pulled him in the jeep just in the nick of time.

As the days progressed and the rockets were flying, I thought to myself that I would much rather be a launcher platoon leader firing rockets than sitting at a desk on the battalion staff. It was exciting, and I put in a request for transfer as soon as we returned to home base. Meanwhile, I had a job to do.

During the second week in the field, it became dreadfully cold, and temperatures dropped below freezing. I was out in a field performing a task when someone suggested we break for lunch. I opened my box of C-rations to find a can of ham and lima beans as my main entree. There was a second can that had fruitcake for dessert, a package of chewing gum, and a package of four cigarettes. All of this was prepared and packaged in 1952. Yummy. I couldn't wait to eat. I opened my can of ham and lima beans with my trusty P-38 can opener, and the food was frozen solid. I stabbed it with my bayonet to break it apart, but it was obvious there was no way to eat it. Someone with more experience than me said, "Let me show you how it's done." He turned the jeep on and popped the hood. Then he set our cans of food on the radiator, and in about 15 minutes we had a hot lunch prepared. There is no end to American ingenuity, especially if you are a soldier. They say that necessity is the mother of invention, but in the Army, ingenuity is the key to survival.

We arrived in Munsterlager toward the end of March, and it was now the first of May. All the fire missions were completed, and all the rockets were spent. It was time to go home. As convoy commander, it was time for me to start praying again. I prayed like a Holy Roller, but this time my prayers would go unanswered. I got the convoy of 35 vehicles lined up. I put the slowest and weakest vehicles in front and the two five-ton wreckers and the mechanics in the rear. "LET'S MOVE OUT`!"

Clippity-clop and clickity-clack, we headed south on the autobahn with 300 miles to go. One-by-one, vehicles would peter out and pull off to the side of the road. The mechanics would show up, kick the vehicle in the ass, and get it running again. However, by the time we were within 100 miles of Mainz, we were down to 30 operational vehicles with five lame ducks. I huddled the five together and left a couple of my best mechanics to work on them. Three hours later, I had the convoy parked in the motor pool and went to report to our battalion commander. He was aware of the condition of our vehicles, and I think he was secretly praying for a miracle and hoping that I could bring everything back without incident.

I told him we had 30 vehicles in the corral, but still had five broken down vehicles sitting on the side of the road near a town called Giessen.

He said, "Well, take the two five-ton wreckers and tow them back."

I said, "Well sir, I would like to do that, but two of the five broken down vehicles happen to be the five-ton wreckers."

With that came a major explosion. The colonel lost it. He slammed down his fist on the desk and yelled, "Dammit lieutenant, I'm sick of your lame excuses. Get out of my office, get those vehicles, and don't come back until you do!" I knew he was frustrated about the sorry condition of our vehicles so when he came unglued, I tried not to take it personally.

"Yes sir." I fired off a snappy salute, did an about face, and marched out of his office.

Now my jeep driver, Sgt. Miller, was standing out in the hallway waiting for me. He said, "Wow, sir. I heard the colonel yelling at you and he sounded really mad. What did he have to say?" I said, "Oh, he wasn't mad, he was giving me a promotion. And by the way, you got a promotion as well."

Sgt. Miller was now very excited. "What kind of promotions did we get?"

Well, I said, "We just got promoted to magicians. I'm Merlin, and you are the Wizard of Oz. Now, go down to the motor pool and check out a jeep. And, while you are down there, pick up a couple magic wands because we are going to need all the help we can get."

Shortly thereafter, the two of us were driving north on the autobahn in total silence. About an hour passed, and we hadn't spoken to each other.

Finally, Sgt. Miller looks at me and said, "Sir, do you have a plan on what we are going to do once we reach those broken-down trucks?"

I said, "I'm thinking. Do you have any ideas?"

He said, "I'm thinking."

Finally, Sgt. Miller says, "I've got an idea. We will use the battalion motto to get those vehicles back."

I said, "Are you crazy? Our battalion motto is, "We support the line." How in the hell are we going to support the line when we can't even support ourselves?"

He said, "Not that motto. The other battalion motto."

I said, "I wasn't aware that we even had another motto."

He said, "It goes like this: We the incompetent, lead the unwilling, to do the impossible. We have done so much, with so little, for so long, we believe we can do anything with nothing."

Once I stopped laughing, I started thinking he may just have something, and we certainly didn't have any other options but to believe in ourselves. As we continued north approaching the town of Giessen, we spotted our little broken-down convoy parked on the southbound side of the autobahn. We crossed over the bridge and pulled up behind our troops. By this time, the mechanics had the two five-ton wreckers running as well as the 3/4-ton communications truck. The two remaining deuce-and-a-half cargo trucks were shot so I had the guys hook them up to the wreckers so that they could be towed. We were back in business!

Now, the Army has another motto that says, "If it moves, salute it. If it doesn't move, paint it." So, I had Sgt. Miller call the men to attention, do an about-face, and give the command to salute the trucks. They thought we were crazy, but they did it anyway. Slowly but surely, we made it back to Mainz. Back in Mainz, I marched into the colonel's office and told him everything was present and accounted for. He was writing a report and never looked up. He tried to hide it, but I could tell he was pleased and grinning like a possum eating shit. He said, "Job well done. I knew you could do it. Now go home and get some rest." I walked into my house, looking and smelling like Hogan's goat. A long shower, a hot meal, and a warm bed made everything all right again.

CHAPTER 26
PREPARE FOR WAR... HERE COME THE RUSSIANS

I must have impressed the colonel with the way I handled the convoy. I requested a personal meeting with him, and we met in his office the next day. I told him that I wanted to become a launcher platoon leader and have a little more action in my life beyond my desk jockey job on the battalion staff. In less than a week, I was the platoon leader for "A" Battery, 2nd Platoon. I had never shot a rocket before, so I had a lot to learn. The massive 27-foot projectile weighing 5,820 pounds made the howitzer cannons feel like shooting a BB gun.

One of the reasons the position became available was the lieutenant before me had just completed his military obligation and rotated back to the States to resume civilian life. Then my battery commander, Capt. Taylor, received orders for Vietnam. His position was to be filled by a captain, but we didn't have one at the time, so they filled it with a first lieutenant.

As the war in Vietnam escalated, and the number of people leaving the military continued, we began to see our staff of officers diminish. Without replacements, those of us that remained would have to wear multiple hats. Soon I would be the platoon leader for two launcher platoons in "A" Battery, fill in for another platoon leader in "B" Battery, and stand by as a back-up battery executive office.

Not only did we feel the pinch in Germany, but things weren't going very well back in the States. The general public was becoming disillusioned about the Vietnam War feeling somewhat deceived. In October 1964 during a campaign speech, President Lyndon B. Johnson promised, "We are not about to send American boys 10,000 miles away from home to do what Asian boys ought to be doing for themselves." However, Johnson increased our military presence in Vietnam to

184,000 troops by the end of 1965. The growth would continue. By April 1969, the number of American military personnel in Vietnam reached 543,000. Broken promises lead to discontent.

The military draft touched the home front of America. Between 1964–1973, the US military drafted 2.2 million men out of an eligible population of 27 million. According to the Selective Service Board, that averaged around 245,000 men per year, with an average age of an infantryman being just 22 years old.

The year 1968 would prove to be the bloodiest and deadliest year of the war with 16,592 American servicemen killed. Had I not been sent to Germany, I would have arrived in Vietnam about April of that year, and I would have been an artillery forward observer with a life expectancy of 90 days. Needless to say, when I got orders for Germany, it was the luckiest day of my life.

The reason 1968 was so bad was the Tet Offensive that began January 31st of that year. Tet was one of the largest military campaigns of the Vietnam War. This was an uprising launched by the Viet Cong and the North Vietnamese People's Army against the South Vietnamese Army. It was a strategy of surprise attacks against military and civilian command centers throughout the south. The enemy showed no mercy to anyone that got in their way.

Meanwhile, back in Germany, trouble was headed our way. We just did not know it yet. In the early morning of August 21, 1968, the Russians along with 200,000 Warsaw Pact troops and 5,000 tanks invaded Czechoslovakia and overthrew that country's leader, Alexander Dubcek. Apparently, the Soviets didn't care for Dubcek's management style and wanted him out of there. The Americans, along with other NATO member nations, feared that this invasion might be the start of World War III. The conventional wisdom was once those troops made it to Prague, they would continue the march into Germany and other countries west of the Iron Curtain.

Supreme Headquarters Allied Powers Europe (SHAPE) is the military governing body of NATO located in Brussels, Belgium. SHAPE put all NATO nations on high alert. In other words, "Prepare for war." Our unit, like all the others, loaded our equipment and headed east to our pre-set combat position which happened to be Grafenworh,

Germany, just four miles west of the Czechoslovakian border. We set up camp in the woods and remained camouflaged as best we could. However, it's extremely difficult to make an Honest John rocket battalion look like it disappeared.

Me near the Czechoslovakian border

CHAPTER 27
BLUEBERRIES AND CHRISTMAS TREES

I loved my new job as a platoon leader. I learned everything I needed to know about the weapon system. My launcher platoon teams were eager to please. They learned what was expected of them, and we cross-trained each member to perform multiple tasks. If we weren't the best, I would challenge anyone to compete with us.

Day and night, we would deploy our launcher platoons from one firing location to another. The strategy was to shoot one rocket, pack everything up, and move to the next location before the enemy could figure out where we were. We practiced and practiced and practiced using the dummy smoke warheads. However, reality was that if the enemy showed up at our doorstep, we would have to use conventional or nuclear warheads. I prayed that I would not be called on to "pop a nuke." Nobody wants that responsibility!

As the days passed and nothing happened, we began to feel confident that the Russians weren't coming after all. Their primary mission was to remove Alexander Dubcek and supervise an orderly transition of leadership. So, the Communist troops sat in Prague drinking beer, eating sausages, and waiting for their next set of orders. And, the Allied forces kept running tactical fire missions as if the Russians were going to show up.

After two weeks of this nonsense, we were exhausted and our battalion commander, Lt. Col. Carl Rucksler, knew it. So, he gathered his team of company grade officers together one Saturday afternoon and told us that Sunday would be a free day. We could sleep in as late as we wanted, and there would be no work assignments. The only stipulation was that we were not allowed to leave the area.

Basically, we were confined to our ten-man tents. We called in a sergeant and gave him a jeep and $40. Then we sent him to town to get us a couple cases of beer in exchange for the six-pack we would give to him for his effort. We ended up having one of the best evenings of our lives. We drank beer, told countless jokes, and laughed our asses off. When our bladders were full, we would leave the tent, walk about 20 yards into the woods, relieve ourselves, and return to the tent for another beer. As the evening wore on and the urge to leave the tent came more frequently, we walked out, stopping at about the 15-yard mark. We would take care of business and return to the tent for more beer and jokes. The third trip was only a 10-yard walk. And when the evening was coming to an end, we just opened the tent flap and took a pee. By about 10 p.m., we were out of beer and jokes, so we called it an evening and went to sleep.

Blueberries were growing everywhere in the area where we camped. They grew like vines that crept along the forest floor, and you could not walk without stepping on them. The Germans invented a little hand rake that looked like a tiny shovel with teeth. It was used to scoop through the vines and harvest the berries that fell into a little reservoir that was part of the tool. It was extremely efficient, and a sizeable stash of blueberries could be collected in a matter of minutes.

Sunday morning Lt. Col. Rucksler went down to the mess tent to have his breakfast and noticed that all the junior officers were missing. So, he asked the mess sergeant if he had seen any of us. The sergeant reminded the colonel that he had given us the day off, and we were probably still asleep in our tents. The colonel, being the good guy that he was, walked over to our tent and said, "You boys have got to get down to the mess tent. Sgt. Stacey is making blueberry pancakes, and they are delicious." We asked the colonel where the blueberries came from. He said, "They are everywhere. Look, here is a bunch just outside your tent." Then he reached down to the ground and scooped up a handful. Before anyone could tell him not to eat those blueberries, he was munching away. Too late. Nobody had the guts to tell him he was eating blueberries watered with recycled beer.

Finally, the day came when the "all clear" signal was given, and we were to return to our home base of operations. There were no officers available to steer the convoy. I had to stay back in the rear party detachment to take care of some administrative issues. So, I told

Sgt. Kyle that he would have to lead the convoy. It would be easy. All he had to do was leave the gate in Grafenworh, turn left, and jump on the autobahn headed west.

Unfortunately, Sgt. Kyle had difficulty identifying left from right, and he turned right instead of left. This led him smack dab into the Czech border. When the border guards saw this convoy with massive rockets coming toward them, they shit their pants. Like us, they thought the crisis was over, and here came an arsenal that could blow them into the next century. The guards justifiably panicked and called their superior officers. That sent off a chain reaction of communication that went all the way back to Moscow. Shortly, the Allied general staff sent a delegation to the scene to straighten out the mess. Eventually, it was all resolved.

Preparing to launch an Honest John rocket

Fire!

As the days rolled forward, I was preparing to become a dad. My daughter, Heidi, was born at the US Air Force Hospital in Wiesbaden, Germany on September 22, 1968. I went to the Air Force PX (the base exchange) and purchased a rocking chair for $12.50. It was the first piece of furniture I had ever bought. It was very high quality, and I still have it and use it to this day. At night, I would hold Heidi against my chest and rock her to sleep. Often, I would fall asleep before she did, and we would both come tumbling out of the chair onto the floor. I would pick the two of us up, dust us off, sit back down, and rock her again. Those were precious moments for me. Heidi and I bonded and became very close.

Me holding Heidi, with the $12.50 rocking chair in the background

After Heidi was born, government housing became available. I thought it would be good for Alice to be close to Americans, so we vacated the German house and moved into the military housing that was provided. This turned out to be a good move for all of us. Everyone seemed genuinely happy. Shortly thereafter, Alice's parents flew over from California for a visit and to see their new grandbaby. This was the first family we had seen since we left home, and it was a great visit.

On December 12, 1968, I was called into battalion headquarters and promoted to first lieutenant. Things were moving fast. Twenty-two months earlier, I had entered the Army as a buck-ass private. Within 10 months, I was an officer holding the rank of second lieutenant, and now I was a first lieutenant at the age of 23. My head was spinning and so was the rest of the world.

Alice befriended 2nd Lt. Lewen Rengle's wife, Lucille. They were the same age, both had recently given birth to daughters, and their husbands were buddies. One morning, Lewen dropped Lucille off at my house. We gave the girls one car and carpooled to work with the other. Alice and Lucille had the bright idea that they were going to go out on the German economy and buy Christmas trees. They asked us how to say, "I want to buy a Christmas tree." The correct answer is, "Ich mochte einen weihnachtsbaum, kaufen." However, we had been living in the country for nearly a year now, and neither one of our wives bothered to learn one word of German. This aggravated Lewen and me that our wives were not more engaged in the wonderful opportunity to live in a foreign country. So, we decided to play a trick. We told them to say, "Ich glaube, du bist ein arschloch." Which means, "I think you are an asshole." Lewen and I drove off to work while the two girls sat in the kitchen practicing their German.

That night, I came home from work and surprisingly Alice had a beautiful Christmas tree sitting in the living room. I was impressed and asked her how her day went. She told me that it was okay; however, she thought the German people were not very nice. I WONDER WHY. Lewen and I laughed our asses off, but never told the girls how we set them up.

157

CHAPTER 28
CAPTAIN HI YA PAL

One of the most interesting dynamics of the Army was how things changed with leadership.

Lt. Col. Carl Rucksler, our battalion commander, was from Texas, and he happened to be one of the sweetest, mild-mannered guys you could ever meet. He walked around with a cigar in his mouth 24 hours a day. He never smoked it. He chewed it. I think he kept it there to look tough. When we approached him with a snappy salute, he would return it with a hybrid salute that looked like a half-wave and half-salute followed by the greeting, "Hi ya pal." Soon we all picked up his habits and casually gestured with the half-wave/half-salute. No longer did the captains and lieutenants segregate themselves from one another. We did salute each other, but it was done in a half-ass way, unlike the snappy stiff salutes we were taught from the day we entered the Army.

The TV series "MASH" offers insight into the way this unit operated. Hawk-eye Pierce, B. J. Honeycutt, and Cpl. Klinger would have been our role models. Their personalities reflected the 1st Battalion, 28th Artillery to a tee. Despite our failure to observe proper military protocol, we managed to operate the battalion with superior efficiency.

However, things changed when Lt. Col. Rucksler received orders for a new assignment in the States. He was replaced by Lt. Col. Darrell Copeland, the polar opposite of Rucksler. To put it mildly, Copeland was one of the biggest piles of shit the Army ever cultivated — so much so that four lieutenants and one captain requested transfers to Vietnam. In a matter of weeks, he destroyed battalion morale and put the unit on a downhill slide.

In mid-1969, we received a replacement among our ranks. His name was Capt. Lewis Gilbert who became the "B" Battery commander. This guy had it together. Lewis was a helicopter pilot that had served in Vietnam and was an airborne paratrooper. Later in life, he was an entrepreneur, a pharmacist, and a lawyer. Basically, he could multi-task with the best in the universe. You could shove a broom handle up his ass, and he could sweep the hallway as he marched toward the battalion conference room with an armful of reports. Immediately, he won the respect of the entire battalion.

As he reported for work on his first day, I happened to cross paths with him walking through the parking lot. I saw him coming and noticed that he was a captain. I fired off our usual "Hi ya pal" greeting with a half-ass salute. He was from the disciplined ranks and not accustomed to this lackadaisical format. He came unglued. His blood boiled, and you could see the steam vaporizing above his head. He was in shock. He tried to say something but choked as he came up dry. Finally, he regained his composure, and words began to form into an audible tone and flowed like hot lava. He screamed, "Hi ya pal? What on earth is this hi ya pal shit? I am a captain, you are a lieutenant, and I certainly am not your pal."

Lewis Gilbert

159

Suddenly, I realized I had struck a nerve and had to recalculate my approach. Immediately, I rewound the clock to my military training. I backed up and tried it again. "Good morning, Sir." I fired off another salute that was more in line with Army expectations. He returned my salute and proceeded to his destination. Meanwhile, I couldn't help liking this guy, and I thought to myself, "He may not think we are pals, but I have a feeling we will be."

I am proud to say I was right, and he was wrong. We did become pals. We became the best of friends, and that friendship lasted until his death almost 50 years later. Every time we got together, we greeted each other with a "Hi ya pal" as a reminder of our first encounter.

CHAPTER 29
NUDIST COLONY SURVEILLANCE

One by one, the captains and lieutenants were disappearing. Some went to Vietnam, and some rotated out of the service and returned to civilian life in the States. One of the first to go was 1st Lt. Ron G. McRaymond. Ron was one of the funniest guys I had ever met. He grew up on a farm outside Enid, Oklahoma. I do not know what the primary business of the farm was, but Ron always complained about how the chickens kept getting in his way. He lived off a lonely country road, and he had to drive a quarter of a mile down a dirt driveway to reach the farmhouse.

As Ron was getting ready to leave the service, we asked him what he planned to do when he returned to the States. He said, "The first thing I'm going to do is race down that driveway and run over 300 chickens." Over and over, we would ask him the same question during his remaining time in the service. The answer was always the same. He was going to run over 300 chickens. His plans for the future never went beyond running over those chickens!

1st Lt. Cutler returned to Florida. The last I heard, he was trying to get hired by the Ford Motor Company. 1st Lt. Brophy dumped his schoolteacher girlfriend and headed for the States. She was furious since she was under the impression that marriage plans were in the near future. Then there was 1st Lt. Robeson who had a German girlfriend looking forward to a free ride to the States. When he announced that he was going back to the US without her, she couldn't accept it and jumped out of a window on the 11th floor of an apartment building.

The old cadre of bachelors cleared out, leaving a lot of heartbreak behind. The newer group of officers were mostly married with an infant, making us a little bit more responsible.

Up until now, our battalion headquarters was located in a suburb of Mainz named Gonsenheim, and our Army post was called Robert E.

Lee Barracks. We shared this post with several other Army units, one of which was the 509th Airborne Infantry Battalion. These guys were certifiably nuts and had the paperwork to prove it.

It was customary on a payday weekend for the German taxi drivers to park on the curb just outside the barracks, waiting for the cash-rich Americans to come off post looking for a ride to town. Typically, the GIs would grab a cab and haul ass to a local bar, hoping to find a pretty little fraulein to help them spend their paychecks. The 509th barracks overlooked the street where the taxi cabs were parked, and for disciplinary reasons, some of the soldiers were confined to the barracks. One night, one of the incarcerated GIs managed to get into the armory and commandeer an M-14 semi-automatic rifle. He thought it would be great fun to use the taxi cabs for target practice. He opened fire from a second story window and killed one of the drivers.

During a second incident, a soldier stole an Army tank, headed downtown, and drove over six parked cars. They were flattened like pancakes.

A third incident occurred on July 4, 1969. A 509th infantryman came over to our battalion headquarters that evening and lobbed a live grenade into the hallway, yelling, "Happy Fourth of July." It exploded leaving our offices partially destroyed. There were a few of our soldiers standing by at the time. When they saw the grenade coming, they yelled and ducked for cover. Fortunately, nobody was injured.

The next morning when our commanding officer saw the damage, he yelled, "That's it. We are out of this crazy place." Shortly thereafter, he relocated the battalion to McCully Barracks in a little town 10 miles west of Mainz called Wackernheim. We called it "Wacky Town." The nickname was more in line with some of the shenanigans that were pulled while we were there.

An Army battalion is run by four departments: S-1 is administration; S-2 is intelligence; S-3 is operations; and S-4 is logistics. Shortly after we moved to our new location, Lt. Col. Copeland called me into his office and told me he needed me to run the S-2 office.

I thought for a moment, "If S-2 is Army intelligence, isn't that an oxymoron?" And now he wants me to be the S-2 officer which is the intelligence officer. Up to this point in time, I could not remember ever doing anything particularly intelligent, unless throwing a cherry bomb in the toilet at school counted. At any rate, if he wanted me to run the S-2 shop, that is exactly what I intended to do. And, I was bound and determined to become the best S-2 officer the Army ever had.

The next day I showed up at battalion headquarters to start my new job. I was there early, so I walked down the hall to the break room to grab a cup of coffee. No sooner had I arrived, when in walked the battalion executive officer, Major Cee.

The primary function of a battalion executive officer is to be a back-up for the battalion commander. He is responsible for ensuring that all company-grade officers (captains and lieutenants) are doing their jobs efficiently, and to make sure they do not do anything that would get them in trouble. To that end, he did a terrific job. He took us under his wing, guiding and protecting us like a mother hen. We had total respect for him and regarded him as our big brother.

Major Cee, AKA Major Chrome-Dome, stood five feet five inches tall. In fact, he was five feet five inches in every direction. He shaved his head right down to the bone, and I think he must have put some wax on his noggin because it shone like a crystal ball.

As the major and I were talking, our battalion commander walked in. We exchanged greetings, and he asked us what was on our agenda for the day. Major Cee immediately responded, saying to Lt. Col. Copland, "Well sir, it's just about the end of the month, so Lieutenant Dolby and I are on our way down to Finthen Army Airfield to get our flight time in. We should be back about mid-afternoon." Copland wished us well, and we took off.

Once in the car, I asked Major Cee, "Why on earth would you tell the colonel I have to get my flight time in. I don't know any more about flying than the man-in-the-moon." Major Cee replied, "Don't worry about it. By the end of the day, I will have you flying like a champ. Besides, you need a break from the office."

A few moments later, we arrived at the airfield. Sitting on the tarmac was an OH-13 helicopter just waiting for us and raring to go. OH stands for observation helicopter, and the OH-13 was a dinky little thing. It had two seats, a joystick, and an instrument panel all surrounded by a glass bubble. Behind the bubble was the rest of the body that looked like an erector set. It had rotor blades on top and two skids underneath for landing gear. We hopped on board, fired it up, and took off.

Army OH-13

It was a beautiful day with calm winds and blue skies, and the temperature was about 75 degrees. Below us was a countryside of rolling hills covered with a densely packed forest of evergreen trees. It was one of those days when you were just happy to be alive. However, that was subject to change. As we were flying along, the major said, "Do you see that orange tower on the hilltop to the right?"

I said, "Yes sir. I do."

Major Cee instructed me, "Fine. Take the controls and head us over in that direction."

I grabbed the joystick and gave it a healthy jerk to the right. The helicopter went ape shit, and we were immediately on a collision course with Mother Earth. I thought we were dead for sure.

Major Cee yelled, "Release." I let go of the controls like I had just picked up a hot frying pan. He took over and got us back on course. Then he said, "Look, these controls are very sensitive. You do not need to go jerking them around. When I tell you to go to the right, all you have to do is think that you want the helicopter to go to the right. Your brain will send out brainwaves that will travel down your arm and onto the joystick, and the correction will take place automatically. Let's try it again."

I closed my eyes and thought to myself, "Go slightly to the right," and I didn't move a muscle. I opened my eyes. The helicopter had changed course, and we were headed in the right direction. The major was excited and yelled, "You got it. You got it." He was genuinely excited, grinning like a possum eating shit.

Next, he said, "Look out to the horizon on the left. Do you see that little clearing in the woods?" I said, "Yes sir." And he said, "Good. Head in that direction." Once again, I closed my eyes and thought to myself, "I want this helicopter to turn slowly to the left." I opened my eyes, and by golly, we were headed directly toward our next destination. Another successful maneuver!

As we got closer to the clearing, Major Cee said, "Okay, I'll take it from here." He began to slow our forward motion. Once we were directly overhead, he completely stopped all forward movement and we were suspended in mid-air, just hovering. He began a slow descent and asked me to tell him what I saw.

"Well sir, naturally I see this nice green meadow surrounded by the forest. There is a pond of water in the middle with a white raft floating on top, lawn furniture, picnic tables, a concession stand, and about 30 to 40 people milling around. Hey, wait a minute. They don't have any clothes on." Major Cee said, "Of course they don't have any clothes on. This is a nudist camp. You know, the Germans are just great sun worshippers, and they've got these nudist camps all over the place."

We were still descending. The Germans were curious about what we were doing there, so they began to gather down below. By this time, we were only about 50 feet off the ground, and the turbulence created from the rotor had sand, gravel, twigs, and everything that wasn't nailed down flying through the air. All the debris was slamming into their naked bodies. In retaliation, they were picking up rocks and beer bottles and throwing them at us. Seeing that we were in harm's way, the major started our ascent to a safe altitude. As we cleared the trees and took off, he was laughing hysterically, and asked, "What did you think of that?" I said, "I thought it was very funny, but quite frankly when I was on my way to work today, I really didn't imagine this was going to be part of my agenda."

We were flying for about 15 minutes when Major Cee spotted another clearing in the woods. "Let me guess. Another nudist camp, right?" I asked. "Yup!" Down we went for a second run. Of course, we were met with the same reception as the first one. After we were run off a second time, I thought it was all over. But the major wasn't done having fun yet, so we stopped to visit a third camp. I was beginning to wonder how long this was going to continue. But about that time, the major looked at his watch and said, "I'm hungry. Let's go into town and get some lunch."

I was asking, "What do you mean, let's go into town and get some lunch? What are we going to do with the helicopter while we are eating?" His reply was, "Don't worry about it. I have a plan." The year was 1969, and there were no McDonald's franchises in Germany at the time. However, had there been, I believe Major Cee was crazy enough to fly the helicopter through the drive-up lane.

We were now flying north along the Rhine River. In the distance on the west bank, we were approaching the quaint little town of Bacharach. Bacharach, Germany is a medieval village built around the 14th century. It was fortified with a wall that was designed to protect it from invasion. Within the walls were the stores, shops, and homes, and outside was farmland that surrounded the area.

The major landed the helicopter in a cabbage field adjacent to the main wall entrance and said, "Let's go. I will take you to a restaurant that serves the best schnitzel you've ever had." I replied, "Are you just going to let this helicopter sit here?" He assured me that he had done this before, and everything would be just fine. We walked into town. He was right about the food. We had a great meal and returned to the chopper, flew it back to Finthen, and returned to our barracks in Wackernheim. It was an unforgettable day, and I had to wonder what was next.

CHAPTER 30
CAPTAIN TOOTH FAIRY

As 1969 was moving along, I had to make some decisions. On December 12 of that year, my military obligation would be fulfilled, and I could return to civilian life. I still had two years of college to complete, and I was trying to time my transition from military life to student so that I could just slide right into one from the other. Also, my wife needed to get back to the States to finish the medical assistant course she was taking prior to her move to Germany.

I developed a plan whereby Alice and Heidi would return to California in November. They could live with my in-laws, and Alice could finish her studies. I would remain in Germany for an additional six months, get out of the service in the summer of 1970, and re-enter college in time to start the fall semester. Everyone thought that was a great plan, so Alice and Heidi departed in November. I moved into the Bachelor Officers Quarters (BOQ).

This turned out to be a smart decision. As a first lieutenant, I had received a pay increase. With the additional income, I was able to save a fair amount of money for college, and with winter just around the corner, I would be able to enjoy a third season of skiing in Europe before returning to the States.

Two buildings from my office was the dental office, and I stopped in for my six-month check-up. The army dentist at McCully Barracks was a guy by the name of Capt. Eric Bogel. He was a jovial person with a magnetic personality. While I was in the dental chair, we struck up a conversation, and he asked me if I skied. I replied, "Yes I do."

Eric went on to tell me that he was part of a German-American ski club that was planning a trip to Kaprun, Austria that weekend and asked if I would like to join them. This sounded fun, and I readily accepted. I asked, "When do we leave?" Eric said, "Thursday evening after work."

I gulped. I told him I had to work Friday and Saturday until noon, so it looked like I would have to pass on his invitation.

"Bullshit," said Eric, "What is your commanding officer's name?" I told him, "Lieutenant Colonel Copeland." He grabbed the phone and called him. "Colonel Copeland, this is Captain Bogel. I have Lieutenant Dolby in my dental chair, and he has a very badly impacted wisdom tooth. I am going to extract it Thursday afternoon. He will be in a lot of pain, so I'm going to send him home with instructions to be on bed rest Friday and Saturday. However, I will make sure he reports back for duty at 6 a.m. Monday morning in time for command reveille." He hung up the phone and said, "Go home and pack. We are going skiing. After all, I'm your doctor. I am also a captain, and you are a lieutenant, so you must obey orders."

"Holy smoke. What just happened?" I thought. I explained to Eric that I did not have any wisdom teeth. I had them all removed several years prior to going in the Army. He told me that it did not make any difference. Wisdom teeth were like having an ace in the hole. They always came in handy when you needed them the most, and as far as he was concerned, I had four brand new ones as of that moment. After all, he was the self-proclaimed Tooth Fairy, and if he wanted to make wisdom teeth magically appear, it was within his power to do so.

As it turned out, we had an excellent weekend. Austria was one of the most beautiful countries I had ever seen. The chalets, farmhouses, countryside, food, and the people were magnificent. Because it was so early in the season, I was concerned about whether there would be enough snow for skiing. We arrived and checked into a quaint hotel in the little town of Zell-am-See. It was storybook perfect. It had a restaurant that served delicious meals. It had a bar with beer that was fantastic. And, our rooms were furnished with big feather beds. However, there wasn't one snowflake to be seen. I asked Eric if he bothered to check the ski report prior to leaving Germany. He told me not to worry about it.

The next morning, about 15 of us assembled at the gondola near the edge of town. Still no snow. But we hopped in and were promptly whisked up the mountain. At the tram stop, another gondola was waiting, and we hopped on that one. Then there was a third gondola that got us to our final destination. By this time, we were well above 10,000 feet, and it was hard to breathe at that altitude. As it turned out, we were on top of a glacier, and this was where the Austrian ski team practiced for the winter Olympics during the summer months. The skiing was great, and I met a lot of new friends. I got home close to 10 p.m. Sunday evening, just enough time to get a good night's sleep and make it to command reveille Monday morning as was promised.

Eric Bogel and me

Several weeks later, Capt. Bogel called me and said he needed to see me right away. It sounded serious, so I walked over to his office. I asked, "What's the problem?" Eric told me that he was reviewing my dental records and discovered another issue. It happened to be a second impacted wisdom tooth. I asked him if he was nuts because we both knew I didn't have any wisdom teeth. He told me that the ski club was going to Grindelwald, Switzerland that weekend, and I just had to make the trip. I went, and it was another successful adventure.

This strategy repeated itself two more times and I finally told Eric, "That's it. I'm out of wisdom teeth, so take me off the invite list for future trips." Then one day a funny thing happened. I walked into battalion headquarters and bumped into the sergeant major. I asked him where Lt. Col. Copeland was as I had not seen him lately. The sergeant major replied, "Haven't you heard? He was transferred to Fort Hood, Texas. He left yesterday. His replacement, Lieutenant Colonel Mac, is due in any minute."

Immediately, I got on the phone and called Capt. Bogel. He asked what was up. I said, "You won't believe this, but I just got four brand new wisdom teeth!"

Shortly thereafter, 2nd Lt. Wally Garvas came strolling into town. Wally was a recent graduate from the United States Military Academy at West Point and was one of the most outstanding athletes of all time to come through the Academy. I believe he held records in football that have yet to be broken.

I was sitting at the bar in the officers' club one evening having a beer, when he walked in and sat down next to me. We struck up a conversation and developed a friendship immediately. Wally wasn't accustomed to drinking alcohol, so as he went from one beer to the next, I watched his face go and glow from white to pink to red. Finally, I suggested we stop drinking fearing his head would explode if we continued. He agreed, and we called it quits with the understanding that we would meet for dinner the next evening.

The following Saturday night, the two of us were invited to a wine tasting in the nearby town of Rudesheim along with four of our colleagues. Rudesheim is famous for the production of white wine, and the new vintage had just become available. As we began sampling the wine, we tried to act like sophisticated connoisseurs, using such language as, "Expresses fruit flavor balanced with oak notes and a rich texture," "Delicate character and a dry complex finish," "Elegant, yet approachable without being complicated," "Distinctive with variable flavors, full bodied, and well balanced," and so on. As we continued this charade, we were getting rather looped. Toward the end of the evening, we asked one of our companions, Greg Collins, to give his assessment of the next sample. He downed it in one big gulp and bellowed, "Great shit. Let's get another bottle." Well, that wrapped it up for the wine-tasting evening. We were asked to leave. So much for sophistication.

Wally didn't know how to ski but wanted to learn, so we invited him to join our group. He was such a good athlete that he caught on immediately. And within about two weeks, he was out-performing everybody on the slopes. Meanwhile, our little German-American ski club was growing in popularity. We had one Austrian by the name of Irving that joined early on, followed by a half-dozen American schoolteachers, and a German couple named Wolfgang and Renate Warner. Before the winter was over, we had about 30 members. Everyone was of the same mindset — ski, eat, drink, party, and laugh until our sides ached. We skied through Germany, Austria, France, Italy, and Switzerland. This was one of the best times of my life, and I developed lifelong friendships that continued to remain strong decades later.

One evening after work, Eric, Wally, and I went to the officers' club for happy hour. We were met at the front door by Wolfgang. Wolfgang loved Americans and wanted to be a member of our gang. He spoke perfect English and had a colorful sense of humor. We accepted him as if he was one of our own. We invited him into the club to join us for drinks. The waiter came up and politely informed us that German nationals were not allowed in the officers' club. I told the waiter, "You do not understand. This is Hauptman Scheisskopf of the German Army, our NATO ally, and he had every right to be here." The waiter apologized profusely and welcomed him with the first round of drinks "on the house."

Wolfgang looked at him as if to say, "Apology accepted, but don't ever make that mistake again." The reality of the situation was that Wolfgang was a civilian and an accountant by trade. He was never in the military, and Hauptman Scheisskopf in English means, "Captain Shithead." He became a regular at the club.

Me, Wally Garvas, and Wolfgang Warner

In December, I was called into a meeting in the battalion conference room. At a long table sat a lieutenant colonel, a major, and two captains. I stood before them at parade rest. They informed me that I was being promoted to captain with a few caveats. I would become a battery commander and have my own 105mm howitzer battery. And, I had to agree to extend my military service for another full year. (By this time, I had not informed them of my intention to extend for another six months.) They approached me, pinned the captain bars on my shoulders, told me to go home and sleep on it, and we would meet again at 7 a.m. the following morning. They all patted me on the back and showered me with congratulations. I thanked them and left.

The next morning, I showed up to the meeting. I had taken the captain bars off and put my first lieutenant bars back on. Now we were in for a heated discussion. "Are you turning down this promotion?" I was asked. Before accepting a promotion, I wanted to know where this battery was that I was to assume command of. They said, "Well, it's in Vietnam." I had a problem with that. By now, we were moving into 1970, and it was obvious we were not going to win that war. I was trying to be as diplomatic with my comments and questions as I possibly could, so I kept that thought to myself.

I told them that I had done some research the night before and discovered the difference in pay between a captain and a first lieutenant was only $28 per month. They came back with, "Yes, but you also get combat pay and that would be an additional $100 per month."

I was thinking, "Let me get this straight. I extend my stay in the Army for another year. I go to Vietnam and get my ass blown off. And, all of this for an additional $128 per month. Math wasn't my best subject in school, but this was definitely not a convincing proposition."

So, I said, "To begin with, when I got drafted, I had a two-year military obligation. I went to Officer Candidate School, and that added almost another year commitment on my part. And, now you want me to re-up for an additional year. This battalion is authorized 29 officers, and because of the war, we are now trying to run it with only nine officers. You are very understaffed. I will tell you what I am willing to do. I will extend for six months. You can keep the captain bars and the extra $28 per month. I am willing to stay on as a first lieutenant providing you keep me here in Germany."

The promotion board went wild. They were excited because, somehow, they thought they had just implemented a brilliant plan. Both parties got something they wanted, we all walked away as happy campers, and I got to be a captain for part of a day.

Meanwhile, Captain Tooth Fairy was plotting our next move. He wanted to take a driving vacation to Ireland, and he wanted me to travel with him. I thought it would be fun, so I put in a two-week leave request, and it was promptly granted. We were off on another great adventure.

When it came to money, Eric was tighter than a flea's ass stretched around a rain barrel. He was not about to spend any more money on this vacation than was absolutely necessary. I agreed to do it his way. So, we loaded his car with a pup tent, two sleeping bags, and a couple cases of C-rations. I asked Eric if we could spring for a hotel every third night so we wouldn't have to bathe in a stream. He had trouble with that idea but was willing to compromise.

Eric drove a beat-up VW that was about ten years old and had four bald tires. In spite of it all, the car managed to hold its own throughout the entire vacation. We took off one evening and drove all night to avoid paying for a hotel. We made it through Germany and France, reached the coast about mid-morning the next day, and drove the car onto the ferry that would take us across the channel to England. Despite the lack of sleep, the ocean was quite invigorating, so I stood out on the deck and sucked in the salt air. By the time we reached the white cliffs of Dover, I was recharged and ready to tackle the new day.

The next challenge was driving on the left side of the road. This scared Eric, so he turned the driving over to me. It scared me, too, but I figured it out and was comfortable after a couple hours. Since Ireland was our primary destination, we powered across England and found a nice little slice of countryside near the coastline of Wales to set up camp. It was beautiful landscape with trees, meadows, and streams. I put up our little pup tent while Eric broke out the C-rations and started to cook dinner.

Eric regarded himself as a good cook; however, his kitchen had only two condiments — ketchup and Worcestershire sauce. He put them on everything -- beef, ham, fish, and of course, all our C-rations, no matter what was in the can. In his mind, this was fine dining. I learned to tolerate it. We sat around the campfire for a while, then turned in for a good night of sleep after being up for two days.

The next morning, I struck camp and loaded everything in the car. Eric was in his gourmet kitchen underneath a tree cooking breakfast on a one-burner stove, fueled by a can of Sterno.

When I asked what was for breakfast, Eric said that he had located some breakfast C-rations containing scrambled eggs and spam packaged June 17, 1954. Sarcastically, I said, "Wow, that sounds delicious." Eric assured me that it would taste great once he doctored it up with his famous secret recipe of ketchup and Worcestershire sauce.

We drove the car onto the next ferry at Fishguard, Wales and crossed the Irish Sea, landing at the seaport of Wexford, Ireland. Heading west, we stopped at Waterford to tour the crystal factory, then drove on to the town of Cork. Once in Cork, we had to visit the Blarney Castle and kiss the famous Blarney Stone. When we arrived in Killarney, we headed north through the city of Shannon. Our next stop would be the Cliffs of Moher. Once there, I approached an old man with a scraggly old mutt. Both man and dog were sucking on corn-cob pipes and wearing green derby hats. This guy looked like he knew the secrets that lay within the cliffs, so I struck up a conversation with him.

He was a grounds keeper and pointed to a little stone house on a bluff where he and his dog lived. It was very quaint, and smoke was coming out of the chimney. I knew that he was about to tell a story, and because it was cold and windy, I was hoping that he would invite me into his house where I could hear what he had to say while sitting in front of the fireplace. That didn't happen. However, he told me that in addition to this being a tourist attraction, it was also a well-known place to come for those contemplating suicide. That caught me off guard.

He went on to tell me that because of the weather, this was a very lonely place to live and people often experienced severe depression. He could tell when someone was about to end it all because they would drive their cars up to the edge of the cliffs and sit there for hours thinking about their next move. Then, after two or three visits, they would arrive and stop their car about 100 meters away from the cliff, fire up the engine full throttle, and go sailing off the edge. Special equipment was used to bring the car and body back up to the bluff. I wondered why they just didn't build a barrier to keep it from happening in the first place.

Our destination for the day was Galway Bay, and we arrived in the town of Galway about 5 p.m. I figured it was about time to take a hot shower and be able to shave without kneeling at the edge of a cold creek. I spotted a quaint hotel overlooking the bay and told Eric that if he wanted to sleep in the woods again, that was his prerogative. I was going to get a room regardless. He opted for a warm bed as well. The hotel had a small restaurant that served a nice dinner, and in the basement, was a large meeting room with a rock fireplace, tables, and chairs.

Located at the mouth of Galway Bay are three islands called the Aran Islands. On Saturday evenings, it was customary for some of the residents of those islands to sail into town with their instruments and perform for anyone who would listen. The night Eric and I were there, the musicians set up their stage in the basement of the hotel where we were staying. It was cold and rainy, so they built a fire in the fireplace and began singing Irish folk songs. Eric and I grabbed a couple beers and sat down to listen to their music. Their ballads were so descriptive that I could visualize myself in the scenes whether they were singing about a farmer tilling the soil, a brave soldier leaving for war, or the fate of a young fishmonger named Molly Malone. Eric and I stayed with the musicians and chatted for a while. I asked them what they did for a living out in the middle of nowhere. They said that the men raised sheep, and the women used the wool to knit sweaters. Then they would bring the sweaters into town and sell them. I asked if they did anything else. They said, "Oh yes, most of our time is spent drinking Irish whiskey." I thought perhaps I would like to go to work with these guys when I separated from the Army.

Captain Tooth Fairy, Eric Bogel

The next day Eric and I packed our car and headed east toward Dublin. I was driving and noticed that everyone was waving at us. After about an hour of this I said to Eric, "Can you believe how friendly these people are. Every time we pass someone, they wave to us." Eric agreed. "Yep, they sure are a friendly bunch." About that time, a big old truck was headed for us, and it looked like we were going to have a head-on collision. I immediately pulled off the road, and then it dawned on me. Holy cow, I had forgotten we were in Ireland, and I was driving on the wrong side of the road. All those friendly people were trying to warn me to change lanes. It's a wonder I didn't get us both killed.

From Dublin, we drove north leaving the Irish Republic and entering the country of Northern Ireland. Our plan was to get to Belfast. At that time in history, Northern Ireland was in a political mess and riddled with hatred between the Irish and the British. Belfast was such a battle-worn city, we decided to get out of there before we got shot. As we were leaving, we were approached by an old drunk. He told a story about how he was in a secret army, and they were on their way to fight the Russians in defense of America. He was asking for a donation so that he and his fellow soldiers could buy some ammunition, as they were running rather low. We knew he was trying to gather enough money to buy a pint or two, but we enjoyed his story so much we decided to give him a couple bucks. We laughed as we watched him make a beeline for the closest bar. Then a real soldier approached us and told us this was a very dangerous place to be, and that we should leave immediately. We did.

We drove onto a ferry, disembarked at Cairnryan, Scotland, and headed toward Loch Ness. We were bound and determined to see "Nessie," the Loch Ness monster, but she was nowhere to be found. So, we doubled back to Glasgow and went into a bar near the university. It was wild with excitement. The beer, the singing, and the laughter made for a fantastic evening.

We completed the loop by returning to London and doing the usual touristy things. Then we took the ferry back to France and worked our way into Germany. We had a few days left on our vacation, so Eric suggested we head north to one of his favorite getaways. I said, "Okay. Where is that?" He said he wasn't going to tell me as it was a surprise, and I needed to trust him on this one. We drove north all the way to the German-Danish border and drove the car up and onto a flatbed train. By this time, it was nightfall, and the train headed west on elevated tracks over the North Sea. I thought to myself, "What on earth is this, and what am I getting myself into?" Eric insisted that I be patient as I continued to question him. After a while, the train came to a stop, and we drove off and onto a road. In the middle of nowhere, Eric says, "This looks like a great place to set up camp." So, we did and got a good night's sleep. The next morning, we drove down to a beach and parked. I said, "Eric, would you please tell me where we are and what we are doing here?" He said, "Welcome to the island of Sylt. This island is one mile wide, three miles long, and you are just going to love it." "Why?" I asked. "We are on a barren island in the North Sea. It is cold, overcast, and windy."

We were walking along the beach, and we were the only ones there. I was wearing a pair of Levi's, a sweatshirt, and a heavy jacket. And, I was freezing. Pretty soon I spotted a girl walking toward us. As she got closer, I said to Eric, "It looks like she isn't wearing anything." Eric said, "She isn't. This island happens to be the largest nudist colony in the world. Enjoy it."

Well, I had never been to a nudist beach, and I had never been naked in public, so I didn't know what to think. As the morning progressed, the temperature began to rise, and more and more people were showing up, and they were all naked. Eric said, "I don't know about you, but when in Rome, do as the Romans," and he shed all his clothes right on the beach.

I had never seen Eric naked before, and when I did, I started laughing hysterically. He asked, "What is so funny?" I said, "Your ass. What on earth happened to it? It looks like the surface of the moon. Did you sit on a grenade?"

So, he began to tell me his story. Before he came to Germany, he was stationed at an Army post in South Korea for about a year. He met this Korean girl at a party, and they hit it off immediately. Chemistry was high, and hormones were flowing. They wanted to be alone, but there was no place to go. Eric spotted a one-man Army sleeping bag, grabbed it and the girl, and took off into the woods. The sleeping bag was only big enough for one person, but Eric was determined he could make this work. He got her all settled in, then climbed in on top. When he tried to zip up the sleeping bag, he could not get it passed his ass. As the night wore on, the temperature dropped below freezing, and when he woke up the next morning, he had a frost-bitten ass that required medical attention to prevent gangrene from setting in. So that was his explanation for an unsightly posterior.

By midday, it was getting hot, and the beach was loaded with hundreds of people who were not wearing clothes, with one exception — me! Now, I was starting to feel out of place, so I sheepishly shed my clothes and became part of the crowd. After about an hour, I was getting used to the idea; however, there was a minor hazard developing that we had to contend with, and that was the oil.

The North Sea is rich in petroleum deposits, and beachgoers must watch where they are stepping because the oil has a tendency to ooze out of the ground and up through the sand. Now we had already identified the fact that Eric had a defective ass, but to make matters worse, he had been sitting on the sand for quite some time, not realizing that oil was seeping up beneath him. When he finally stood up, his pocked-marked ass was coated with a thick layer of sand and tar. This stuff didn't come off easily, and there was no way he could put his clothes back on.

We made it back to the car. Fortunately, we carried a spare can of gasoline in the trunk. Between the gas, an old rag, and a lot of rubbing, Eric finally got himself cleaned up, but we were careful not to light any cigarettes for a couple hours.

After two weeks on the road with Eric, it was time to end the trip and return home. We had a fantastic vacation with just a few hiccups along the way.

As we moved into the summer months, my tour of duty was coming to an end. I drove my car up to Bremerhaven, Germany and had it shipped to Bayonne, New Jersey because I knew I would be processing out of the Army at Fort Dix. My car would be waiting for me there, only a short cab ride away.

Sadly, I said good-bye to all my friends. I had so many of them and hated to leave them behind. But I left, taking 30 months of fond memories with me. I was very lucky to have met all of them, and fortunately over time, I was able to reconnect with all of them. It was time to become a civilian again and start a new chapter in my life.

Once at Fort Dix, I was provided a nice clean room at the BOQ. I was exhausted and went to bed immediately. The next morning, I met the pay officer at the quartermaster's office. He calculated my pay and paid me off in cash. He gave me my honorable discharge papers and sent me on my way.

My in-laws agreed to babysit Heidi while Alice flew back to New York to meet me. We would have two weeks to get reacquainted as we drove from the East Coast to California. Along the way, we stopped to visit with friends and relatives. All-in-all it was a pleasant and exciting trip. Having been out of the United States for two and a half years made me realize how much I missed home.

CHAPTER 31
BACK TO CIVILIAN LIFE

In September 1970, I re-entered college. I was a business major, and originally, I had planned to return to UCLA. However, by the time I got back from Germany, UCLA had closed its undergraduate School of Business. When that happened, the faculty and staff transferred to California State University in Northridge, a suburb of Los Angeles in the San Fernando Valley. I did the same.

Financially, the plan was for Alice to get a job. However, she decided that she would rather stay home with Heidi. So, the only income we had was from the GI Bill, and that wasn't going to cut it for a family of three. I joined the Army Reserves, and that brought in some extra cash. I also got a job loading trucks at night for UPS. And during the summer months, I worked for a painting contractor during the day. I stayed focused on school and work, determined to complete my college education as quickly as possible.

I had stayed in contact with my college roommate from Arizona State University, Cliff Rifkin. He called one evening to announce that he was in town and asked if I could come down to his hotel near Los Angeles International Airport to meet him for a beer. We had not seen each other for the past four years, so it was a great opportunity to get caught up. I asked him what brought him to town. He told me that after he graduated from college, he got this really great job with Trans World Airlines (TWA) as a Director of Customer Service or DCS as they were called.

He was based at Kennedy International Airport in New York, and his job was to manage Boeing 747 flights around the world. I thought to myself, with all the places I had lived, and with my passion for travel, this was exactly what I wanted to do as well. However, I was in school and that had to be my top priority.

After nearly two years, I was getting close to graduation. I didn't have much time for extra-curricular activities. However, I did join the American Marketing Association and assumed an officer position as vice president of the college campus chapter. The Dean of the School of Business and I befriended one another, and he encouraged me to go to Harvard for my MBA once I earned my undergraduate degree. I explained that I didn't have the mental capacity to compete in education at that level, and I sure didn't have the $10,000 per year to finance the tuition. He explained to me that my brain was just fine and how well I would fit in once I got there. That was encouraging, but what about the $20,000 I would need to complete the two-year program? He had all the answers. He told me he would sponsor me to get into Harvard and help me apply for scholarships to pay for it. This man was wonderful, and I am eternally grateful for the interest he took in me.

Corporate recruiters began arriving on campus scouting for talent among the graduating class. Also, on campus was an employment office of sorts with a bulletin board for posting jobs. During my final year of college, I would stop in there to review my options. One day I stopped by, and the lady behind the counter told me that TWA was hiring flight attendants, and she asked me if she could set me up with an interview. I preferred the Director of Customer Service position but figured if I got my foot in the door and became a flight attendant, it would get me one step closer to the job I really wanted. She wrote down on a piece of paper, "Interview, 4:30 p.m. Friday, TWA hangar, Los Angeles International Airport."

I arrived ahead of schedule and checked in with the receptionist. I told her I was there for a 4:30 interview. She said, "Oh, are you interviewing for the DCS position?" Holy crap, I didn't even know they were interviewing for that position. My head was spinning, and my mind was racing. I thought, "Quick Steve, recalculate and react."

"Yes," I said.

She invited me to have a seat, and she let the interviewer know that I had arrived. In a couple minutes, Mr John Warren approached me and apologized, saying there must have been a mix-up because he did not see my name on the list. I pulled out a slip of paper from my shirt pocket and said, "See. The note said to be here at 4:30." I sure wasn't going to tell him I was there to interview for a different position. Mr Warren said, "Well, as long as you are here, let's spend a few minutes together." The interview went well, and I was invited to go to Kansas City for a second interview.

I could not believe what had just happened. My dream job just popped out of nowhere. I was so excited I could not sleep all weekend. I called my buddy, Cliff Rifkin, and told him the good news. He said he was unaware that TWA was planning to hire more DCSs but wished me good luck with the interview. The next thing I knew, I was on a Boeing 707 headed east. Nervously, I took a seat and buckled up. A few seconds later, a guy by the name of Carl Rogers sat down next to me. He seemed very personable, and we easily struck up a conversation. He asked me where I was going, and why. As it turned out, we were both interviewing for a DCS position. When we landed at Mid-Continental Airport in Kansas City, we wished each other well. However, secretly we were each hoping to out-interview the other.

The interview was exactly as I expected. There was a panel of five men, professionally dressed in business suits, well-groomed, and confident. They all sat on the same side of the table, opposite me. So, from the get-go, I am on an uneven playing field, outnumbered five to one. They had a game plan, and it was well rehearsed. I had no game plan and did not know what to expect. They were intimidating. I was intimidated. They planned it that way, and I felt it. They asked a series of questions one might expect during an interview. After a while, one of them said they had conducted so many interviews that they all were getting very bored, so could I please humor them with a funny story.

I started in with a story about a skiing trip I was on in Germany during my time in the service. About a quarter of the way through, I could tell this was a set-up, and these guys were not going to laugh even if Bob Hope was telling the story. This was just a continuation of the intimidation process as I watched their expressions solidify into ice. So, I stopped and explained to these five zombies that I was there to interview for a job and not to tell stories. I went on to say that I had developed strong leadership and managerial skills in the military, and if they were looking for someone that could lead and react in tight situations, then they were looking at the right person for the job. They thanked me for my time, and I thanked them for theirs and left.

Back at the airport, I jumped on a return flight to Los Angeles, and my fellow passenger coincidentally just happened to be Carl Rogers once again. We had about a three-hour flight ahead of us, and that gave us plenty of time to talk and compare notes. He asked me how my interview went, and I told him I did not think it went well at all. I went on to say that the interviewing panel was so poker-faced that I just could not get a read on how good or bad I did. Carl said he felt the same way. We both sat there headed west at 35,000 feet in doubt and lacking self-confidence.

About a week later, I received a letter from TWA offering me the job, along with instructions to report for training at the Breech Training Academy in Overland Park, Kansas on May 8, 1972. I GOT MY DREAM JOB`!

Now, I had a new challenge. College graduation was set for June 15, five weeks after my start date with TWA. So, I arranged a one-on-one meeting with all my professors and explained my situation. I told them about my good fortune with TWA. They were genuinely excited for me and agreed to give me my final exams on a schedule that accommodated my TWA agenda. Job offers for graduating seniors at that time were paying starting salaries of about $800 per month. TWA was starting me at $1,100 per month. That was 37.5 percent above the norm.

Carl Rogers

I flew to Kansas City to get settled into my new surroundings. Upon arrival, I ran into a familiar face. It was Carl Rogers. "You made it. Congratulations," I yelled. We were genuinely happy for each other. Now, we were classmates.

I lucked out getting a fantastic roommate by the name of Doug Trevor. We had a lot in common. We were about the same age, as were our wives and daughters. Doug had a great sense of humor and was always up for anything at any time. He wanted to have fun and expected me to be part of it. I had to explain early on that I liked to have fun as much as the next guy, but I was still in school and had to use every spare minute to study for my final exams. He wasn't happy about that, but I promised that if he was patient with me, I would make it up to him once we graduated.

Doug was already a TWA employee as were several of my other classmates. They knew the company, the industry, and the unique language associated with the airlines. For me, it was a whole new world. In the beginning, I felt like a foreigner that just stepped off the boat at Ellis Island. At night, I would tell Doug that I heard an unfamiliar word or phrase that day. "What does that mean?" I would ask. He would provide me with answers, and slowly I became one of them.

Breech was laid out like a typical college campus with classrooms and dormitories all on the same property. This would be my home for the next five weeks.

In the evenings after dinner, most of the group would go to a bar for a couple beers or get together to study and socialize. I went to my room and spent about an hour reviewing all that I learned that day. Then I would spend a couple more hours studying for my college exams. Doug would tease me with the thought of going out for a pizza and some beers. As I was studying, he would say, "Let me build you a pizza. First, we start out with a high yeast dough, smothered with rich, tangy tomato sauce, then covered with cheese, and topped with plenty of pepperoni." He was a great salesman and painted an image of the most beautiful pizza in the world. Sometimes I would end up saying, "Okay, let's go."

I worked out a schedule with my professors at California State University. Each Friday night, I would fly back to Los Angeles. Then on Saturday mornings, I would meet one of them at their house and take an exam. I would fly back to Kansas City on Sundays to begin a new week of training. I did this every week, and when it was finally over, I graduated from college and TWA training within a couple days of each other. It was a grueling schedule. I was exhausted, but I got it done.

When my class of 40 graduated, we would be assigned to a domicile in New York, Chicago, Los Angeles, or San Francisco. Doug and I were hoping for New York because that was the departure city for most international destinations, and that was our primary interest. Fortunately, the dream came true for both of us and Carl Rogers as well.

I left Kansas City and returned to California to prepare for my move to the East Coast. Doug was originally from Kansas City. He was already packed and ready to go. He took off for New York immediately with the understanding that I would catch up to him in a couple days. We hoped he would find us a good place for our families to live by the time I got back there.

I arrived home late Friday night and told Alice we were moving to the East Coast. She asked, "When?" "As soon as I wake up tomorrow morning," I said. I called the Mayflower Moving Company at 8 a.m. and told them if they could be at my house by noon, they had the job. They arrived by 11 a.m., got us packed, and they were out the door by 5 p.m.

Sunday morning, Alice, Heidi, and I drove to Los Angeles International Airport. My first stop was the TWA cargo terminal. I dropped off my car, and they loaded it onto a Boeing707 cargo jet. Then we grabbed a cab to the passenger terminal, barely making a 9 a.m. flight to New York. We were off on another great adventure, and to start a new chapter in our lives.

Prior to joining TWA, I had many discussions with Alice about me working with hundreds of flight attendants. I wanted to know if she had a problem with it. If she did, I would pass on the job. She assured me over and over again that this was not a problem, and I should move forward with my new career. She thought it was a great job with unlimited travel benefits, and she seemed genuinely excited.

We were on our flight to our new home, and a flight attendant came up to us and introduced herself. She was very attractive and had the personality to match — a downright nice person. I introduced myself as a new TWA employee, and she enthusiastically welcomed me aboard the world's greatest airline. She went on to tell me how proud she was to be a TWA employee, and how I would be, too.

I could tell that Alice was intimidated by her, and considering everything, I could understand why. I tried to explain to Alice that making passengers feel welcome was part of the job. However, I could tell she was taking notes and parking them in the back of her mind. These thoughts would resurface in the months to come.

CHAPTER 32
WELCOME TO NEW ENGLAND

We arrived in New York that evening and checked into the Hilton Hotel. The next morning, Doug met us. He had been house hunting for the past three days and told us he had found the perfect place to live.

One of TWA's rules was that we had to live no further than a 100-mile radius from our domicile, Kennedy International Airport. Doug instructed us to follow him, and we drove exactly 100 miles north to the town of Brookfield Center, Connecticut. Doug had indeed found the perfect location. I signed the lease and received the keys to our new home. I was moving at lightning-speed, starting in Kansas City Friday, to meeting the movers at my home in California on Saturday, to a flight to New York on Sunday, and moving into my new home in Connecticut on Monday.

Our new home was in a complex of townhomes nestled in the woods. The units were more like condominiums and were later sold as such. Doug, the salesman that he was, recruited other TWA classmates, and soon two more, Ted Cannon and Andy Thorton, joined us. As new tenants continued to arrive, we formed a very cohesive neighborhood. In the coming months, several other TWA DCSs moved into the surrounding area. We would get together frequently for barbecues, and on Mondays, the guys who were in town took turns hosting Monday night football parties with hamburgers and beer. The wives joined in, and block parties became a weekly event. The camaraderie created a feeling of family.

All our homes had fireplaces, and in the fall, we would organize a firewood harvest. The surrounding woods had many fallen trees that made it easy to collect enough firewood for the winter. There was a small pond on the property, and when it froze, we would haul logs down to the pond and build bonfires to keep us warm while we were ice skating.

Fall was a fantastic time of the year. With the leaves on the trees changing, New England came alive with spectacular colors. I loved to hike and explore the hundreds of years of history that time left behind for me to enjoy. Walking down the road kicking through the piles of leaves would eventually lead me to some old, abandoned graveyard. Early settlers cleared the land of rocks and trees to create fields for planting crops. The rocks were removed from the fields and used to build walls for a variety of structures. Often, they were used to create the perimeters for graveyards. Stacked with precision, these old grey stones were covered with moss that added a bit of charm to an already idyllic country setting. I would push through the rusty, sagging gates that were sandwiched between walls of stacked stone and start reading the inscriptions chiseled on the grave markers. "Here lies John Smith, born 1752, died 1796. Fought for our country during the Revolutionary War." "Here lies Sarah Miles, born 1803, proud mother of five children, died of smallpox 1857." And so on.

I would spend hours reading grave markers and pondering what life must have been like for these people. Often, time and weather had taken their toll, and the gravestones were worn down to the point where they could barely be read. The winters were harsh, so I knew life must have been very challenging for those that preceded us.

Brookfield Center had only 700 residents, with a general store, church, school, and a library. It was charming, beautiful, peaceful, and a great place for a family. I drove around the small village and marveled at all the color. Having spent so many years in the Southwest, the Northeast offered a whole new perspective on life. In the springtime, there were daffodils blooming along with cherry trees, dogwoods, and burgundy-colored Japanese plum trees. Everything was so different from the environment I left behind. It was exciting and refreshing.

I had a 10-speed bike with a child's seat mounted on the back. On my days off, I would take Heidi on bike rides through the countryside. There was one route I particularly enjoyed because there was a grist mill on the side of the road. It probably had been there for 200 years or more. Heidi and I would sit nearby and imagine all the activity that must have taken place there at the time it was first built.

Doug Trevor and me

In the mornings on the days Doug and I were both at home, we would go for a three-mile run just to get the blood pumping. We were both in good shape and equally competitive athletes. In the evening after dinner, we would often grab our fishing poles, go to a stream or river, throw a line into the water, open a couple beers, and get our exercise doing 12-ounce curls.

I planned day trips with Heidi and Alice. Our favorite was to take a drive up Route 7 through the Berkshire Mountains. This two-lane country road was loaded with charm. There were many antique stores to visit and fruit stands along the way. We passed vibrant red covered bridges and waterfalls cascading down the rolling hillsides of dense forests. This was a drive that just made us happy to be alive.

CHAPTER 33
HAULING MAIL AND MOVIE STARS

My new employer had a unique and colorful history. It began in 1930 through a merger of three companies, Transcontinental Air Transport, Western Air Express, and Pittsburg Aviation Industries Corporation. The newly formed company would go by the name Transcontinental & Western Air (T&WA). These companies merged at the recommendation of the Postmaster General, Walter Brown, who was looking for bigger airlines to handle airmail contracts.

Each of the three companies contributed significant talent and assets to the merger. Transcontinental Air Transport contributed the expertise of Charles Lindbergh, Pittsburg Aviation contributed mail contracts, and Western Air Express offered the expertise of aviator Jack Frye.

Frye approached Howard Hughes in the late 1930s to invest in the new venture. Hughes agreed, and by 1939, he had acquired control of T&WA and would eventually own 78 percent of the airline. Because of Hughes' influence as a movie producer and his close ties to the entertainment industry, the carrier soon became known as the "Airline to the Stars." And if a Hollywood movie star or executive was going to fly anywhere, chances were good that they were going to fly the airline Hughes made famous.

Under his leadership, Hughes expanded the airline to serve Europe, the Middle East, and Asia. They began trans-Atlantic service to Europe in 1946. Flights reached Cairo in 1946, Bombay in 1947, Ceylon in 1953, and Manila in 1958. Routes continued to expand to include Bangkok and Hong Kong. Then in 1969, the trans-Pacific segment opened to complete round-the-world service.

In 1950, the company changed its name from Transcontinental & Western Air to Trans World Airlines or simply TWA. Passengers and employees would humorously come up with alternate names for the acronym such as Teeny-Weeny Airlines, Try Walking Awhile, Travel With Angels, and The Wrong Airport.

On April 7, 1967, TWA became one of the first all-jet airlines in the United States. From 1967–1972, TWA was the world's third largest airline by passenger miles, behind United Airlines and Aeroflot. In 1969, TWA carried the most trans-Atlantic passengers of any airline. In 1970, TWA was the first airline to offer Boeing 747 service in the U. S.

TWA assisted in structuring Saudi Arabian Airlines, Ethiopian Airlines, and Lufthansa. Airlines from around the world sent their pilots to TWA for training. TWA had become one of the largest airlines in the United States and was the "go-to-airline" for aviation-related resources.

Sadly, the company was acquired by an outside investor who took the company private in 1988. TWA became heavily burdened with debt and underwent chapter 11 restructuring in 1992 and again in 1995. In 2001, TWA filed for a third bankruptcy and was eventually acquired by American Airlines.

What a tragedy for a company with such a rich and glorious history.

CHAPTER 34
JUMBO JETS

Throughout the years, TWA and the Boeing Company had an excellent relationship. In the 1960s, the workhorse for TWA, and other airlines as well, was the Boeing 707 aircraft. Its contribution to aviation history is well recognized. It moved people and lots of them. Passenger capacity was 140-200 people, depending on the airline and the specifications they requested. TWA's 707 was configured to carry 170 passengers.

About the time commercial aviation began growing at a rapid pace, Juan Trippe of Pan American Airways approached the Boeing company and urged them to build an aircraft twice the size of the 707. He suggested that a larger aircraft would be the solution to the congestion at airports, reducing the number of airplanes required to move the same number of people.

Boeing responded by designing and building the 747. It was the first wide-bodied airplane ever produced and was nicknamed the "Jumbo Jet" and often referred to as the "Queen of the Skies." The maiden flight took place on February 9, 1969. The first commercial flight took to the airways on January 22, 1970, flown by Pan Am from New York to London. TWA was the second airline to launch operations and began service on February 25, 1970, with a coast-to-coast flight from Los Angeles to New York, making it the first transcontinental US service by a 747.

Boeing was off and running, and by March 1970, a new 747 was coming off the assembly line every three days. The original version was two-and-a-half times the size of the Boeing 707. TWA placed an order for 19 of these Jumbo Jets with a seating configuration designed to carry 346 passengers at a cost of $22 million each. Over time, Boeing would produce four variants of the 747. In accordance with each airline's specifications and requirements, the 747 was designed to accommodate up to 600 passengers. The Boeing 747 held the passenger capacity record for 37 years until the Airbus A380 was built.

The primary purpose of the aircraft was to carry passengers, but it was also being built as a cargo plane. Boeing designed it in such a way that the passenger version could easily be converted into a cargo plane. They did this because they thought the industry was moving toward supersonic transportation for passengers, and if that happened, they wanted to be able to make the conversion as quickly and inexpensively as possible without having to scrap the airplanes. Furthermore, it was thought that the 747 would become unpopular in time, so Boeing's original plan was to build no more than 400 of them. However, much to their surprise, orders continued coming in, and the number built as of April 2018 was 1,544 planes. Obviously, demand exceeded critics' expectations.

It is difficult to discuss with specific accuracy the dimensions and capabilities of the 747 because it continued to change with each new variation, and because each airline demanded certain modifications for their unique needs. However, for general discussion, the first version, the 747-100, had a length of 231 feet which was longer than the Wright Brothers' first flight. The wingspan was 195 feet, and the tail height was 63 feet. The aircraft was equivalent in height to a three-story building. The maximum take-off weight was 735,000 pounds. The fuel capacity was 48,445 gallons, with a range of 6,100 miles, and the typical cruising speed at 35,000 feet was approximately 600 miles per hour.

I recall in 1970, when I was in the Army stationed in Germany, we received word that Pan Am was flying into Frankfurt with their new Boeing 747. Frankfurt was only a 30-minute drive, so a couple buddies and I drove over to Rhine-Main International Airport to observe the landing. It was amusing to watch the 747 with a height of a three-story building pull up to the one-story terminal building. It was hard to imagine anything that big at that time, but the plane got bigger with each new variation. The 747-8 series would be the fourth and final variant. It was the largest 747 version, the largest commercial aircraft built in the United States, and the longest passenger aircraft in the world.

TWA 747

During that first encounter with a 747, it never crossed my mind that someday in the near future, my first job as a civilian would be to manage the in-flight services on these big birds, flying internationally through Europe, the Middle East, and the Far East.

CHAPTER 35
TWA's DIRECTORS OF CUSTOMER SERVICE

As we transitioned from narrow-bodied jets into the wide-bodied jet era of aviation, the airline industry went through a tremendous transformation. Because of that, the Director of Customer Service job was born.

Before acquiring the 747 aircraft, TWA filled the skies with Boeing 707s. On board were three pilots in the cockpit, five to six flight attendants in the cabin, and 170 people spread out between two passenger zones, first-class and economy. There was a single aisle running down the center of the airplane with two to three seats on each side of the aisle, four lavatories, a couple galleys for meal service, and a couple magazine racks for entertainment.

With the Boeing 747, there were three to four pilots in the cockpit. In addition to the captain, first officer, and the flight engineer, some long-haul flights would require the addition of a fourth pilot, designated as the international relief officer.

International flights could have a cabin staff of up to 14 people — a service manager, a purser, and as many as 12 flight attendants. The main deck was divided into five passenger zones. There were two aisles that ran the length of the airplane, and the seats were configured in rows of nine across — three on one side, four in the middle, and two on the other side. Each zone had a large movie screen and projector with the capacity to show different films in different zones. There was an upper deck designed as a lounge for first-class passengers accessed by a spiral staircase. It was equipped with a cocktail bar and two lavatories. There were an additional 10 lavatories located on the main deck for a total of 12 on the aircraft. Four galleys were used to prepare two in-flight meals for 346 passengers.

The first-class service included champagne, caviar, appetizers, cocktails, and cordials. There were five entrees to choose from that usually included lobster and chateaubriand. In the economy section, the passengers received menus with a choice of three entrees. Wine, beer, and cocktails could be purchased for a minimal price. The meal services on TWA's 747s were beautifully presented, resembling a flying five-star restaurant.

As glamorous as it was, it came with a price — not in terms of money, but in terms of a management system required to keep it all running smoothly in an age when computers were not commonplace, and cell phones had yet to be invented.

TWA realized that with all the extra benefits and services on these giant aircraft, they needed to put a management representative on board — one that would assist and coordinate putting the flight together at the departure station, travel with the flight to troubleshoot and solve problems as they developed in flight, be able to take it apart at the down-line arrival station, and ensure that all the services TWA promised their customers were fulfilled. That position was given the job title of Director of Customer Service or DCS as we were usually called. The airline had a DCS on every wide-bodied flight. The program was a success and enhanced customer relations and satisfaction immensely. So successful was the program, that TWA soon initiated a similar program by putting DCSs on the narrow-bodied aircraft as well.

TWA, like most airlines, was impacted by labor unions. There were three of them. The pilots had one. The flight attendants had one. And the mechanics had one. Each union was opposed to management intervention. The DCS program was 100 percent management driven and faced an uphill battle for acceptance. TWA was bound and determined to get their DCSs on board one way or another. The pilots were the biggest hurdle. Egos got in the way. The captains' philosophy was, "I am the captain of this ship, and I am ultimately responsible for what happens. Therefore, I do not need some smart-ass kid coming onboard usurping my authority." In the beginning, some of the captains kicked the DCSs off the airplane before the flight.

The flight attendants' union regarded the service manager as being the one in charge of them and responsible for everything that happened in the passenger zones of the aircraft. And the mechanics' union supported whatever the other two unions were fighting for. Painfully, the battle dragged on, but over time, the DCSs were slowly accepted by most of the union employees.

The DCSs did a lot of public relations work with both groups to smooth the way. On layovers, we would go out to dinner with the pilots. As they got to know us, the adversarial relationship started to fade, and they began to think of us as part of the team that could add value to making TWA a better airline. We would go out to dinner with the flight attendants as well. As their trust in us grew, so did the working relationship, and they began to rely on us as the "problem solvers." Got a problem? Turn it over to the DCS, and the flight attendant won't have to deal with it. Of course, there would always be a few sour grapes left in the two groups, but they were easy to identify, and we learned to work around them as well as could be expected.

The job was exciting, rewarding, frustrating, and exhausting. For me, a typical monthly schedule involved five round trips to a specific European city and back home, with three days on and three days off. So, I might be flying to Paris five times one month and making five trips to Madrid the following month. The cockpit crew changed after each round trip. However, the DCS would stay with the same cabin crew for the entire month. The cockpit crew and the cabin crew wore uniforms, but the DCSs wore business suits. TWA wanted the DCSs to have a unique presence, so we all wore the same suits. TWA provided the suits for us and furnished us with a half-dozen dress shirts and a couple ties. Every other year, they would buy us a new wardrobe of a different style and color. We were identifiable by our consistent appearance.

The days were long, and a DCS might be on duty for 14-24 hours depending on whether the flight was routine or not.

A typical trip for me would start with the 100-mile drive to the airport from my home, so I allowed myself two hours to get to work. Check-in was three hours before flight departure time. I would go to my office that was in the TWA hangar building, read my mail, and meet with my supervisor. The next stop was the dining unit to inspect the meals for quality and ensure everything that was needed for the flight was present and accounted for. Back at the hangar, I would go into flight operations and introduce myself to the cockpit crew. This gave us a few minutes to get acquainted and have an opportunity to discuss the flight plan. We talked about the route we were taking, the weather, alternate airports if we were unable to land at our primary destination, and any political issues we needed to be concerned about at the down-line station that could impact the safety of passengers.

From there, I would go over to the terminal building and meet the cabin crew. The service manager would hand out the work assignments to the flight attendants. I would inform them about the passenger load so that they could plan the meal service accordingly, and then we conducted a safety briefing before we headed to the airplane. Once on the airplane, I would do a general walk-through inspection. When that was completed, I would meet with the station manager and/or the employees working the ticket counter. Here, I would find out if I had any VIPs traveling with us or if anybody needed special assistance in one form or another. Since there were no computers for our use at the time, everything had to be done manually, and trying to move 346 passengers in the right direction was a challenge. It was very important for me to work closely with the ground personnel to insure an on-time departure.

Most international flights departed from Kennedy Airport in New York between 7 p.m. and 8 p.m. So, I might have three to four hours of work under my belt before we rolled out to the runway. If I was working a flight to Rome, for example, that meant I had at least another eight and a half hours of work to do before we landed.

Once we were airborne, I would get on the public address system and introduce myself to the passengers, explaining the various ways I could be of assistance to them. I worked my way through "A" zone and shook hands with every single first-class passenger. Then, I would methodically work my way to the back of the plane, one row at a time. Meal service and the movies were critical elements of the flight, so it was important that they both ran smoothly and on-time. The service manager, purser, and flight attendants saw to that, and I stayed out of their way unless there was a related problem.

In addition to coordinating in-flight service activity, DCSs had the ability and responsibility to offer additional services such as making hotel and car rental reservations while airborne. Also, we could sell future airline tickets and give advice relating to connecting flights. TWA contracted with Hertz and Hilton, so if a passenger needed to rent a car or needed a hotel room, we would make sure it was waiting for them upon their arrival. The most time-consuming activity was advising passengers regarding their connecting flights. Typically, the conversations would follow a similar pattern: "When we arrive in Rome, we need to connect to a Turkish Airline flight to Istanbul. How do we do it? Once we get inside the terminal building, where do we go? What time does our connecting flight leave? Will we have enough time to make the connection?" In essence, we assumed the role of a ticket agent/airport ambassador, and each conversation took about five to 15 minutes. It wasn't too bad for a routine flight because we may have that conversation with about 25 people. However, if the flight was delayed and landing late, we may have that conversation with 100 people, and that was exhausting.

TWA was very savvy when it came to sales and marketing. As DCSs were reviewing airline tickets with passengers during the flight, we had the opportunity to see their flight itineraries. If their return trip was on any other airline, we were trained to suggest they fly back with us. Usually they would say, "Sure, okay." We would rewrite the ticket, and the revenue would go to TWA. I don't know how much we enhanced the bottom line, but with several hundred DCSs in the air, it was probably significant.

We finally arrived at Rome's Fiumicino International Airport, for example, the following morning. The pilots and flight attendants bade the passengers farewell, and a bus took them to their hotel. The DCS stayed behind with the passengers to ensure tour groups got hooked up with their liaison, the VIPs got connected with their chaperones, and others found their way to the baggage claim area. Inevitably five to 10 bags would be missing once everything was up on the conveyor belt. The DCSs worked with the ground personnel to put tracers on the lost luggage with a promise to deliver the bags to the hotel where the passenger was staying. The DCS was now free to leave, taking an hour-long bus ride into the city, followed by a 15-minute walk to the hotel. By this time, the DCS had been on duty for about 14 hours, assuming the flight was routine.

In Rome, we stayed downtown at the Hotel Mediterraneo, and in the lobby was a bar. I would check in at the front desk, get my room key, and head straight for the bar. I was so dehydrated that I would suck down two beers in as many minutes. Then I would go to my room for a much-needed nap. I was exhausted.

My supervisor in New York taught me a little trick. He told me, "When you get to your European destination, go to bed, take a two-hour nap, force yourself to get up, and that will put you on European time. Then, you can explore the city, have a nice dinner, and go to bed for a good night of sleep." That made sense, so I tried it. Waking up from a two-hour nap after working 14 hours was painful. I did it, but I was miserable during the entire layover because I was so tired. At night, I would go to bed and fall asleep immediately. Unfortunately, I would wake up within a couple hours because my internal clock was still set on New York time. I would lay there, tossing and turning for the next six hours until I received my wake-up call that usually came around 6 a.m. on the third day of the trip. By this time, I had about five hours of sleep collectively and had to prepare for a full day of work that required adding six hours to the day due to the time zone change. It was brutal! Six o'clock in the morning in Rome was still only midnight in New York.

I showered, shaved, packed my bag, and grabbed a cab to the dining unit. It was time to reverse the trip. The next incoming DCS from New York brought in my 747. I would meet the flight and the DCS on the tarmac, and we would exchange information. I would tell him about all the problems relative to Rome. He would tell me everything that was wrong on the 747 he had just jockeyed in. We had a limited amount of time to make the corrections. I would take his information to the flight engineer and explain that this was wrong and that was broken, so the mechanics needed to get on it ASAP and fix the problems before we took off to New York. Sometimes the issues were corrected, and sometimes they were not. Once in flight, we had to make do.

The usual problems were passenger seats that would not recline and movie projectors that malfunctioned, but the worst was clogged lavatories that had to be taken out of service. When one went down, it put a burden on the others. One-by-one, the lavatories went out of commission, so that by the time we made it back to New York, we may only have four lavs out of 12 to accommodate 346 passengers. Because of the headwinds, the flight back to New York was an hour longer than the eastbound flight. This added additional stress to passengers and crew members.

Equipment malfunctions were only one category of problems. Meal service was another. If we had a lot of babies on the flight, it was conceivable that we would run short of milk. If we had a lot of Jewish passengers on the flight, we could run short on Kosher meals. If we had Muslims on the flight, they might want to hold a prayer meeting in a section of the aircraft that was prohibited. If we had people from Pakistan, they may want to bring their goats and chickens into the passenger cabin. This list could go on forever.

Temperature also was a big factor. In the summer months, we had to get out of town before the runway got too hot. The hotter it was, the more fuel would be required to get the 747 off the ground. The amount of fuel we burned during take-off would determine whether or not we had enough to make it to our final destination or had to divert to another airport to refuel. If one thing went wrong, it had a ripple effect that could transform a routine flight into a non-routine disaster.

Upon return from Rome, assuming the flight was routine and landed on-time, I would guide the passengers through the passport control/immigration gates and into the baggage claim area. Passengers would retrieve their luggage, pass through customs, and go on their way. If they had connecting flights, it was my responsibility to make sure they made it to their connections. This process took about an hour. Then I would hop on a bus to the office in Hangar 12 and log in the reports relative to the flight. That took another hour. So, if the flight arrived in New York at 4 p.m., I could be in my car by 6 p.m. for my two-hour drive home.

By the time I got home, I was a basket case. I had been busting my hump for three days and probably had a total of five to eight hours of sleep. I had dinner with my family and tucked Heidi into bed. She always wanted to hear a bedtime story, so I would read to her for a while. She listened patiently, and when I was through, she would tell me that wasn't the story she wanted to hear. So, I asked her what she had in mind. Heidi would say, "Tell me a story about how the airplane got broken." She must have overheard me talking to Alice as I told her about my various trips. Frequently, a mechanical problem would develop, so Heidi just assumed that any time I went somewhere, the plane would break down, and she just loved those stories. There wasn't anything entertaining about a mechanical malfunction, so I would have to invent stuff to make the story exciting. It worked, and the requests kept coming. On my two-hour drive home from the airport, I had time to think and would conjure up stories for Heidi. It became a ritual, and we had fun with it.

With Heidi asleep, one would think I would be so exhausted that I would drop into bed, but I had been working at such a frantic pace during the previous 72 hours, I couldn't just stop and go to sleep. I had to unwind and slowly decompress. I would go into the living room with a fire roaring in the fireplace and enjoy a glass of wine as I listened to my wife tell me about all the events that took place while I was gone. Now relaxed, I could go to bed. I didn't just go to sleep, I went into a deep coma and stayed in a catatonic state until about 10 o'clock the next morning. Refreshed, I now had three days off before my next trip.

During my days off, we would head for the hills and go camping in the woods, or we would take a drive and explore all the interesting sights and destinations New England had to offer. There were so many things to see and do that it was hard to decide which direction to go. When the three days were up, it was time for my next trip to Europe which was equally as exciting as my days off. I thought to myself, "How many people love their job so much they can't wait to get to work?" No matter where I was going, I couldn't wait to get to work, and at the end of the trip, I couldn't wait to get home. Every day was an adventure, and I always had something to look forward to. As I drove to work, I thought to myself, "My job is so much fun. I can't believe I am actually getting paid to do this. If I could afford it, I would have worked for free."

The job, however, had its limitations. We were alerted to the fact that the job was so physically, mentally, and emotionally challenging that a DCS would burn out after two years. I thought to myself, "Not this kid." Little did I know how right they were. When I started flying, I was 26 years old. One day, when I was working a flight to some foreign destination, a passenger engaged me in conversation. (This happened a lot, as they were often curious about my position). He asked me, "How did a young man, such as yourself, get such a wonderful job?"

I would respond with the question, "Just how old do you think I am?"

He came back with, "22?" (At the time, I really did have a baby face.)

"No, I am actually 26." A year later, passengers would ask the same question. By this time, I was 27, and I would reply, "How old do you think I am?"

They would say, "Oh, I don't know. Maybe 27."

"Yep. You are right on." By the time I was 28, passengers were guessing me to be 40. I was shocked. In the eyes of the public, I went from age 22 to 40 in just three years. That was when I realized what a physical toll this job had taken on me.

From a mental perspective, DCSs had to be alert, creative, and forward-thinking because every flight was like a chess game. Whatever the situation, the DCS often had to make split-second decisions to correct problems, and we had to think them through to determine what sort of ripple effect our decision may create down the road.

The emotional aspect of the job was also very challenging. We were high-profile employees, and everyone had their eyes on us. Some passengers and fellow employees looked for reasons to turn us in for the slightest infraction, real or perceived. We all felt the insecurity from time-to-time, wondering if we would still have a job when we returned to our home domicile from our trips.

In all fairness, we weren't all lily white either. Most of us were mavericks, which is why we were hired in the first place. We re-wrote the rules as we went along, and our supervisors confessed that we were an uncontrollable group. However, it was that spirit that enabled us to get the job done. "We kicked ass and took names!" Every time we made a decision to do something, we were putting our jobs on the line, but we had to forge ahead and hope that whatever we did was the right thing to do.

Every day was an adventure, and every flight was a challenge. One day, my supervisor called me into the office to have a chat. He was pleased with my performance and recommended me for a job at our downtown office. It was a job as a senior analyst, and he set me up for an interview. I took the train from Connecticut to New York for the meeting, and I was not impressed with the two-hour one-way commute. The interviewer was a very patient and nice man several years my senior. As he explained the job, I envisioned myself sitting on that train for two hours each workday to get to work, sitting at a desk counting beans and putting them in a jar for another eight hours, and then another two-hour ride back home every night. I became disenchanted very quickly.

He read my body language and changed the direction of the conversation abruptly. He said, "You know Steve, I am offering you a job that will substantially increase your salary, and I am sensing that you are not interested in it. What is your take?"

I looked at him and said, "Bob, I really appreciate you taking an interest in me. However, the more I learn about this job, the more I appreciate the one I have. The money is attractive; however, the excitement of what I am doing right now seems far more rewarding." I thanked him for his time and suggested that he interview other candidates. On the train ride back home, I realized how much I appreciated being a DCS.

Shortly thereafter, I was working a flight to Paris and making my rounds to meet and greet all the first-class passengers. I approached a distinguished looking gentleman wearing a very expensive grey business suit. He was sitting by himself and invited me to sit down and join him. Chatting with passengers was part of my job. We wanted them all to feel welcome and important. I loved doing this, and I did it well. It gave me an opportunity to hob-nob with the big-wigs. This particular individual told me that he was a vice president with General Motors in charge of automobile design. He went on to tell me that he had been with his company a long time and was compensated extremely well. Financially he was set for life. I congratulated him on his success and inquired as to why he was telling me all this. His response was, "Quite frankly, I have been watching you work, and I am so impressed with your job, I would be willing to throw my whole career away just to be able to do what you are doing. However, the fact of the matter is, I am way too old now, so I will just sit back and envy you." I thanked him and told him how lucky I realized I was. And it reinforced my decision not to have taken that analyst job.

This would be one of many passengers I would meet. There were the good, the bad, and the ugly!

CHAPTER 36
PASSENGERS FROM HEAVEN, HELL,
PLANET EARTH, AND PLUTO

Passengers came out of the woodwork from every direction. I looked forward to meeting them all, never knowing what to expect. Those appearing to be mild and meek could turn out to be raging maniacs. The ballistic personalities could turn out to be my strongest allies.

Because TWA was considered the "Airline of the Stars," we had many celebrities on our flights. For the most part, they were wonderful people. I met the actor, Dick Wilson, who played Mr Whipple in "Please don't squeeze the Charmin" commercials. He was a pleasant guy that raved about his wife, whom he adored. He was as down-to-earth and as uncomplicated as the rolls of toilet paper he promoted. What a great guy!

One day, I was working a flight from London to New York. Doug McClure, a lead actor in the TV series *The Virginian* was sitting alone. He invited me to sit down next to him, and we struck up a pleasant conversation. He was very handsome, successful, and wealthy. Many people with those assets were arrogant. Not him. We talked for a half-hour like long lost buddies. He kept patting his chest as though he was looking for something. I finally said, "Can I help you?"

He said, "You wouldn't by any chance have a cigarette, would you?" I had half a pack of Marlboros in my shirt pocket, so I gave them to him. I quit smoking in 1978. Apparently, he did not quit, and sadly died of lung cancer in 1995.

I met Willard Scott, the well-known *Today* show weatherman. He came on board the aircraft with a grin from ear-to-ear and walked up and down the aisles greeting people as if he was running for President. Everyone loved him, and he exuded warmth toward everyone. Some of the older passengers would tell him how many years they had to go before they turned 100, expecting him to remember to put their picture on the Smucker's jelly jar when that day arrived.

Sammy Davis, Jr. did the same thing — smiling and shaking hands with other passengers. Not only was he a great entertainer, but he was also a great human being.

There was William Conrad. He was a World War II fighter pilot, actor, producer, and director. He starred in the 1970s TV series *Cannon* where he assumed the role of Frank Cannon, a detective with the Los Angeles Police Department. On a transcontinental flight from New York to Los Angeles, we sat together engaged in a long and enjoyable conversation. He talked about his weight problem, saying that he ate like a bird, but the weight kept piling on no matter how hard he tried to lose it. Meanwhile, his wife could eat whatever she wanted and never gained a pound. He thought the world of her, and justifiably so. Her name was Sue Randall, a fashion model and actress. She is remembered for her role as the kindly Miss Alice Landers, Theodore Cleaver's grade schoolteacher on the TV series *Leave it to Beaver*. She died of lung cancer in 1984, and William Conrad died of heart failure in 1994.

On a night flight from Los Angeles to New York, I had the pleasure of welcoming Dick Clark, the host of *American Bandstand*. He sat in first-class, and the seat next to him was empty, so he invited me to sit down with him. Soon I would learn the reason for him wanting company. He hated to fly and was very uncomfortable about it. He needed assurance that everything would be okay and that we were not going to auger into a cornfield somewhere in Nebraska. I assured him that if I thought for one minute this flight wasn't going to make it to New York, I would be the last person to get on board. I remained cool as a cucumber because I was sure we had nothing to worry about. That helped, but not enough. I told him I had recently read an article saying that the human mind was not capable of thinking about two things at the same time. So, instead of thinking about the airplane going down, I asked him to please tell me about his life and outstanding career. He smiled and started talking as he reminisced about his past. Eventually, I had to excuse myself to attend to my duties but assured him I would return shortly. By the time I got back, he was sound asleep. When we arrived in New York the next morning, he smiled and winked at me as he exited the aircraft as if to say, "Your strategy worked. Thanks." What a delightful passenger he was!

The following month, I was working a flight from Frankfurt, Germany to New York. Sitting in first-class was a most distinguished looking gentleman, and I felt compelled to meet him. "Hi, my name is Steve Dolby. I am the Director of Customer Service on this flight, and I want to introduce myself to you. Incidentally, you look familiar. Have we met before?" He said he did not think so and introduced himself as Warner Klemperer. I said, "Holy smokes, it's you! You are Colonel Klink on *Hogan's Heroes.*" This television sitcom aired from 1965–1971 and was one of the funniest shows I ever saw. I continued watching the re-runs well into the 1980s. It was about a German POW camp during World War II that housed American, French, and British prisoners of war. Warner played the part of Col. Klink, a bumbling, inept German commandant in charge of running the camp known as Stalag 13. Klink's right-hand man, Sgt. Schultz, was played by the actor, John Banner.

Warner Klemperer, son of a Jewish father, was a German-American television actor born in Cologne, Germany. His family immigrated to America in 1935, and he served in the US Army during World War II. After the war, he became an actor, performing on and off Broadway and on television. John Banner was born to Jewish parents in Vienna, Austria in 1910. He, too, immigrated to the States in 1935, served in the US Air Force during World War II, and went on to become an actor as well.

So, I asked Klemperer what had brought him to Frankfurt. He told me John Banner had just passed away, and he was returning from attending his funeral that took place in Vienna, the place where he was born. He had come through Frankfurt to catch his connecting flight back to New York. He went on to tell me that he and Banner were both Jewish. I did not know that, so the information threw me off guard a bit. I responded by asking, "Given the Holocaust and all that happened during that era, why would a couple of Jewish actors take on the roles of playing Nazi soldiers?" He smiled and said, "Steve, think about it for a minute. Every week for six years, we produced a new episode that was a complete mockery of the Nazi regime. Can you think of a better way to get even?" I replied, "Point well taken." I had just spent another half-hour of my life with a wonderful human being and regretted that I did not have the opportunity to meet John Banner before his passing.

The crew and me posing with Spiro Agnew

Shortly thereafter, I was assigned the New York to Athens run. It was a hot summer day in 1974, and I had worked for the past 15 hours getting this bird from the US to Greece. The crew and I laid over at the Athens Hilton. I relaxed by taking a swim in the hotel pool shortly after we arrived. Several of the crew members sitting at the edge of the pool pointed out Spiro Agnew sitting in a poolside cabana. I glanced in his direction, verified the target, and went about minding my own business. The next day, as we were preparing to fly back to New York, I was notified that Spiro Agnew would be on my flight and I was instructed to extend preferential treatment to him.

He was the first passenger escorted onto the plane, and the crew and I posed for a photo with him. During the flight back to New York, once the meal service was completed and the movies were started, I sneaked into the upper-deck lounge to log in my flight reports. Usually, it was empty and quiet, affording me time to get some administrative work done. Soon, Mr Agnew meandered up the stairs, ordered a drink, and sat down to relax. He was patient, watching me work. But when I was done, he motioned me over to join him in conversation. He wanted to talk, and I was eager to listen. We spent an hour together. I remember he complained about "the people." He told me that both sides always wanted something that the other party was not willing to give. As a result, it was impossible to satisfy all the people all the time, and that was the dilemma of being a politician. In spite of the accusations against him and all that had happened, he was an enjoyable conversationalist. As a 28-year-old kid, I was just sitting there shooting the shit with the former Vice President of the United States. Many news reporters would have loved to be in my position!

One day, I was working Flight #901 from Madrid to New York. Tex Ritter was sitting in coach with his beautiful wife. Born Woodward Maurice Ritter, he was an American country singer and actor starring in many western movies from the mid-1930s through the 1960s. He was inducted into the Country Music Hall of Fame in 1964. As a kid, I regarded him as a "hero" as I heard him sing his songs and watched him ride his horse across the silver screen at the local movie theater. He was also the father of John Ritter, best known for his comedic acting role in the TV sitcom *Three's Company.*

Ritter flagged me down as I was walking through the aisle of the aircraft. I don't remember what prompted the conversation, but we had a great talk. I told him how much I regarded him as my hero when I was a kid growing up. He was humble and appreciative. I also told him how much I liked to listen to his songs. He told me that he had just released a new album, and if I gave him my business card, he would send me an autographed copy. I promptly did so, but never received anything. I was very disappointed. I later learned the reason why. He died shortly after our meeting at the age of 68.

I met so many great celebrities I could go on forever with stories. However, there was an unfortunate flip side to my experiences. Not everyone was as cordial. They all had their own reasons, but I think the biggest one is they just didn't want to be bothered. One such person was Lucille Ball. She traveled first-class and had a female companion that I will label "her assistant" for lack of an official title. As I walked up to introduce myself, Ms Ball gave me a quick glance, then looked at her assistant as if to say, "Take over and do your job."

Her assistant instructed me, "This is how it works. You cannot talk to Ms Ball directly. If you have something to say, you must say it to me. Then I will tell her. If she wishes to reply, she will reply to me, and I will relay the message back to you." I had never experienced anything like this before.

It was extremely rude, awkward, and uncomfortable. What I wanted to say was, "Tell her to take her attitude and shove it up her ass." That would have cost me my job, so I just said, "Tell her I just stopped by to say welcome, and I hope you both enjoy the flight." Then I walked away.

On a flight from London to New York, as I was making my rounds glad-handing the passengers in first-class, I ran into the actor, Roger Moore (007). I extended my hand. "Welcome on board." He looked at me as if I was the creature from the Black Lagoon holding a dead rat in one hand and a sack of rat shit in the other. He cringed in his seat and didn't say a word. A little voice inside of me said, "Ignore it and just walk away," which is what I did.

Then there was the movie actress, Gloria Swanson. Born in 1899, she made her film debut in 1914. She started her acting career in silent movies, and later she made the transition to "talkies." Swanson skyrocketed to stardom and became one of the most sought-after actresses in Hollywood. By her own account, she had an affair with Joseph P. Kennedy, father of President John F. Kennedy. In her lifetime, she had been married six times before her passing in 1983. I met her on a night flight from New York to Paris. She sat alone in first-class eating bean sprouts from a plastic container. I thought to myself, "Why would you be eating that crap when TWA was serving steak and lobster?" Later, I would learn she had become a vegetarian around 1928 and was an early health food advocate who was known for bringing her own meals to public places in a paper bag.

As I was flying to Paris that evening, a female DCS colleague of mine was working the New York to London flight. When we returned to New York two days later, we ran into each other and swapped stories about our experiences during the past 72 hours. I told her about Gloria

Swanson, but she one-upped me. On her flight was a very beautiful and famous movie star from the 1940s. I won't mention her name, but apparently, she had a drinking problem. By the time the plane landed at Heathrow International Airport, this passenger was so drunk she had a difficult time walking off the airplane and fell over right at the exit door as more than 300 passengers were trying to get off the plane. The DCS and others tried to help her up, but in the process, she peed all over them. What a way to end a flight. My colleague had worked all night, was dead tired, and now needed to find a dry cleaner before she could work her return flight back to the States.

Some of the most colorful stories were generated by non-celebrity passengers and unique flight situations. I think that was a primary reason TWA management told us that we would burn out as DCSs within two years — we were under tremendous pressure to deal with unruly passengers. During our first year on the job, we were naive and eager to please. However, as time marched on, we became less tolerant. We still performed our mission as goodwill ambassadors in a very professional way. However, it took more and more effort to maintain the level of decorum expected. Quite simply, some wore out and others just lost patience for the job. Even so, most of us loved the job so much that few were willing to throw in the towel. We consoled ourselves and said, "Let's just give it six more months." The months grew into a year. And the year grew into five years. It became a dilemma because we knew we had to get out, yet we couldn't imagine any other job with the adventure and enjoyment we got from being a DCS.

The DCSs loved to get together and share stories about their experiences. One story was rather sad though because it cost Terry, one of our DCS colleagues, his job. He was one of the nicest guys you could ever hope to meet. He was also a former Marine and tough as nails. So, the last thing you wanted to do was to get on the wrong side of him. He was working a flight from New York to Los Angeles. When the plane landed and passengers began to exit, Terry stood at the door saying good-bye and wishing them well. One passenger was upset about something that happened during the flight, and as he walked out the door, he turned around and slugged Terry so hard that it knocked him off his feet. Terry stood up and dusted himself off, and the guy came back at him, knocking him down for a second time. Terry picked himself up again and warned the passenger not to do that. The passenger came after him a third time. Terry doubled up his fist and hit the passenger in the brainpan with the force of a Sherman tank. He sent this guy flying through the air, and he landed about five feet short of the Pearly Gates. He laid there out cold for a couple minutes. The other passengers that were watching cheered and applauded Terry for defending himself, but that wasn't acceptable behavior by TWA standards. When Terry returned to New York, he was called into the office and fired. Management's rule was that you never hit a passenger for any reason.

Along the way, we met a cast of characters. I secretly labeled them, "The Clowns." One was an Army soldier stationed in Germany. We were flying from New York to Frankfurt. He was drunk and wanted to pick a fight. He took a swing at me but missed. I held up my hand motioning for him to stop and told him I was an officer in the Army Reserves, and if he hit me, I would have the flight engineer radio ahead and have the military police waiting to meet the flight. The possibility of a court martial motivated him to put the brakes on his bad behavior and quickly return to his seat.

Another clown showed up on the New York to Frankfurt flight several months later. He was sitting in coach toward the rear of the airplane. Several passengers came to me to say what a rude jerk he was. Everyone around him was upset with his behavior, so they wanted me to speak to him. I approached the individual and asked him to settle down. He basically told me to "go pound sand." I asked him what his favorite cocktail was, and he told me, "Rum and Coke." I had the flight attendant deliver several complimentary drinks to him that he greedily accepted. Since it was a night flight, my intention was to put him to sleep. He took off his shoes and placed them under his seat. After a couple drinks, he was out like a light. The passenger sitting behind him, and the one that complained the most, stole the shoes while the half-hammered guy was sleeping. When I walked down the aisle to check on things, the guy that stole the shoes proudly displayed his catch to me.

Then he got up, went into the lavatory, and dumped the shoes into the trash.

About the time we entered German airspace, the captain called me to the cockpit. He reported, "Frankfurt is completely socked in with fog. We cannot land so we are going to divert to Dusseldorf, put the passengers on the train, and send them to Frankfurt." I made the proper announcement to the passengers, and everyone seemed comfortable with the plan. The only shortcoming to the plan was there was snow on the ground, and Dusseldorf did not have jetways at the time. This meant that we had to park on the tarmac, and everyone had to hike to the terminal building.

It was about 7:30 in the morning when we landed, and Numb-nuts woke up to find his shoes missing. Angrily, he called me and demanded that I locate them for him. I told him I had a lot of responsibilities on the flight, and I could not be held accountable for a passenger's shoes. He was on his own with his crisis. As he walked across the tarmac in the snow in his socks, other passengers laughed and made fun of him. Silently, I did too — nothing like a little vigilante justice to make things right!

Another clown had nothing to do with TWA, the flight crew, or the passengers. However, he deserves an "Honorable Mention." We had an on-time departure from New York, and everything was operating in our favor. Strong tail winds pushed us into Frankfurt almost one hour ahead of schedule. Everyone on board was happy and excited. The problem was that it was winter, and the fog was so thick you could have cut it with a knife. The captain called me to the cockpit and explained the situation. We had plenty of fuel but could not land. We needed 400 meters visibility, and we only had 100 meters. So, we joined a queue at about 20,000 feet over the city as the tower put us in a holding pattern. The idea was that we would stay there until the fog burned off so we could land. I grabbed the fourth seat in the cockpit and put on the headphones so I could monitor what was going on between our cockpit and the tower. Then I got onto the public address system and explained the dilemma to the passengers. They understood and remained seated, as they had no other choice. Soon, we were joined by KLM, Pan Am, Lufthansa, and British Airways. From the cockpit, we looked like a giant circus carousel going around and around in a circle. We started to get dizzy, a little bit air sick, and low on patience.

Finally, the captain on the Lufthansa flight had enough and called the tower. Speaking in German he said, "Frankfurt, this is Lufthansa flight #8613. We are low on fuel, and we are coming down." The tower responded saying, "Lufthansa #8613, when communicating with the tower, please use the appropriate international language, which is English." The Lufthansa pilot responded with, "I am a German national, flying for a German airline, landing in a German city. Why do I have to speak English?" About that time, the pilot on the British Airways flight piped in and said, "Because you lost the war." I lost it, as did everyone else on the frequency. We laughed our asses off. However, having lived in Germany and understanding the nature of the German people, I don't imagine the Lufthansa captain found any humor in the comeback.

Back in New York preparing for a flight to Paris, I walked by the ticket counter and observed a passenger acting rudely to a ticket agent. The agent was a friend of mine, so I approached him and asked if I could help. He said, "Let me introduce you to Jean-Claude Ciserelli. He is on your flight tonight." I could tell immediately this guy was trouble, but I introduced myself to him and gave a warm welcome. As the two of us walked away toward the departure gate, the ticket agent gave me a wink and a smile. I knew something was up.

At any rate, we arrived in Paris the next morning, and I escorted the passengers through the terminal building into the baggage claim area. Everyone's bags came up except for Jean-Claude's. He was justifiably upset. I asked to see his luggage claim ticket, and when he presented it to me, I noticed that the ticket agent in New York had checked his bag to Hong Kong (sweet revenge for bad behavior). Now Jean-Claude really had something to bitch about.

Paris was great. We stayed at the Meridian Hotel in Port Maillot, a subway stop about a mile west of the Arc de Triomphe on the Champs-Elysees. Behind the hotel, down a narrow ally, was a quaint family-owned restaurant called the Entrecote. They served a fantastic steak dinner at near McDonald's prices. Along with the steak, they served a salad with a homemade mustard dressing. It was so good I asked for the recipe. They gave it to me, and I use it to this day.

On a subsequent trip to Paris, my old friends I had met during my Army days in Germany drove to the hotel to pick me up for dinner. They had recently moved to a small suburb five miles from downtown Paris called Villeijuif. They were excited to show me where they lived, and the wife, Christina, had a nice home-cooked meal waiting for me.

The husband, Paul, handed me a beer shortly after we finished dinner. I told him I was getting very tired and asked if they could take me back to my hotel. He said, "Sure, grab your beer and you can drink it along the way." As we were crossing the street and about to get into the car, a French paddy wagon came screeching up alongside us and four policemen jumped out. We were surrounded and detained. I asked Paul if we were stopped because I had a beer in my hand. He talked to the police, and they explained that they stopped us because a minute before, someone was shooting at another police officer.

They took us down to the station, and we waited in a holding room several hours before we could be heard. When it was our turn, the interrogating officer asked me what I was doing there. I told him I was on a business trip and just arrived earlier that day. He asked to see my passport, and I explained to him it was back in my hotel room. Of course, this delayed my release for another hour or two. Finally, as the sun was just beginning to break over the horizon, the police caught the man they were looking for and let us go. When I got to my hotel room, the phone was ringing. I answered it, and the voice at the other end was a recording of a rooster crowing, followed by "Bonjour Monsieur Dolby. This is your wake-up call." Holy cow. So far, I had only a two-hour nap, and now I had to face a new workday that included working an eight-and-a-half-hour flight back to New York. Another 16 hours would pass before I would see my own bed.

One of my most memorable trips related to confrontational passengers started on a hot summer day in Rome. I was working TWA flight #841 destined for New York City. This was a very long flight with extra time for things to go wrong and passenger tempers to flare. The flight was full, with over 300 souls on board. Soon after take-off, I was approached by several passengers complaining about a demanding, loud, and obnoxious family sitting in the forward section of the economy zone. They asked me to get them settled down so that others could enjoy the flight.

I approached the family patriarch. I explained that people were complaining and asked him to please control the family and tone things down a bit. This infuriated him and inspired him to coach the family to become more militant than they were before.

By this point in my career with TWA, I had learned how to deal with uncooperative passengers. I could create strategies that produced painful results yet left me completely exonerated.

So, I cornered the spokesman for the complaining group, pulled him aside, and told him I could not get the jerks to settle down. However, if they could tough it out for the remainder of the flight, I would make it up to them once we reached New York. He was eager to hear my plan.

Somewhere, somehow, word got out that people overheard the misbehaving family talking about drugs. I do not know if this was true or not, but it got the wheels turning in my mind to develop a story for the customs officials once we arrived in New York.

I told the leader of the aggrieved passengers to meet me in the customs hall along with all the passengers that were inconvenienced by the asshole family once we arrived in New York. He did not know what was about to unfold, but he knew it wasn't going to be good for the assholes.

I went to the cockpit and told the flight engineer to radio ahead to New York and alert the customs officials that we had a potential problem. As soon as we arrived at JFK Airport, I bolted off the airplane, ran down the escalator, ran through passport control, and hooked up with the customs officials on the other side. I explained to them that a family would be coming through the gate very shortly, and during the flight, they were bragging about how they were smuggling drugs into the country. Whether it was true or not, I did not know, but I had a moral obligation to bring it to their attention. The fangs of the customs officials came out, and they were eagerly awaiting the confrontation.

Next came the nice passengers that were inconvenienced by the asshole family. As they cleared passport control, they gravitated toward me waiting for instructions on what the game plan would be. I told them to mill around customs inspection Table #1 and enjoy the show. Despite exhaustion from an international flight, they were as excited as kids in a candy store.

A few minutes later, Mr and Mrs Asshole showed up with their entourage of asshole offspring. The customs officials were waiting and pounced on them like a buzzard sitting on a fencepost waiting for a wounded rabbit to crawl by. They grabbed them and their luggage and went to work.

In shock, the family was required to open their suitcases and dump their dirty laundry on the table. The customs officials went on the attack. They looked like a pack of pit bulls as they ripped through one bag after another. We watched the inspectors take out box cutters and slit the lining of the luggage. They tore the bags apart and showed no mercy. The father gave me a dirty look, as if to say, "I know you are behind this, but I can't prove it, and that makes it even more irritating." They were delayed an hour and a half on a routine check that would normally take about 15 minutes.

The good passengers enjoyed the performance, cheering through the inspection. As they exited the customs hall, several of them came up and patted me on the back to thank me for the show and a job well done. When my job was complete, I left the inspection area. I looked over my shoulder, and the room was empty except for the customs officials, the assholes, and a pile of shredded luggage.

One evening, as I worked TWA flight #740 from New York to Frankfurt, the passengers seemed anxious and restless. It was unsettling to be around them. I paid a visit to the cockpit, and the pilots asked me, "How are things going down below?" I explained the situation. They smiled and said they had an easy fix. The flight engineer flipped a couple switches and turned a couple dials. Shortly thereafter, I went downstairs and did a walk-through of the passenger cabins. Everybody was sound asleep. I reported back to the cockpit and asked how they did it. The flight engineer explained it was an old pilot trick. They simply raised the temperature and lowered the oxygen. I never forgot this, and on future flights when things got edgy, I would visit the cockpit crew and asked them to raise the temperature and lower the oxygen. It was more effective than the Sandman and always worked like a charm.

I never really understood the political aspects of the situation, but there were thousands of refugees in Cuba during the 1970s seeking asylum into the United States. The Cuban government, under the dictatorship of Fidel Castro, refused to let them go. However, he was willing to release some of them, mostly the sick and the old, so they would no longer be a burden to his country. The catch was that they were not allowed to go to the States. So, they all booked flights to Spain. Once in Spain, they purchased airline tickets from Madrid to New York and then down to Miami. TWA packed them in by the hundreds.

I woke up one morning in Madrid and prepared to work my flight, TWA # 901, back to the US not realizing that it was about to become one of the most joyous days of my life. Once we were airborne, I started my normal routine by making an announcement on the public address system that I was the Director of Customer Service that would accompany them on the flight.

As I walked down the aisle, a Cuban and his wife waved for me to come over. They were so very gracious. The husband was eager to tell me that they were on their way to America to become US citizens. They were proud and excited. He noticed that I was wearing a little metal lapel pin of an American flag on my suit jacket. He asked how he could get one. I took mine off and pinned it on his shirt. He was so humbled he started crying. Seeing his heartfelt emotion brought tears to my eyes as well. This experience caught me completely off guard. Then I remembered, "I've got work to do and can't be walking around the airplane crying." I quickly curbed my emotions and resumed my duties. However, I will never forget that day, and I was so happy that such a small gesture could bring so much joy into another person's life. From time-to-time I have thought of him and hoped all his dreams came true once he arrived in America.

Passengers frequently wanted to buy airline tickets at economy prices and receive the comforts of first-class. That is human nature and understandable. However, it rarely happens that way. One day I was working a flight to Tel Aviv. A flight attendant approached me and said there was a passenger and his wife bitching about their seat assignments and wanted to be relocated to first-class. By now, I had encountered these clowns a million times. I had learned how to handle them. I asked the flight attendant where they were sitting and realized for an economy priced ticket, they were seated in a very comfortable position in an exit row with ample leg room. Any other economy passengers would kill for their seats. At any rate, I had developed several scenarios to combat the situation. The flight attendant gave me the seat numbers, and I headed in that direction.

I walked past them, did a double-take, and backed up. With a shit-eating grin on my face, I approached him and said, "Welcome on board. Can I ask you a personal question?"

He said, "Sure."

I said, "You look like you should be sitting in first-class. What are you doing back here? May I please see your tickets." He was excited, expecting that the bitching would reap a reward. I looked at the tickets. They were priced as an excursion fare, the lowest fare short of traveling in the cargo compartment. In a tone that came short of asking him why he bought such cheap tickets for such a long flight, I told him they were the type of people we normally find traveling first-class. I explained that I would be happy to move them to the forward cabin, but unfortunately, it was full and there was no room for them.

I told the couple that I was going to buy them drinks to make this flight more comfortable if they make a promise to me. They said, "Sure, what is it?" I told them to never fly on TWA again unless they were prepared to purchase the first-class tickets they deserved. They felt like they were being shamed and embarrassingly promised they would not make the same mistake again. Then to make them feel more empowered, I told them about a trick they could use to get into first-class on their return flight. I explained that flights this time of year were overbooked, and when economy class was oversold, they took the late-comers and bumped them up to first- class. So, when they checked in for their return flight, I instructed them to do so at the last minute. I did not know if this would work or not for them, but they felt like they had insider knowledge that others didn't know about.

Two weeks later, I was back in Tel Aviv and working the flight westbound to New York. Once we were airborne, I heard a man yell, "Steve." I turned around and sitting in first-class were Mr and Mrs Cheapskate. The husband shook my hand and gave me a bear hug. He said, "We took your advice, and the plan worked beautifully. When you have a few minutes, please stop by and I'll tell you all about our vacation." He was as happy as a pig in shit, and I'm sure I made him a TWA passenger for life.

The following month I was working the New York to London route. My flight into Heathrow International Airport went smoothly, and by 10 a.m. the following morning I was checked into my room at the Sheraton Skyline Hotel. I laid down and took my standard two-hour nap, then took the subway into London to enjoy the city. That evening, I decided to hit the sack early and get a good night of sleep before heading back to New York the next day. The plan failed. I could not get back to sleep, so I laid awake all night until the phone rang. "Good morning Mr Dolby. This is your crew call. It is 7 a.m. Have a nice day." I thought to myself, "How will I ever make it through this day. We haven't even gone anywhere yet, and I'm exhausted." Things were about to get a lot worse.

The departure was routine, and as soon as we reached cruising altitude, the flight attendants started the meal service — not the box lunch meal service you get on today's flights. TWA served hot dinners with three entrees to choose from. Cocktail service was first, followed by the meal and perhaps a glass of wine. It was a lavish presentation. While meals were being served, a flight attendant approached me and said there was a passenger traveling with his wife in the aft cabin creating a disturbance and asked that I come back and get him settled down.

I approached the individual and saw that he was completely out of control — someone must have shit in his Cheerios for breakfast that morning. He carried his grudge onto the airplane, and he was meaner than a rattlesnake with a broken fang. I explained to him that all the passengers around him were complaining about his behavior and asked that he please control his frustrations. I also told him that it was having an effect on the flight attendants' ability to perform their duties. His behavior constituted a federal offense that could bring severe consequences.

My conversation with this clown was interrupted when another flight attendant grabbed me and said, "The captain needs to see you right away." I bolted toward the cockpit. The captain told me that a warning light came on indicating that there was a fire in the cargo hold. As a precaution, it was necessary to stop at the airport in Shannon, Ireland to get it checked out prior to crossing the Atlantic Ocean. He told me not to say anything to the passengers at that particular point in time. My lips were sealed.

The captain asked me if the cabin attendants had started the meal service. I informed him that "Yes, they had." He told me to have them confiscate the meals, stow them back in the ovens, and secure the aircraft for an emergency landing.

Meanwhile, the flight crew began dumping fuel. This procedure, known as fuel jettison, was a procedure used in certain emergency situations to reduce weight and reduce the chances of a major fire upon landing. There are valves located close to the ends of the wings, and when they were opened, it allowed the fuel to be disbursed.

Usually, when things started to go wrong, they had a ripple effect on the rest of the flight. I could tell immediately this was going to be one of those days. First, I was operating on very little sleep, and I was dog-tired. Then, I found out I had a problem passenger on board. And now, we had a mechanical problem with the aircraft. Lady Luck was not on my side for this trip! If I had fallen into a barrel full of titties, I probably would have come up sucking on a thumb.

The flight attendants were snatching meal trays away from passengers about the time they were ready to take their first bite, and passengers looking out the window could see hundreds of gallons of fuel being dispensed into the atmosphere. We did not want the passengers to panic, but it was obvious that something was wrong. One passenger, sitting next to a window, called me over and asked, "What's all that black stuff coming out of the wing?" I explained that we took on too much fuel at Heathrow, and we had to dump some of it to lighten the load. Other passengers started yelling at the flight attendants for snatching their meal trays.

In addition to all the chaos that was going on, one of the flight attendants working the aft cabin told me that the obnoxious passenger I talked to previously continued to raise havoc, and the surrounding passengers were becoming increasingly upset. I walked up to this clown and told him to knock it off or I would have him thrown off the airplane. (At this point in time, none of the passengers knew that we were going to be stopping in Shannon.) He started yelling at me. He said I could not throw him off the airplane because he was a full-fare passenger, and since this was a non-stop flight to New York, there was no way that was going to happen. I said, "That's it," and grabbed the closest intercom telephone. It just happened to be hooked to the flight attendant jump seat right in front of him. I pretended like I was calling the cockpit and talking to the flight engineer. I told him to land the airplane and get rid of this guy. The clown said, "That's bullshit, and it's not going to happen." In essence, he was calling my bluff. I hung up the phone and proceeded to the cockpit. I asked the cockpit crew for an update. They told me we were scheduled to land in about 20 minutes. I asked the fight engineer to call ahead for the authorities to meet the flight and remove this unruly passenger.

By this time, the captain had received clearance for a non-scheduled emergency landing. He got on the public address system and announced to the passengers that we had to stop in Shannon to get something checked out, but not to worry because everything was okay.

I had never flown into Shannon before. Fields of grass were growing between the runways. On the grass, were hundreds of sheep munching away like a herd of four-legged lawn mowers completely oblivious to the aircraft that were taking off and landing. The fire trucks were waiting, and we were escorted to a hard stand away from the terminal building as a safety precaution.

Once it was determined that there was no fire, standard procedures required that the entire cargo compartment had to be unloaded and inspected before we could proceed. The airplane was guided to a gate at the terminal building. We opened the door, and two policemen were waiting to apprehend the nasty passenger. I suggested they follow me and escorted them to where the clown was sitting. He was in shock and had several shit-hemorrhages before he could comprehend what was going on. They picked him up, one under each arm, and escorted him off the airplane. His wife became outraged and demanded that we return him to the aircraft. In a calm voice, I asked her if she wanted to join her husband in Shannon or if she would like to proceed to New York. She chose New York. So, I told her to return to her seat and keep her mouth shut for the next seven hours. She did so, and we never heard another word.

We informed the rest of the passengers about the delay and suggested that we would be on the ground for about an hour. If they wished to do so, they could disembark and go shopping at the duty-free shops in the airport. While the cargo hold was being inspected, I ordered 340 fresh meals to be delivered to the aircraft. Shannon did a beautiful job with such short notice, and they got the job done in record time. When it was time to board, I walked into the terminal building to gather all the passengers. Standing against the wall with the two police officers was the jerk I kicked off the airplane. He motioned for me to come over and talk to him. By this time, his demeanor had changed dramatically. He was meek, mild, and gentle as a lamb. He asked me if we were going to send him to jail. I told him it was up to the local authorities and walked away.

With passengers, cargo, and fresh meals on board, we taxied out to the runway. We made several turns and several more unexpected turns. I ran back to the cockpit to find out what the problem was. The cockpit crew informed me that the warning light was on indicating that there was a fire in the cargo bay. We had to return to the terminal for a second time.

Everything checked out, so we got ready for take-off once again. But things wound down. I looked out the window and saw those stupid sheep again. We returned to the terminal building because the fire warning signal came on for a third time. By now, I had made so many announcements, none of the passengers wanted to hear from me any more. The captain had to say something with a voice of higher authority.

Once the inspection was completed, it was determined that there was a faulty warning light, and we were good to go. The captain made the announcement, and we were finally on our way. Originally, we were supposed to land in New York at 3 p.m. Our new estimated arrival time would be 9 p.m. Once we left Shannon, I spent the next six hours consulting with passengers. There were about 30 of them that would be missing their connecting flights, and they had to overnight in New York. TWA put them in a hotel and bought them dinner. They were tired and frustrated, but appreciative.

I knew all the international flights would have come and gone by the time we arrived, and the ground personnel would be down to a skeleton crew as many of the employees would have left the airport for the day to be home having dinner with their families. I could not move that many passengers through the terminal building by myself.

So, I had the flight engineer call ahead, contact the DCS duty officer, and see if he/she could round up any DCSs that could help me out. The DCSs were a loyal group. One for all, and all for one. Our job got us into some really tight situations, and we had to rely on each other to overcome the problems we were faced with. I always came to my colleagues' rescue, and they came to mine. Together, we survived and always overcame our challenges victoriously. When I arrived at JFK, three DCSs were standing in the customs hall waiting to help and do whatever needed to be done.

When it was all over, collectively, we went back to the employees parking lot. In my suitcase, I had a bottle of Johnny Walker scotch that I purchased at the duty-free shop at the airport. I invited them to join me for a drink at my makeshift car bar. They eagerly accepted, and we all piled in about 11 p.m. We sat in the car, passing the bottle around, telling jokes and war stories for the next two hours.

It was time to call it quits for the evening, but I was in no condition to drive all the way home. I went into the TWA hangar/office building, marched into the pilots' rest area, laid down in a lounge chair, and fell asleep for 12 hours. That was one hell-of-a-trip.

CHAPTER 37
LAST FLIGHT OUT

I loved flying to Greece. The flights were brutal because they were long and exhausting, but I volunteered to work them because I had so much fun when I got there, and the people were some of the nicest I had ever met.

I befriended two of the Athens male TWA ground personnel, Alex and Faden. They were customer service agents and always helped me process the passengers through the terminal building upon my arrival. They themselves were good friends, and I often invited them to join the crew and me for dinner. Obviously, they knew the city better than I did, so I suggested they pick the restaurant. They showed up at the hotel in their chartreuse VW minivan, and we headed to the Plaka, the city's ancient marketplace. We would usually end up in some obscure little hole-in-the-wall that the regular tourists did not know about. Singing, dancing, breaking plates, and eating exotic Greek food was the bill of fare. Lots of laughter and good times were had by all. However, things were about to change.

On July 20, 1974, all hell broke loose over the island of Cyprus. Cyprus is a small island with a long history that spans 10,000 years, making it one of the oldest civilizations in the Mediterranean. It is located south of Turkey, east of Greece, and west of Lebanon. It is mostly inhabited by Greeks and Turks, and both countries like to believe Cyprus belongs to them. As a result, they had been duking it out for years.

Whenever there is a conflict between the two countries, it creates a problem for the United States because both Greece and Turkey are our allies and members of NATO. For whatever reason, Turkey invaded Cyprus in an effort to gain control. During the struggle, the Greeks felt like the United States was taking sides with the Turks. This made them mad, and hostilities arose. This warm and peaceful nation developed a roaring case of the ass against the Americans. I brought my 747 into Athens, and we landed on July 21. A militant crowd awaited. They were spitting on and throwing rocks at Americans, including me. Since I had been airborne for the previous 10 hours, I was not expecting the reception we received.

I sequestered myself in my room and ordered room service. I kept a low profile for the remainder of the layover. The next day, I made it to the airport. Sympathetic ground personnel helped me get my pre-flight chores done.

Then I met the pilots in flight operations to develop contingency plans if necessary. Rumors were rampant that we might encounter trouble trying to leave Athens. There were no jetways to accommodate 747s at that time, so the aircraft had to be parked on the tarmac, and the passengers were bussed to and from the terminal.

Heat was also a problem. Our flight was scheduled to depart at noon. We needed to be airborne immediately thereafter because as temperatures rose, every minute delay required additional fuel to get us off the ground. With such a long distance to go, we needed to conserve as much fuel as possible to insure we could make it to our destination in New York.

We started a routine boarding procedure that required moving people from the terminal to the airplane. That meant 346 sets of cheeks that needed to be placed in seats. As we started the process, the captain called me to get to the cockpit immediately. He told me that he just got word from the tower that there was a militant group of soldiers en route to the airport. They were driving a jeep equipped with a 50-caliber machine gun and their intent was to destroy our plane. We needed to get everyone on board ASAP and get the hell out of there.

We scrambled and literally pushed people up the stairs and onto the plane. The captain started the engines the second everyone was on board. We took off like a teenager in a hot rod on a Saturday night, as we could see the jeep coming up behind us. We were out of range, but the jeep was closing in fast. We lifted off just as they began to fire. This was like a scene from the movie, *Last Flight Out*.

Me on the tarmac at Athens airport,
moments before learning about the impending attack

We burned so much fuel in the process that there was not enough to make it to New York. We would have to stop in Goose Bay, Labrador; Gander, Newfoundland; or Bangor, Maine. Bangor was selected. Somehow, the press got ahold of the story and alerted the citizens of the city that we were coming. The people of Bangor had never seen a 747, so when we arrived, the whole town was lined up along the runway to see what this big bird looked like. They went berserk. However, my passengers were exhausted, and all they wanted to do was get to New York. We were a little late in arrival, but everyone made it in safe and sound.

In addition to the Cyprus incident, Athens was a hotbed for terrorist activity in those days. My first brush with death was in 1953 when I was eight years old and nearly died from an appendicitis. My second brush with death was hours away on the day I took TWA flight #880 into Athens, landing in the morning of September 7, 1974. The pilots, flight attendants, and I were exhausted and made a beeline to our hotel rooms for much-needed sleep. We agreed to meet for drinks at 5 p.m. We were staying at the Athens Hilton. On the roof overlooking the city was an outdoor bar. It was the perfect place to relax.

Everyone showed up and ordered a drink. Within a couple minutes, I got an incredible abdominal pain and excused myself to go to the restroom. Along the way, I realized things were quite serious, and I opted to go directly to my hotel room. I became very ill. I must have ingested something during the trip that was not agreeable. Without going into gory details, I ended up spending the entire night sleeping on the bathroom floor to be close to the toilet.

By the next morning, I called flight operations at the airport and announced that I was too sick to work flight #881 back to New York. I was told that they were just getting ready to call me because the airplane that I was to take back to New York had a mechanical problem, and my flight was cancelled. Flight operations was in the process of calling all the crew members to tell them we did not have an airplane, and we would have to stay over in Athens an extra day.

We were held up in our hotel rooms, but our passengers were stuck at the airport. TWA had another flight, #841, coming in from Tel Aviv to New York via Rome. They stopped in Athens and picked up all the passengers that would have normally gone on our flight. We had European flight attendants based in Rome, so they could work the flight in lieu of our team.

Thirty minutes after take-off, the airplane blew up and crashed in the Ionian Sea killing everyone on board. It was believed that a bomb had been placed in the cargo hold in Athens, and that was the cause of the tragedy. Holy smoke, that was supposed to be my flight. However, due to food poisoning and a mechanical problem, my life was spared once again. It took a while for all of this to sink in before I realized how close to death I had come.

On the other hand, this incident did not stop me from wanting to make the Athens run. Every layover I had was a memorable one, so I kept returning over and over again.

One of the reasons I liked flying to Athens was the fact that I enjoyed the people so much. They were always friendly and accommodating. After my duties were completed at the airport, I would grab a taxi and head for the Athens Hilton. I was always met by a doorman that was close to my age. He opened the cab door and greeted me with a warm, "Hello. Welcome to Athens." Recently I had purchased a suitcase. It was cheap but looked like it was made of expensive leather. When the doorman was helping me with my luggage and escorting me to the check-in desk, he admired my suitcase and asked if I could get one for him.

On my return trip the following week, I presented him with his request. He was excited and beside himself. "Thank you, thank you, thank you. How much do I owe you?"

I said, "Nothing. This is a present from me to you." He insisted that he pay me. I gave him a pat on the shoulder and told him to just enjoy it. We became good friends, and my gift paid dividends many times over well into the future. I asked him what his name was. He told me several times, but I could not pronounce it, and I could not remember it. I asked him, "Can I just nickname you Zorba?" He laughed and said "Sure."

On future flights, I would arrive at the Hilton, and Zorba was there to greet me. When I pulled up to the hotel, he would grab my luggage and take it to the check-in counter. He would tell the clerk I was a high-ranking official with TWA, and if a luxury suite was available, she should give it to me. That worked some of the time, and I was in the lap of luxury for the next 24 hours.

Zorba carried my luggage to my room and refused to take a tip. One time, I arrived and told him that the pilots, cabin crew, and I were going to meet later in the day for a drink at the top of the Hilton, and I invited him to join us. He told me it was a Greek holiday, and all the stores and bars were closed. I expressed my disappointment since the crew and I were looking forward to a de-briefing, a term we used for a social get-together commonly held after such a long flight. Sometimes I would attend these get-togethers to strengthen relationships for team building between management, cockpit crew, and the cabin crew. Zorba told me that he would secure a conference room on our behalf and take care of everything. He had a brother-in-law that owned a grocery store. When the get-together started, Zorba showed up with wine, cheese, and all sorts of party snacks. We had a successful gathering, and it did not cost us a dime.

CHAPTER 38
HOME NOT SO SWEET HOME

On my days off, I enjoyed the solitude of being home with my family and living in a small town. The hikes, picnics, and bike rides in the countryside were so peaceful and relaxing after dealing with big cities and hundreds of passengers during the previous few days.

However, life was not without its challenges. When we first arrived in Connecticut in 1972, Heidi was about to turn four years old. Alice and I noticed that she was becoming extremely hyperactive, and her behavior was becoming more and more concerning. She could not sit still for more than a couple minutes, and she could run faster than an Olympian. When she bolted, Jessie Owens would have had a hard time catching her. So, we started taking her to the University of Connecticut Medical Clinic. Many trips were made over the months for testing. We tried drugs, therapy, and anything else that would help us get to the root of the problem. Nothing seemed to work, and Heidi became increasingly difficult to manage. When she turned five years of age, we enrolled her in kindergarten at a public school that was only three blocks away.

She would wet her pants, and the school would call for us to come and get her. This went on for the first three days of school. I brought her home and asked her what the problem was. I explained to her that she was a big girl now that she was in school, and that big girls did not wet their pants. She looked at me and said, "I don't want to be a big girl, and I don't want to be in school." This is when we began to realize that she had additional problems. After considerably more testing, it was determined that she had learning disabilities and special education had to be arranged. She could not compete in a normal school environment where the other kids began to pick on her. We could not find a facility adequate for her needs, so we decided to keep her at home for the time being.

My daughter's hyperactivity was wearing on Alice, so I suggested that she get a friend to watch Heidi so she could go to Florida and park it on the beach for a while or take trips to Europe with me. She declined the offers many times over. Then I suggested she get a part-time job and hire a babysitter so that she could get a break. She thought that was a good idea and landed a job as a receptionist at the nearby Marriott Hotel. She purchased a new wardrobe and started her new career. Immediately, I noticed a positive change in her demeanor, and I was genuinely happy for her. The plan seemed to be working.

The hotel manager was a guy named Dennis. He was married, and he and his wife, June, were expecting their first child. We invited them over for dinner from time-to-time and played board games after dinner as a form of entertainment. They seemed like a nice couple. I never realized that while we were playing board games on top of the table, my wife and Dennis were playing footsie underneath the table.

One time, I came home from a trip, and the next day my daughter and I drove to New York to visit an Army buddy of mine. Along the way, my daughter said, "You know, Mommy has a new boyfriend."

I said, "Really. Who is it?" She said it was the guy she worked with, the one whose wife was going to have a baby. I laughed it off and thought, "No way." I immediately dismissed it as I never thought for a second my wife would have an affair.

Shortly thereafter, I noticed that a half-dozen of my dress shirts were missing along with a couple ties. I asked my wife about it, and she suggested that the cleaners must have lost them. After I raised hell with the cleaners, my wife confessed that her boss at the hotel needed shirts and ties, so she gave him some of mine. I said, "Are you crazy? You can't go giving my business clothes away without my permission. I need them for my job."

Then, Alice announced that she needed a break from my daughter and asked me to help. I called my parents that were living in Santa Barbara, California at the time and asked if they could be of assistance. They still had kids at home, but said, "Sure, bring Heidi out, and she can stay with us." The two of us flew out together. I spent a couple days with my parents, left my daughter with them, and returned to New York in time to work my next flight.

By the time I got back from my three-day European trip, I called my parents to see how things were going. They were livid and told me to get to California and pick up my daughter. They hadn't realized what a handful Heidi was when they agreed to keep her.

I called my wife and asked her if it was okay to bring my daughter home. She said, "Absolutely not." So, I called my mother-in-law in northern California to see if she could help. She said, "Sure, bring her up." So, we flew up to San Francisco where we were met by my mother-in-law. She was living in a small town called Red Bluff, about a three-hour drive north of the bay area. I explained to her that I had to get back to New York for work, but I would return in four days to pick my daughter up.

Because of all the running around, I never had time to get home. I had not seen my wife for nearly two weeks. When I returned to California, I was informed by my mother-in-law that she and Alice had agreed that my daughter would be spending an undetermined length of time there, and my mother-in-law was going to enroll her in school. I thought this was crazy. "Are you both out of your minds?" It was then I realized something was dreadfully wrong. My heart fell to my stomach, and I grabbed a flight back to the East Coast. When I got home, I sat down with my wife and said we needed to have a serious talk.

Calmly she informed me that our marriage was over. She and Dennis were in love, and they were going to plan a new life together. I asked, "What about me?"

She replied, "Oh, I'm sure you will find someone else." I reminded her that we had been together for seven years. We had gone through and overcome many hurdles such as my time in the military and then college. I had a well-paying job, a new car, and I was getting close to paying off my college loans.

I said, "We are finally getting out of the woods. Why would you want to leave at a time like this?" She did not seem to have a clear-cut explanation other than the fact that she thought she was in love with this guy. I looked deep into her eyes and could see there was nothing on the other side. I felt like I was trying to reason with a terrorist.

My line of logic was clearly not going to work, so I tried a different approach. I mentioned our handicapped daughter and asked if she had given any thought to how we were going to deal with that issue? She said that her mother would take care of Heidi until she got settled. Another brilliant plan! "Just how long do you think that will last?" I queried. She didn't have a clue.

I asked, "What about Dennis's wife, June? Does she know her husband is about to run off with another woman?"

Alice replied, "I'm not really sure."

"June is eight months pregnant. What's the plan for that one?" was my next question.

"Dennis said he would handle it," she replied.

"What does that mean?" I prodded.

"Uh, I'm not really sure."

"Does he have a plan to divorce her?"

"Yes."

"What is the plan?"

"Uh, I'm not really sure, but he said he had it figured out."

The back and forth between us continued.

I asked, "When are you planning to leave?"

Another less-than-concrete answer, "I'm not really sure, but I think within the month."

"Where are you planning to go?"

"Vermont."

"What the heck is in Vermont?" I demanded.

"Well, we are going to work the pumpkin harvest, make a lot of money, and use that to finance our way out west, job hunting along the way." I had to laugh. I reminded her that I had known her since she was 18 years old, and she had never done a day of manual labor in her life. How on earth was she going to harvest pumpkins? She started laughing as well because deep down inside she knew she wouldn't make it through the first day.

In reality, they had no plan, but they would figure it out one day at a time. I shook my head in disbelief. I just could not understand what prompted her to do this. Then one day, the lights came on. It went back to the very first day we got on a TWA flight from Los Angeles to New

York and that attractive flight attendant walked up and introduced herself to us. At that point, Alice must have felt that with my new job, I would fall in love with a beautiful flight attendant, run away, and leave her high and dry. So, she devised a plan whereby she would find a guy and beat me to the punch. Wow. That was never my intent; however, in her mind, that was exactly what she envisioned.

After hearing all of this, I think most men would have kicked their spouse out of the house right then and there. But I was determined to salvage this marriage, and if they were not planning to leave for another month, I could use the time to talk some sense into her. Between my trips to Europe, I would come home on my days off and try whatever was necessary to see if we could patch things up.

On one trip, I unexpectedly arrived back in New York a day early. I took a nap in my office at JFK, awoke about 3:30 a.m., and began the two-hour drive up to my home in Connecticut. It was a Sunday morning, and I arrived at home around 6 a.m. I pulled into the driveway and opened my garage door. Dennis's car was parked inside, and I had to park out in the street. I walked to the front door and put my key in the lock but could not budge the door open. I went to the living room window and looked inside. The two little lovebirds had slid a huge trunk up against the door. So, I ran around to the back of the house and tried to gain entry through the sliding glass door. It was locked, and I did not have a key to get in.

By now, I was really getting pissed. I ran back to the front yard and hollered up to the bedroom. Alice, dressed in her nightgown, opened the window. I told her to open the door because I was coming in one way or another. She was buying time while Dennis was trying to get dressed. Finally, the two of them walked down the stairs. She employed diversionary tactics while Dennis headed to his escape route, the back door. As he was unlocking it, I was on my way in. When he saw this freight train coming toward him, he panicked, ran back into the living room, and crawled underneath a desk. He knew he was going to get the crap beat out of him, so he thought if he could find refuge under the desk, I would not be able to get a good swing at him. This guy was so quick I couldn't help thinking, "He has done this before. This was not his first rodeo."

I dragged him out from under the desk, put some knots on his head with my fists, marched his scrawny butt out to his car, and told him to never, ever take my parking spot again. He put up no resistance, didn't say a word, and hauled ass down the road.

Back in the house, I walked up the stairs with my wife trailing me. She said, "I do not know why you are so upset. Nothing happened."

"If nothing happened, what was Dennis doing here at six in the morning?"

"He was on his way back from Hartford and just stopped by to say hello," Alice replied.

"Oh really. How do you explain the empty pizza box, empty box of Oreo cookies, and the empty quart-size bottle of Coke in the bedroom?"

"Well, he thought that I might be hungry, so he picked up a pizza," she blurted. Gee, quick thinking on her part! How on God's green earth did she think I was going to buy that line of bullshit? "He would have had to pick it up at 5 a.m. Do you know of any place making pizza at 5 a.m.? He must have purchased it at the donut shop."

"Oh yeah. Maybe that is where he got it," she said hoping that could really happen.

I fumed, "So, he arrived here at 5:50 a.m. I show up at 6 a.m. And during that ten-minute interval you devoured all this food and fell asleep out of pure exhaustion. Is that correct?"

"Uh. Yes. I guess so."

"Listen to me. Your story line is developing at a rate 50% slower than your ability to belch out lies. I want some truthful answers."

Nothing.

About that time, lover boy calls. He told my wife he had a problem. They talked things over, and she hung up the phone. She was visibly upset and mad as a hornet as she explained, "Now look what you have done. That was Dennis on the phone. He said you hit him so hard that his head is full of lumps, and he is embarrassed to go to work because he looks so bad."

I sat her down on a chair like a schoolteacher talking to a third grader. "Now, listen to me. You have no right to be upset. But I do. How would you feel if you came home from work and found me in our bed with another woman? I don't think you would be a happy camper.

Secondly, Dennis should not be upset about his appearance. He should be grateful that he is not dead."

One day, I finally told her I had tried everything in the book to keep the marriage together and could go no further. I would let her go without any further resistance on my part.

I took off on my next TWA trip to Madrid, and Dennis took off on a trip of his own. He purchased a package deal that included round-trip airfare from New York to Bermuda, a welcome cocktail, hotel room, 18 holes of golf, and a quickie-divorce for an all-inclusive price of $500.

While he was on his journey, I was in my hotel room in Madrid. I laid there wide awake all night long. Something in the back of my mind told me to get back to New York as soon as possible. Upon arrival, I drove home only to find all of Alice's clothes gone. They finally made the "Great Escape." I felt like I had been kicked in the gut.

Apparently, the man Alice couldn't live without returned to the States from Bermuda and went home to pack his things. June was in the hospital giving birth. Once he loaded his car, he drove to the hospital to meet with her. She said, "Where have you been? I went into labor, took a taxi to the hospital, and gave birth to a baby girl. Would you like to see her?"

He said, "Not really. I just stopped by to give you these papers. We are officially divorced. Good-bye and good luck. I'm taking off with your friend, Alice." He then walked out of the room never seeing his newborn. June was stuck. This poor gal was laying in the recovery room after just giving birth. Her husband left her. Her friend left her. She had no relatives close by. And now she didn't even have a car. (I learned all this several months later.)

I did not have a clue where Dennis and Alice had gone. She mentioned Vermont, but I had no way to verify that. I called my mother-in-law to check on my daughter and asked if she knew Alice's whereabouts. Either she truly did not know, or she just wasn't going to tell me. With Alice gone, I figured that I had to pack up and start a new life.

I called my TWA buddy, Carl Rogers. Carl and I had gone through training together and developed a good friendship. I learned that he and his wife were separating as well, so I thought I would call and see if he was looking for a roommate. He told me he was renting a three-bedroom house with another colleague of ours by the name of Jack, and I could take the third bedroom. They lived on Long Island in the small town of Long Beach, New York. It was a short commute to the airport, so I thought this was a good deal. I put all my furniture except my bed in storage and moved in.

The next day I had to work a flight to London. When I returned three days later, both Carl and Jack had gone on their respective trips, leaving me with the house to myself. I was dog-tired and crashed for about 12 hours. When I awoke, I was starving. I went to the kitchen and found eggs, ham, and cheese in the refrigerator and decided to make an omelet. I got everything in the skillet. Then I opened a cupboard door and found several jars of spices. First came the oregano. I dumped some in the eggs. Then I found some basil and dumped some of that in as well. Then I found a jar of chopped parsley, so I put that in, too. I noticed that all the spices looked alike, but I really didn't think much of it at the time.

As I ate my breakfast, I started to get light-headed. My immediate thought was that jet lag was catching up with me. However, jet lag had never affected me like this. I went back to bed and slept it off. The next day, Jack and Carl returned. Jack went to the cupboard and said, "Who the hell has been stealing my pot?" That is when I realized he was hiding all his marijuana in spice jars. No wonder I got high. I had never used pot before, so that was a complete surprise. I had just eaten the omelet from outer space.

Shortly after I moved in, the lease was up, and the landlord asked us to leave. I really liked Connecticut and suggested we move back there. Carl and Jack thought that was a great idea, so I took it upon myself to find our new home. I found a beautiful four-bedroom house in the town of Westport just up the road from the home of Paul Newman and Joanne Woodward.

It was very quaint, tucked in the woods with a stream running through the backyard. Every morning the deer would come down to get a drink of water, and the entire environment was tranquil and relaxing. We all loved our new abode. The house had two fireplaces. One was on the main floor. The other was in the basement. The basement became our TV room and den. We chopped firewood from fallen trees on the property and set up a refrigerator and bar on the lower level. No matter how bad the winter wind blew, or how much snow fell, we were warm and cozy in our little nest with a roaring fire blazing away in the fireplace. We raked leaves in the fall and built snowmen in the winter. We were all genuinely content.

Carl got a new girlfriend named Victoria. Jack got a new girlfriend named Gracey. And, I was still licking my wounds from my failed marriage. One day, I woke up and said, "I've had enough of this crap," and decided to get on with life. I tried to date, but it wasn't easy at first. All the flight attendants knew when I was married so they left me alone. However, when they found out I was available, some slowly began to gravitate toward me, and me toward them. I was back on the market. Not with a clear head, but at least I was making an effort.

CHAPTER 39
DISCO BILL

In the Fall of 1974, all DCSs were called to the office in New York for a special meeting. The corporate office decided to close the flight attendant domiciles in Hong Kong, Rome, and Paris. They feared that once this decision was made, the flight attendants would rebel and try to sabotage the flights. To combat the situation, management assembled teams of DCSs to relocate to strategic locations around the globe and monitor all overseas flights.

Bill Gernal

I was assigned to the Lisbon team. There were five of us, and our team leader was a good friend of mine by the name of Bill Gernal. Bill was originally from South America. He was very talented and spoke a number of languages. Bill moved to the United States in the mid-1960s and became an international purser for TWA. He was a good leader and always maintained a great sense of humor.

Our base of operations was the Tivoli Hotel, and we were to monitor flights from Lisbon to Madrid, Rome, Athens, and back again. So, back and forth we went. When we returned to Lisbon, we were always granted a couple days off, and we used that time to explore Portugal. We rented a car and headed to a new destination every time we had a break. The explorations were fun and adventurous. We visited the ancient walled-city of Obidos and drank their famous "fire-water" called Agua Dente.

We visited the town of Estoril and had fantastic lobster dinners. But perhaps the greatest pastime was horseback riding. We discovered an equestrian riding academy that rented horses. We mounted up, and with the assistance of a guide, we rode through olive orchards that ran along the cliffs overlooking the ocean. Our guide would sing songs as we rode along, and our team leader, Bill, would do the same. He knew the language and had a beautiful singing voice.

One Saturday evening, Bill suggested the two of us go bar hopping. I pushed back, telling him that I was still rather depressed because of my recent marriage break-up and preferred to stay in my room at the hotel. He said, "Bullshit, you are coming with me. It will cheer you up." Not only was Bill a good salesman, but he was a prankster and always knew how to have a good time. Reluctantly, I went.

We walked into a disco where the music was loud and lively. Bill spotted a couple attractive girls and suggested we move in for the "kill." The music put me in a good mood, and I said, "Let's go for it." We approached the girls and the four of us hit it off immediately. About the time things were getting hot-and-heavy between one girl and me, Bill inserted himself between the two of us and said to me, "What are you doing, messing with this girl? I thought you told me you were married." Upon hearing this, the girl became upset and went stomping off. I asked Bill why he would make such a stupid comment. He laughed as though it was the funniest thing in the world. "Come on Steve, there are plenty of other discos, so put it behind you, and let's move along," he instructed.

Within three blocks, we came upon another lively hot spot and went in to investigate. Bill found two more girls that caught his eye and suggested we go over and introduce ourselves to them. We did. And once again, the four of us hit it off. I was so proud of myself because I was moving away from my depressed mood and into a happier state of mind. The girl I was with was very easy to talk to, and I was glad Bill suggested we go out on the town that evening. I was genuinely having a good time. Suddenly, Bill walks up between the two of us and says, "Hey Steve, what are you doing with this lady? I thought you said you were married." She got mad and stomped off.

"Damnit Bill, how many times are you going to pull this trick on me?" He started laughing his ass off again. He thought this was the funniest prank he'd ever pulled, especially since he did it twice in the same evening. I told him I had enough and headed back to the hotel. By this time, I wanted to kick him in the nuts, but I didn't. To this day, we remain the best of friends, and we often laugh and reminisce about that evening.

The next day we headed to Rome, laid over for the evening, and ended our trip in Athens the following day. Bill suggested we meet for dinner that evening. The Athens Hilton had a beautiful restaurant on the lower level. There was a pond in the middle, nicely landscaped, and full of colorful fish and turtles.

The hostess seated us at a table next to the water. The atmosphere was delightful, and Bill and I ordered top-of-the-line entrées, a couple cocktails, and a nice bottle of wine. The waiter brought our salads, and as I began to eat, this little turtle swam up, climbed onto a rock, and watched us while we were eating. Her eye-contact was so intent, it was like we invited her to join us for dinner. She just sat there watching us as if she was sitting at our table engaged in conversation.

At first, I thought it was cute. However, shortly thereafter, a second turtle showed up with lust on his mind. He climbed up on the rock and started humping the first turtle about the time the waiter brought our entrees. Turtle number two was in seventh heaven with his eyes glazed over and having a ball. Turtle number one was rather lethargic, and I was finding the whole thing rather repulsive. I lost my appetite, excused myself, and went to bed. As I left, I looked over my shoulder, and caught a glimpse of Bill grinning at turtle number two encouraging him to "Go for the gold."

CHAPTER 40
PUMPKIN HARVEST

When I returned from the European assignment, I was granted one-week of personal time off. It was good to be back home in Connecticut and in my own bed. Having been gone for quite some time, I had a stack of mail to get through. One envelope caught my attention. It was from the Franklin County Courthouse in Vermont. When I opened it, it turned out to be a notification that I was being sued for divorce because of "cruel and abusive treatment" toward my missing wife. She had been gone for quite a while, and I didn't have a clue as to where she had disappeared.

Ironically, she called me at the exact moment I was reading the letter. I was shocked at the letter, and shocked that she called me. I asked her why she was suing me for divorce based on cruel and abusive treatment because we both knew that was not the case. She told me when she filed for divorce, there were only two reasons for a divorce to be granted. One was cruel and abusive treatment, and the second one was adultery. Alice said, "I knew you weren't adulterous, so I chose the other one."

I was justifiably irked since I didn't fit into either cause for divorce. I decided to get in a dig of my own when I asked, "By the way Alice, just before you left, you mentioned that you would leave your wedding ring on the nightstand, but I never found it. What's the deal on that?"

She said, "Well, that was my intent, but Dennis told me to bring it along. He said we would be getting married shortly, and since he could not afford to buy me a ring, I should just go ahead and wear the one you gave me." This guy was proving to have no lower limits, and her expectations were meeting his ability to deliver.

Feeling the need to make Alice squirm a little more, I asked, "How did the pumpkin harvest go? Did you make a lot of money to finance your job-hunting trip west?"

"No. Not really."

"Oh. What happened there?"

"Well, when the big day came, we didn't feel like carrying pumpkins, so we just slept in."

"For the whole harvest?"

"Yes."

"Well, you started the job-search migration in Vermont, and you are still there. When do you plan to start heading west?"

"We are not going any further because Dennis got a job flipping burgers at a local fast-food restaurant."

"Okay, so let me get this straight. You moved to Vermont as your starting point to head west to California. You made it a grand total of 12 miles, and that's it?"

"Yes."

"Where are you living?"

"In a little town called Fletcher."

"Do you have a home there?"

"We rented a trailer, and it is located in the woods just outside of town," she explained. It was painted dark green so that it blended in with the trees, and the owner took the wheels off. He hoisted the trailer up and set it to rest on top of a cinder block foundation to keep it from flooding during the rainy season.

Alice had started a business taking in ironing which lasted a short time until her iron stopped working. This was all starting to unfold like a bad romance novel. I shook my head in disbelief, feeling the need to get on with my life as quickly as possible.

Shortly thereafter, I received another call from Alice. Wow, two calls in less than a month. "What is going on this time?" I wondered. Apparently the two love birds got into an argument, and Alice claimed that Dennis had beat her up, and she wanted to know if I would consider taking her back. But, a couple days later, she called again, said they resolved their differences, and I should just forget about the last phone call.

Then, I received another call. Alice claimed she had yet another problem. I asked her what the new dilemma was. She told me they just went through a very bad snowstorm and the weight of the snow caused the roof on the trailer to cave in during the night. When she reached down to pull up the covers, all she came up with was a handful of snow. The trailer literally snapped in two, so they had to look for another place to live. All I could do was wish them good luck. The phone calls started coming in on a regular basis. The physical abuse continued, and the romance was being challenged.

I went to the mailbox one day, and there was a bill for $700 from the Franklin County Hospital in Vermont. I thought to myself, "What in the hell is this all about?"

Alice called me, and I confronted her about the bill. She said, "I forgot to tell you, but I got pregnant. Then on Thanksgiving Day I had a miscarriage and had to go to the emergency room for treatment."

We did not have any money, so Dennis said, "Technically, you are still married to Steve, and therefore it is his responsibility to pay the bill." It became obvious that this guy had more balls than brains.

Like an idiot, I submitted the bill to the insurance company, and since the policy was in my name, they sent the check to me instead of the hospital. I was about to forward the check to the hospital when a little voice entered my head and said, "Listen numb-nuts, you have been more than generous with these two knuckleheads. Just keep the money." That was exactly what I did.

About a month later, I received another letter from the Franklin County Courthouse stating that my divorce was being processed, and if I did not contest it, I would be giving up all my rights to do so. I did nothing. A month later I received another letter from them stating that my divorce was final and properly recorded.

That week, Dennis and Alice went to the Justice of the Peace and were united in unholy matrimony. The wedding ring I bought her years ago shone brilliantly that day, I am sure.

CHAPTER 41
KEEP YOUR PANTS ON

After several months of domestic flying, I was sent back to international flight status. Tel Aviv would be my next assignment. TWA had a unique flight schedule for the DCSs traveling to Tel Aviv. For us, it was a five-day trip. We left New York on day one arriving in Rome on day two. We laid over in Rome, and on day three, we continued east with a stop in Athens, then on to Tel Aviv where we spent a second layover. On day number four we returned to Rome via Athens and had a third layover. Finally, on day five, we returned to New York. That was one hell-of-a-trip. By the time I got home, I was so tired I felt like I had the lead role in *Night of the Living Dead*.

TWA had flight attendant domiciles in New York, Los Angeles, San Francisco, Kansas City, Chicago, and Boston. Internationally, they also had flight attendant domiciles in Paris, Rome, and Hong Kong.

I left New York with an American crew. After an overnight layover in Rome, they returned to New York the following day, and I inherited a crew of European flight attendants domiciled in Rome. Together, we would continue the journey east to Athens, then onto Tel Aviv. We would overnight in Israel and return to Rome the next day.

On my first experience with this route, I went into the briefing room and introduced myself to the flight attendants. I told them this was my first trip to Tel Aviv, and I would really appreciate any assistance they could give me. These were spunky, fun-loving girls, and my admission of my lack of knowledge regarding where we were going got their wheels turning. They immediately began to plot a practical joke on me.

We left Rome, had a two-hour layover in Athens, and headed for Tel Aviv. En route, two of the flight attendants approached me in one of the galleys. They had talked it over among themselves, decided I was a good guy, and invited me to join a group of six for dinner that evening. I accepted their invitation. Our layover hotel was the Tel Aviv Hilton, and we planned to meet in the lobby. From there, we took a couple of taxi cabs to King Herod's seaport city of Jaffa. The taxi driver dropped us off at an obscure beach, and we traipsed across the sand to a rather large tent. Once inside, the sand was covered with exotic carpets, and this would be our dinner table.

The menu was fish, followed by more fish. If you didn't like fish, you were out of luck. The fish were netted and hauled in from the Mediterranean Sea. There was no refrigeration at the restaurant, so they preserved the fish with garlic. We sat on the carpet, and dinner was served. I am not a big fish eater, but the dinner was fantastic. When it was all over, we left the restaurant, intending to catch a couple taxi cabs back to the hotel. However, none came.

By now, it was midnight, and one of the flight attendants suggested that since it was such a beautiful evening, it might be more enjoyable to walk back to the hotel instead of taking a taxi. We all agreed and began the three-mile hike to the Hilton.

We were walking along the esplanade heading north. The Mediterranean was to our left, sand was on either side of the sidewalk, and a major thoroughfare was to the right of that. Because Israel was either at war or preparing for war, the military was constantly on the move day and night. As we were walking, the Army was conducting field exercises on the thoroughfare next to us with armored personnel carriers, followed by squads of foot soldiers armed with their semi-automatic weapons. It was most impressive. Had I not already been in the military myself, I might have been somewhat intimidated.

As we walked, one of the girls said, "Isn't this a beautiful evening."

Another agreed and said, "Oh yes, and look, we have a full moon."

A third said, "It is such a warm evening, and the water is so calm, this would be the perfect time to go skinny-dipping."

I was now a bachelor, and I was getting interested in how this conversation was developing. The girls agreed and began taking off their clothes. One undressed at lightning speed and went racing out into the surf. I followed and was the second one in the water. Meanwhile, the others slowly went through the motions, pretending to get undressed. I lost sight of what was going on around me. Soon, I looked around and noticed that we were the only two in the water. I asked my companion what happened to the rest of the girls? Puzzled, she looked at me and said, "I don't know. Perhaps we should go back to shore and see what is going on."

When we got back on land, the other girls were gone and so were our clothes. I panicked and said, "Now what do we do?"

She said, "I have no idea. Perhaps we should just walk back to the hotel."

I knew that wasn't going to work. We were standing in the middle of nowhere with no clothes on. We had hundreds of military troops running alongside us with semi-automatic weapons. It was at least another mile before we got to the hotel, and what were we going to do once we got there? I could not see myself walking into the lobby naked.

Panic raced through me from every direction. If TWA got wind of this back in New York, I would be fired immediately. How on earth did I get myself into this situation? And what on earth was I going to do to get out of it? The two of us started walking. I was sweating bullets. My mind was trying to think about various strategies, but I was getting nowhere. My brain began to atrophy. About the time I was at my wits end, we began to hear some giggling. It was the rest of the crew. They jumped out from behind some bushes and threw our clothes back to us. Their ruse was a success. As for me, I was eternally grateful.

By the time I got back to my hotel room, I double-locked the door and fell sound asleep after saying many prayers of gratitude. The next day, the girls came up to me one by one, telling me what a good sport I was. "Welcome to the club." Apparently, I was not the first DCS to go through this ritual. In spite of it all, it was a successful flight, and I would return to Israel many more times.

CHAPTER 42
STREAKING THROUGH THE SKY

The following month, I was flying the New York to Rome route, affectionately referred to as "The Ravioli Rocket." It was eight hours over, and eight and one-half hours back. This provided plenty of time for things to go wrong. And they did. The biggest issue was that the toilets would clog up and had to be taken out of service. Another issue was the fact that the passengers would get restless over time, leading to crankiness among the ranks.

One night flight proved to be anything but boring. "Streaking" came into vogue in the early 1970s. It started out on football fields, then to basketball courts, and finally onto airplanes. We had just finished the meal service and were ready to start the movie when a team of young men in their early twenties put their plan into motion.

The 747 had two restrooms located toward the front of the airplane, four more at mid-section, and another four grouped together in the aft section. Streaking was a team sport that took some logistics planning — two guys would secure a specific lavatory in the back section, and one guy would occupy a lavatory near the front section, take off his clothes, and hand them to a relay man. The relay man would march the clothes to the back lavatory and hand them to the two guys that were waiting there.

The relay guy would slowly meander up to the front lav where the naked guy patiently waited. He would crack the door open and give last-minute instructions to him, plotting his course and alerting him to any congestion along the way. "GO, GO, GO, GO, GO!" Naked man takes off and runs the entire length of the airplane with a final stop at the aft lav where his two partners-in-crime with his clothes were waiting. Upon his arrival, they exited the restroom, handed him his clothes, and returned to their seats. Naked man got dressed and casually walked out like nothing happened. Meanwhile, the passengers were trying to put together in their minds what had just happened and determine if they really saw what they thought they saw. It happened so quickly that everything rapidly returned to normalcy before anyone could figure out who the real players were. Flights that were traditionally painfully long and dull could become a source of in-flight entertainment.

Male passengers were constantly hitting on the flight attendants. For the most part, the flight attendants found these passengers to be obnoxious and stupid. On one flight to Rome, I was standing next to the first-class galley when a passenger came up to a flight attendant and said, "My oh my. You have beautiful legs. Do they go all the way up?"

Calmly, she said, "Yes, they do, and when they reach the top, they turn around and make an ass out of themselves." When I heard this, I started laughing uncontrollably. I thought it was one of the cleverest "think-on-your-feet" responses I had ever heard. The guy was not expecting this, got embarrassed, and returned to his seat. We never heard another word out of him for the remainder of the flight.

That evening, the flight attendants, the pilots, and I went out to dinner, and the story was retold at the dinner table. We all had a good laugh. By then I was divorced, and one of the flight attendants said, "Hey Steve, we get hit on by so many passengers, and also by your fellow DCSs, but we never get hit on by you. Why is that?"

Calmly, I said, "I watch all the others make their stupid moves. You have been hit on so many times there is not a single line you haven't heard a thousand times before, and none of them work. I do not want to be put in the same category as all the other idiots. I figured if you were interested in me, you would let me know in your own way."

They responded, "Wow, good answer." That strategy worked out well for me in the long run.

One flight I took to Rome had me landing on December 31. I was warned to be careful because on New Year's Eve, the Italians were known to get a little crazy. I went out to dinner that evening and headed back to my hotel. At precisely midnight, the shit hit the fan. The Italians had a tradition on New Year's Eve — if they had items in their apartment that they thought brought bad luck, or if they had old items they no longer wanted, this was the time to discard them. So, at midnight, the windows went up and out flew the crap. Walking along the sidewalk below, I could see it coming. It started out with harmless things like bits of clothing and trinkets, followed by household items, and finally the big stuff like bookcases and even kitchen stoves. It was a wonder nobody got killed. I made a run for it and arrived at my hotel unscathed.

Rome is a beautiful and exciting city. The history and sights to see are endless, and one could never get bored with all there is to do. Italian food is some of the best in the world, and the people are most accommodating. When I worked flights back from Tel Aviv to Rome with the Rome-based flight attendants, often they would offer to show me their city even though they were back home and off-duty. We would go sightseeing in the daytime, and in exchange, I would take them out to dinner in the evening. I got to see things and go places that tourists would never know about. It was an exciting time!

CHAPTER 43
ITCHY FEET AND DIVINE INTERVENTION

In the Spring of 1976, I became restless and started missing life on the West Coast. I requested a transfer to the TWA domicile in Los Angeles, and my request was granted. I found a beautiful apartment in Marina del Rey, a newly developed beach community and just a short commute to the TWA office at the airport.

Now that I was in Los Angeles, I only worked domestic flights, and layovers in Chicago and Cleveland were not as exciting as London and Paris. I was growing bored, and the glamour of the job was beginning to fade.

Yvonne

One evening, I had a layover in Phoenix and called some friends who lived there. They suggested we meet for a cocktail. They were aware that I was now divorced, and they wanted to introduce me to their friend, Yvonne, who was also recently divorced. Yvonne was easy to

Yvonne and me on the ski slopes

Yvonne and me sailing in Marina del Rey

Yvonne on one of our bike rides in Marina del Rey

Yvonne on my apartment balcony

talk to, and we seemed to have a lot in common. I called her the next time I was in town for a dinner date. Our relationship took off like a freight train, slow to start but picking up steam along the way. The next thing I knew, we were moving down the tracks at lightning speed.

At first, I was a bit apprehensive because I was 30 years old, and Yvonne was only 21. I had never dated someone with that big of an age difference and wondered if it would have an impact on our relationship. However, that concern was dispelled quickly as I got to know her. She was wise and mature beyond her years. She was beautiful, intelligent, and energetic. We had a lot in common and liked to do similar things.

If I suggested a bike ride, off we went. If she wanted to go for a jog or enter a 10K race, we were on the trail. Camping, hiking, fishing, snow skiing, she was up for anything. We did it all, and I was very excited and appreciative of her enthusiasm. My flight schedules kept me hopping about, but on my days off, she would fly over to see me in Marina del Rey, or I would go to Phoenix to see her. Yvonne and her three-year-old son, Jason, were living with her parents. They had a five-bedroom house with plenty of room, so I stayed with them when I visited.

I liked going to Phoenix on my days off because it was such a nice city with many things to do. We rented horses and did trail rides during the day. At night, we would go over to the Arizona State University campus and play tennis. In the summer, when the daytime temperatures showed no mercy, we would go to one of the many resorts in Scottsdale and meander out to the pool area, swim, sunbathe, have a glass of wine, and leave at our leisure.

One weekend we hiked the Grand Canyon. We went down on Saturday morning choosing to walk by ourselves. We were met several times by caravans of mules transporting people up and down the trail. The mules were fascinating to watch. It is my understanding that they are in training for seven years before they can carry a passenger. They know every inch of the way, and they are trained to handle just about any situation including rattlesnakes. On our way down, about ten mules and riders passed us, but before they cleared our path, they came to an abrupt halt. Not one of them flinched a muscle as if they were stopped at a red light. We kept walking, and once we caught up to the lead mule, we could clearly see the problem. There was a rattlesnake crossing the path. The mules froze, as they were taught to do, and patiently waited for the snake to pass. Once they felt that it was at a safe distance, they started up again as if a gate had been lifted at a railway crossing. It was fascinating to watch them. Obviously, the training paid off.

Yvonne and me on our Grand Canyon Hike

We got to the bottom of the canyon and spent the night on the banks of the Colorado River at a camp called Phantom Ranch. The camp included several wooden cabins, a mess hall for eating, and two dormitories, one for men and one for women. What struck me as interesting is that most of the Phantom Ranch occupants were Germans. Americans were outnumbered three to one. Although this was a long way from Berlin, these folks were feeling right at home, laughing, singing, and having a good time. About 10 p.m., Yvonne and I went to our respective dorms for a well-earned rest.

It was recommended that hikers take four quarts of water each for the journey to the top, but we only had two each. Our game plan was to hit the trail early and beat the heat. I woke up at 4 a.m. and knocked on the window next to Yvonne's bunk. She was already up and raring to go. We started our trek, and it was so dark down in the canyon we could barely see our own hands in front of our faces. Nobody else was around. We had the world to ourselves. The trail was rather spooky at that time of day. We heard strange noises but could not see anything. As the sun slowly crept up to the crack of dawn, we could faintly see hundreds of bats flying overhead. There were so many we proceeded with caution. By now we had about 20 percent visibility and could make out the images of deer grazing in the narrow meadow that laced the banks of the Colorado.

We had taken the Bright Angel trail down to Phantom Ranch but chose the Kaibab Trail for our ascent. It was steeper, but about three miles shorter. As we climbed higher, so did the sun. The break of dawn was a beautiful way to start the day. By 10 a.m., we were at the top, thirsty, but feeling a sense of accomplishment. The memory of that day will stay with me for the rest of my life.

Back in Phoenix, we had plenty to do. This had to be the restaurant capital of the world. You could not visit them all in a lifetime. I really enjoyed the city and the state of Arizona. I did not realize it at the time, but someday in the future, it would become my final destination.

CHAPTER 44
UNDER SIEGE

During the summer of 1977, TWA was faced with two serious challenges. One had to do with finances. Like most other airlines at the time, TWA was strapped for cash. The second issue had to do with the flight attendant union. Their contract was just about up, and serious negotiations were taking place between management and the union. TWA could not afford a strike as it would be financially devastating to the company. The union knew this, so they were the ones that held the bargaining chip.

At the 11th hour, all items of contention were settled, and it looked like both sides were ready to sign off on the deal. During the previous seven years, a militant faction in the flight attendant union fought vigorously to keep all management personnel off the airplane; specifically, they wanted the DCS program abolished. With minutes to go before the strike deadline, management agreed and conceded to cancel the DCS program. The next morning, I got a call at 4 a.m. from my supervisor. He said, "I've got some good news and some bad news. The good news is that we averted the strike. The bad news is that we had to cancel the DCS program, leaving several hundred of you without jobs."

A special meeting was called for 8 a.m. the following Monday morning. Our managers encouraged us to review the job posting board daily and try to find a new home within the company. I did this religiously but came up empty-handed. Every position that became available was either boring or located in a place I did not want to be.

After careful consideration, I decided to end my career with TWA and turned in my resignation. It had been a wonderful experience to work with such a fine airline; however, it was time to move on.

CHAPTER 45
CLIPPED WINGS

One day, my college roommate called me to tell me he was getting married and invited me to his wedding. He was living in Seattle at the time, so I flew up to the Northwest a couple days before the festivities began. This gave us a little time to spend together and get caught up.

He mentioned that he was selling clothing apparel for a company that recently went bankrupt. The company had a warehouse full of inventory, and he proposed we form a partnership to liquidate the entire lot with the idea that we could make a substantial profit.

With TWA clearly in my rear-view mirror, I accepted his proposal, returned to Los Angeles, put my furniture in storage, and moved to the Northwest. I rented a small studio apartment that suited my needs, and we went to work. Not knowing anybody, I was rather lonely, but kept busy with the job at hand. In the evenings I would fill my time with jogging along a five-mile trail that gave me time to commune with nature, followed by a good night's sleep.

One evening, as I was jogging down a country road minding my own business, something hit me in the head like a sack of bricks. It was Mr Cupid reminding me that I had found the girl of my dreams, and I needed to ask for her hand in marriage. If I was any sort of a salesman at all, I had to close this deal. Rejection was not an option.

There was a phone booth sitting out in the middle of nowhere at the end of my jogging trail. So, I stopped and called Yvonne to tell her she must get up to Seattle immediately. I would have an airplane ticket waiting for her at the airport in Phoenix.

Upon her arrival, we went to a beautiful French restaurant, and we were assigned the perfect table, along with an outstanding waiter. He did everything he could to make the evening go well. I proposed, and Yvonne said, "Yes." Deal closed!

Having just gotten engaged, it was difficult to drive Yvonne back to the airport to catch her flight. We were excited to tie the knot and set up housekeeping. However, we both had things to do before that would happen. I decided to immerse myself in work and get the project done that I had gone to Seattle for in the first place. And, Yvonne returned to Phoenix to plan the wedding along with all of her other responsibilities.

My job was to "sell." I traveled the highways and byways along the I-5 corridor of Washington from Oregon to the Canadian border calling on every clothing store I could find. This was turning out to be a bigger task than I imagined, and I soon realized that it was not going to be an overnight success. I kept plugging away at it as did my partner. Having been in the clothing business, my partner was very well connected. We decided that he would work with the big department stores and chain stores with multiple locations, while I would handle the small mom-and-pop stores scattered about Washington, Oregon, Wyoming, Idaho, and Montana.

Meanwhile, Yvonne and her mother worked diligently planning the wedding, and I flew down to Phoenix a couple days early before the big day on September 30, 1978. The wedding took place at the Registry Hotel, an upscale resort located in Scottsdale. My parents flew in for the wedding, my TWA buddy, Carl Rogers, and Yvonne's sister, Debbi, were the witnesses, and Yvonne's son, Jason, was the ring bearer. The minister arrived on his motorcycle. The ceremony was small but memorable with our closest friends and family members. For a wedding present, Yvonne's parents gave us an all-expenses paid honeymoon on the island of Maui.

Above: Me, Jason and Yvonne on our wedding day
Below: Me and Yvonne at our wedding reception

CHAPTER 46
LIFE REIMAGINED

Once on Maui, we rented a car and drove to the Inter-Continental Hotel on the west shore. This hotel was paradise. We drove around the island taking in all the sights there were to see.

Me and Yvonne in Hawaii on our honeymoon

We snorkeled, jogged on the beach, played tennis, and did everything a tourist would do. One day we chartered a boat to go deep sea fishing. We were joined by a dentist and his two sons.

The morning started slowly with no bites and no excitement. Suddenly, Yvonne hooked a 400-pound marlin, but it snapped the line. A few minutes later it struck again, and Yvonne was strapped into the fighting seat. The dentist and his two boys laughed hysterically as my 112-pound wife took on this monstrous fish, but it snapped the line for a second time.

Finally, Yvonne hooked a 25-pound Ono and brought it in. The boys kept laughing at her fighting the fish with her skinny little arms, but at the end of the day, she was the only one onboard to catch anything. When we arrived on shore, we gave the fish to a vendor and called it a day. That evening, we went to the restaurant at the hotel for dinner. The "special" for the evening was Ono. Out of curiosity, we ordered it, and it was an excellent meal. The irony of it all was that we paid $300 for the fishing trip, gave the fish away, and then spent another $50 to buy it back again as our evening meal. Everyone was making money off this deal except us.

The weather in Hawaii was so warm and sunny that it was difficult to return to Seattle. Yvonne's parents drove Jason to Seattle from Phoenix, and we moved into a quaint three-bedroom house in the Seattle suburb of Redmond. At the time in 1978, this was a sleepy little community, before Microsoft moved into town and really put Redmond on the map.

Jason and I hit it off from the time we first met when he was three years old. I was a stranger to him, but he gravitated toward me with total trust, and we bonded in many ways. We spent a lot of time together, going to movies, going out for a hike or a jog, playing ball, and doing things that guys like to do. One day Yvonne and I asked Jason if he would like me to adopt him. He was excited, so we went to the King County courthouse to find out what the procedure was.

We learned that Yvonne and I had to be married for a year. Once the probationary period was over, we were free to start the adoption process. Yvonne's ex-husband (Jason's natural father) agreed to the adoption without resistance.

By the time the year was up, we arranged for another meeting with the court. The judge asked us a lot of questions, then excused Yvonne and me so that he could have a one-on-one with Jason. At this juncture, I think most kids would be intimidated. But Jason handled it like a champ. Once that meeting was over, the judge invited Yvonne and me back into the courtroom to congratulate us. He had approved the adoption. With the paperwork completed, Jason Brown became Jason Dolby.

As was required by the process, we submitted the adoption paperwork to Maricopa County back in Phoenix where Jason was born. They issued a new birth certificate reflecting that I was Jason's father.

The trace of his past as a Brown was erased. According to his new birth certificate, Jason was officially born a "Dolby." We all went out to dinner to celebrate. The family was now complete.

CHAPTER 47
RED BUTT AND MARSHMALLOWS

Living in Seattle was wonderful. The countryside was populated with alder and hemlock trees, and I felt like I was living back in Germany. However, there were concessions that had to be made. One was the weather. Grey skies and drizzling rain day-after-day got the best of us at times. One weekend when we were fed up with the gloomy dismal days, we went to a movie filmed in Hawaii just to see the sunshine. It was an adjustment for Yvonne who had spent most of her life in Arizona.

One pleasant sunny weekend day, I suggested we sit out in the back yard with a couple lawn chairs and enjoy the weather. We weren't out long when a big black cloud rolled our way, coming from the southwest. I said to Yvonne, "I'll be damned. We finally get a break in the weather, and here come the clouds." As it turned out, it wasn't a cloud at all. Mount St. Helens had erupted, and we had an 11,000-foot plume of volcanic ash headed our way.

As we were settling into our life in Redmond as a family, I was enjoying the benefit of a marriage partner in a way that Yvonne could not appreciate. I have always had trouble sleeping and get bored during my hours of insomnia. Yvonne, on the other hand, can sleep through an earthquake. We went to bed one evening, and she slipped into her eight-hour coma. As I was trying to count sheep, mental hyperactivity would take over. I would lay awake and think of ways to entertain myself.

Yvonne was my source of entertainment during my restless hours. I would take her arm and hold it up in a vertical position until the blood drained from her arm, and her arm went to sleep. The irritating tingling sensation woke her up, and she would have to shake her arm to get the feeling back. I would lay next to her laughing until the whole bed shook.

Another time, she was sleeping soundly, and I was awake. I went into the bathroom and got a bottle of her fingernail polish, pulled back her panties, and painted little red dots all over her bum. The next morning when she went into the bathroom, I heard a blood-curdling scream. I yelled, "What's wrong?" She answered, "I've got a terrible rash on my butt." About that time as she looked in the mirror, she noticed that all the little red dots were perfectly symmetrical, and she realized a real rash would be more random in its pattern. I was busted.

One Saturday night, we went to bed and decided there would be no alarms on Sunday morning. We were going to sleep in. As usual, Yvonne went fast asleep, and I laid awake trying to figure out a way to occupy time during my sleepless hours. I got out of bed and went into the kitchen, spotting a bag of marshmallows in the cupboard. I opened the bag and took it to the bedroom where I started loading marshmallows into Yvonne's panties. I got about half the bag stuffed in her underwear and returned the rest to the kitchen. Sometime during the middle of the night, Yvonne rolled over and realized there was more than just herself in the underwear. She reached in, grabbed a handful of inventory and yelled, "What on earth is in my underwear?" She unloaded everything, throwing the marshmallows on the floor, and went back to sleep. Early the next morning, Jason walked into the bedroom, saw the irresistible treat and yelled, "Marshmallows!" Before Yvonne or I could stop him, he was down on his hands and knees stuffing his mouth with marshmallows. This was not a kid who normally ate off the floor, but this was just too much temptation!

As we acclimated to life in the Northwest, the clothing liquidation project was nearing completion. Meanwhile, Yvonne enrolled at the University of Washington to finish her college degree. During summer break, she took a temporary job as an administrative assistant at a local executive recruiting firm. One day, she came home from work, and during dinner, she told me that she discovered a company that was looking for salesmen. The current salesmen were making about $60,000 per year. In 1979, that was a lot of money. Then she came home to tell me she made a mistake; the salesmen were making more like $100,000. As a point of reference, I thought I was making good money while I was at TWA earning $13,000 per year. My ears perked up, and I decided I needed to pursue this opportunity.

I bypassed human resources, busted down the door, and went right to the top of the food chain. I told the guy I talked to that he better hire me because I wasn't leaving until he did. He must have been impressed with my moxie and said, "Okay, you are hired. There is only one catch. You must relocate back to California and work out of the Los Angeles office." I really did not want to go back to L.A. but agreed to do so if they would pay for my move. They agreed. So, after two years in Seattle, we were headed to Southern California.

CHAPTER 48
CITY OF ANGELS

The company I went to work with was a general partner that raised investment capital to finance oil and gas drilling ventures through limited partnerships. It was 1981, and oil prices were going through the roof. The investment objective was to produce financial gain through the discovery of new-found domestic oil reserves and to utilize tax incentives created by the federal government's tax reform act to help pay for it. In other words, it was a tax-sheltered investment opportunity designed to stimulate oil and gas production in the US in order to reduce our dependence on foreign oil.

My job was to go out and find investors. In order to become a successful salesman, I had to figure out four things. One, I had to learn about the oil and gas industry and how it worked. Two, I had to learn about taxation and the tax laws that made this an attractive investment. Three, I had to figure out a way for investors to pay for their investment utilizing their tax obligations to fund it. Four, I had to figure out a way to find the "right investor" that could afford to do this.

So, I lubricated my brain with a couple shots of WD-40 to get the cobwebs out and set up a well- disciplined study hall. Every night, I went home from work and burned the "midnight oil" until the wee hours. Eventually, the lights came on one-by-one, but ever so slowly. Along the way, I developed a powerful sales presentation and became the "top rookie salesman" of the year. I was proud of my accomplishments and started to make a respectable income.

The marketing strategy was to make 100 phone calls per day and talk to at least 10 people. Of the 10 people I talked to, I had to get at least one appointment. And of every 10 people I met, I had to close at least one sale. That required eating a lot of rejection, but on the other hand, it was the ticket to success. It worked.

Everyone I met told me they would run it by their CPA or attorney. If their professional advisor felt it was a prudent investment, they would tell my prospect to proceed. The problem was that none of the advisors understood the investment, so they simply told my prospects to "pass on the deal." Also, the advisors had everything to lose and nothing to gain. If they recommended the investment and it went south, the client would fire the advisor, and he/she would lose a client through no fault of their own. That was a dilemma I had to overcome.

The advisors were the "deal killers," and I had to find a way to get them on my side. So, every time I met with a prospect that told me they had to "run it by their advisor," I told the prospect to call the advisor right then and there, and I would make the presentation to the advisor in person. This way, the prospect made the appointment with the advisor for me, bypassing any further rejection.

I needed to get the advisors on my side. So, when I met with them, I approached with compassion. I would tell my story, and once they understood it and liked it, I explained to my prospects that their accountant or attorney could only verify that the tax advantages were in place, but the prospects had to make the investment decision themselves and not hold the advisors accountable. The advisors really liked that approach because it got them off the hook right up front. Often, I would suggest the three of us all meet just to ensure we were on the same page.

This strategy made all the difference in the world, and I started getting referrals from the advisors instead of rejections. My conversations with them improved over time as I began to speak their language. One of the advisors went so far as to ask me where I took the CPA exam and wanted to know how long I had been in practice. I explained that I was an investment salesman and not a CPA. He said, "Well, you sure sound just like one of us." I was very flattered. Then he made me an offer. He told me that he was a member of The California Society of CPAs and asked me if I would like to attend one of their breakfast meetings as a guest speaker to talk about the tax benefits associated with investing in oil and gas limited partnerships.

Would I? WOW! This was the opportunity of a lifetime, and I jumped all over it like flies on a horse turd. I started meeting more

CPAs and got more referrals. My client base grew, and my career raising investment dollars took off. I was very happy with the way things were going. Unfortunately, two issues developed that would impact my new career.

First, it was becoming apparent to me that the company I was working for could not find oil if they were standing underneath a grease rack at Jiffy Lube. Second, the oil and gas industry was about to experience a major downturn.

Companies in that industry were banking on oil prices to continue rising. However, oil prices are governed by supply and demand, and supply is controlled by the Organization of Petroleum Exporting Countries (OPEC). This cartel was created to administer policies for the sale of petroleum. The 15 countries that made up this organization accounted for 44 percent of global oil production and held 81 percent of the world's proven oil reserves, giving OPEC major control of oil prices.

OPEC developed a strategy to tie oil prices to the rate of inflation and add 10 percent. In effect, this would give them a net increase in revenue of 10 percent each year. I am not quite sure what precipitated it, but in 1982, one of the largest members of the cartel decided to buck the system, turn on the spigots at the well-head, and flood the market with oil. Oil prices plummeted, and the market collapsed. Many oil producers in the US watched as their profit margins dwindled to nothing. Rising production costs began to exceed market price, and one-by-one, producers began to shut their doors. This had a major impact on my business, and it was only a matter of time before the company I worked for would go tits up.

Seeing the writing on the wall, I began to look for another opportunity before the roof caved in. I really hated to leave. My Seattle-based company did a lot for me. First, they taught me how to dress like a professional. We were required to report to work every day looking like Mr GQ in our three-piece suits and ties. They taught me how to prospect for appointments. They taught me how to sell and overcome objections. They taught me how to analyze situations and present solutions. I cannot say enough good things about this firm. But the fact remained, I had to move on. I am glad I did. The company folded soon thereafter.

As I continued my search, I found a company and a whole new industry. The company was called Santa Ana Wind Resources, and they were in Tehachapi, California. Tehachapi is a small town located between Bakersfield and Edwards Air Force base. It was sparsely populated, primarily because it was in a mountain pass, and the wind blew so hard that nobody wanted to live there. It was like being on the back side of the moon. Santa Ana Wind Resources was a start-up company, and they were building a "wind farm."

"What on earth is a wind farm?" I asked myself. It was a new concept. The US federal government was trying to develop ways of producing energy domestically in order to reduce our dependency on foreign oil. Since much of the electricity used in the US came from oil and gas fired generating plants, the energy department thought it would be prudent to produce electric power using renewable resources as opposed to burning hydrocarbons that were in limited supply. In order to fund this concept, Congress passed a bill in 1978 called "The Public Utilities Regulatory Policy Act," otherwise known as PURPA.

PURPA was designed to attract entrepreneurs and investors to stimulate and support the renewable projects. It was sugar-coated with every bell and whistle imaginable, encouraging entrepreneurs to embrace the vision by creating companies that would use natural renewable resources such as wind and solar to produce electricity. In return, the government guaranteed a purchase price at a rate equal to "avoided cost." Avoided cost is the price a utility company would pay for their most expensive source of generation. So now, these entrepreneurs were guaranteed the highest market price for their electricity, and the utility companies were required to buy 100 percent of it.

Developers came up with the concept of building "wind farms." Much like a farmer that was starting an orchard of fruit trees, the developers would install wind turbine generators in lieu of trees. These "windmills" would harness the kinetic energy from the wind that passed through the turbine blades, producing electricity. The wind turbines were connected to a substation that would collect the electricity, and through a transmission line, transport the power to the local utility company.

Of course, the developer needed to raise money to fund the operation. To do so, they sold wind turbines to investors. The developers would act as the operating company for the farm, sell the electricity to the utility company, keep a small profit margin for managing the project, and pass the remaining revenue on to the owners of the windmills.

PURPA also made things very attractive to investors. Through a series of tax incentives, to include investment tax credits and accelerated depreciation, it was possible for investors to recover up to 87.5 percent of their investment through tax savings alone within a five-year period of time. The higher the tax bracket the investor was in, the quicker they recovered their investment. Therefore, it was important to find investors who were making a substantial income and had a hefty tax lability.

One of our California wind parks

The remaining 12.5 percent of the investor's capital was recouped in the form of revenue from the sale of electricity to the utility company. Selling the electricity to the utility company on a 30-year power purchase agreement generated income that would pay out quarterly and continue for three decades into the future.

Wind turbines, completely installed and operational, sold for $150,000 each. Rather than having the investor write a check for that amount, I would meet with the investor and their banker to arrange a line credit to be issued for the total amount. The tax savings and the revenue generated from electricity sales exceeded the debt service, so that the investor was never out-of-pocket any money. Once the debt service was retired, the investor enjoyed an additional stream of income for the remaining 25 years of the power purchase agreement. In essence, I applied some of the techniques I learned from my previous employer and developed a marketing program that turned a tax liability into an income-producing asset.

By this time, I had developed a strong working relationship with a number of CPAs, so I began calling on them to explain the tax incentives associated with the investment. Then, I simply asked them if they had a few of their clients that were paying $50,000 or more in taxes each year. They usually did. So, I suggested that the CPA set up a series of meetings for me and him/her to meet with their clients individually to do some tax planning. With one phone call from the CPA to his client, he was able to set the appointment for me. Now that I was seated in front of my target investor, I told my story. When I was done, most clients agreed that they needed the investment. Without the CPA's involvement, I would have to make hundreds of phone calls on my own just to make one sale. This strategy expedited the process, and my closing rate jumped from 10 percent to 80 percent.

When I first began this venture, I was an independent contractor starting my own marketing company. On a handshake contract, I negotiated with Santa Ana Wind Resources to pay me a commission on the investment dollars I raised for them. They agreed and instructed me to do my job quickly because their cash flow was not healthy. If they were going to remain in business, a large part would depend on my ability to perform.

I didn't have personal wealth to sink into a risky operation; in fact, I was borderline broke by this time. One day while looking for office space, I met a man that ran an executive recruiting firm, and he was about to retire. He asked me if I knew of anyone that would be interested in subleasing his office. It was perfect, completely furnished with multiple desks, chairs, and phones. I told him I would like to take it over but could not afford to pay him right away. However, I explained that if he would trust me, I would pay him back as soon as I could. Surprisingly, he agreed. I moved in and went to work the very next day. At the time I was driving an old Datsun B-210. I had a half tank of gas and a five-dollar bill in my wallet.

I will never forget that day. It was Friday, December 31, 1982. I started making phone calls and secured a 1 p.m. appointment. The prospect I was to meet had a significant tax problem, and today was the last day of the year to handle it. I called the office in Tehachapi and told them to send down the paperwork immediately. One of the company's officers jumped in his car and made the three-hour drive to my office in Los Angeles. I grabbed the application forms and beat a hot path over to the investor's house arriving five minutes ahead of schedule. I explained the investment to him and what tax relief he would realize from it. He loved the concept and wrote me a check on the spot. By 3 p.m., I was back in my office and handed off the paperwork to the officer from the company, and he drove it back to Tehachapi. Mission accomplished. I called my wife and told her to scrub up the kids because we were going out to dinner to celebrate my success. I had just made a substantial commission on one sale that exceeded an entire year's salary with TWA.

That night, I went to bed and made my New Year's resolution. My goal was to make $100,000 in 1983. Things went well that year, and I far exceeded my goal in the months to come. I contacted a friend of mine who I had worked with in the oil business the year before. He joined me, and we became business partners forming a marketing group that would continue raising money for the wind farm developer. As 1983 came to a close, we had 12 salesmen working for us, plus another dozen independent contractors. By the end of our first year in business, collectively we raised $25,000,000 of investor capital.

My decision to represent Santa Ana Wind Resources was based on faith and due diligence. If investors were to invest their money through me, I had a responsibility to make sure I was working with a reputable organization. Prior to starting my marketing company, I spent six months researching and meeting with other start-up companies that would ultimately create this new industry. I chose to represent Santa Ana Wind because the founders were honest, hardworking, committed to being successful, and invested their own money in the company. This was a wise decision on my part as their executive staff performed brilliantly. I decided to open a second office in Orange County, California. My partner agreed to run the Los Angeles office as I set up a second office further south between Los Angeles and San Diego.

My partner and me getting ready to take a flight to Tehachapi

Originally, Santa Ana Wind had been trying to align themselves with a major Wall Street firm to raise all the money they needed to grow the company. The problem was that they did not have the track record to make that happen. Now that we had raised $25,000,000 and the first wind farm was successfully operational, it caught the attention of the major brokerage houses. They were becoming receptive to the idea of getting involved. A major wire house stepped up to the plate and committed to raising $30,000,000 for us.

Between them and our internal sales force, we brought $60,000,000 to the table in 1984. We could have done much better except for the fact that the equipment manufacturer could not make turbines fast enough to meet our demand. By September, we were sold out, and we had to turn away investors. All we could do was gear up for the following year.

The success of this business was dependent on the tax incentives that attracted investors. However, the tax laws as they were written were due to expire at the end of 1985. So, everyone in sales realized from the get-go that we would be unemployed at that time, but our philosophy was to work hard, sell hard, and make as much money as possible in the time available.

With nothing to sell, I spent most of fourth quarter 1984 gearing up for our final year. I designed marketing brochures and sales literature to knock the socks off any potential investor. The campaign was powerful and effective. When the flag went up January 2, 1985, our sales team was ready and stormed the market like Grant going through Richmond. The Wall Street firm we worked with the year before was ready to go as well, and between the internal and external sales teams, we raised another $100,000,000. We sold up to the last minute, and at midnight December 31, 1985, I called everyone into my office. We opened a couple bottles of scotch and toasted to our success. During the past 36 months collectively, between the two sales teams, we had raised $185,000,000. That was something to celebrate!

Now that all the tax incentives no longer existed, those of us on the sales team were hoping that Santa Ana Wind Resources would come up with a plan to carry us into 1986. Unfortunately, that did not happen, and we were all left to our own devices to come up with a plan to continue making a living. Eventually, the sales team disbanded, and everyone scattered in their own respective ways.

Santa Ana Wind continued to grow. The company was split into two divisions. The first one was the development company that oversaw building wind parks and selling them off to other entities such as power producers, utility companies, and municipalities. These projects were positioned in California, Iowa, Minnesota, Texas, and the British Isles to name a few locations. The second division became the technology company. Their mission was to develop and build newer, bigger, and more powerful wind turbines. Up until 1985, the company had relied on one manufacturer, The Vestas Company, located in Lem, Demark, to supply them with wind turbines. Santa Ana Wind decided to design and build their own wind turbine generators and became very good at it. The size and capability of these future models were most impressive. The industry started out with 10Kw wind turbines. This quickly grew to 65Kw machines, followed by the 125Kw wind turbines. In subsequent years, these machines continued to grow in size and power output. Today, manufacturers are building 2.5Mw — 5.0Mw windmills.

For a perspective on what that means in energy production, a 10Kw machine can supply enough power to sustain one average household. A 1.5Mw wind turbine can supply enough energy for 500 homes. The evolution of this industry continues in such a manner that it is making a major impact on our nation's ability to become "energy independent."

Santa Ana Wind Resources was expanding and growing in many ways. As a result, it became very attractive to other companies looking for acquisitions. A Houston-based power broker made a successful bid to acquire Santa Ana Wind. In 1997, the transaction was completed. I was very proud to be part of the company's history — what a great chapter in my life as well as the lives of the executive team that excelled in building that organization.

CHAPTER 49
MOONSHINE THE PARTY DOG

When Yvonne, Jason, and I relocated from Seattle to Los Angeles, we moved into a three-bedroom condominium on a hillside in Redondo Beach that overlooked the entire Santa Monica Bay. In the evenings after work, Yvonne and I would grab a glass of wine, sit on the balcony, and enjoy the sunset. It was a very relaxing way to end the day. It only took ten minutes to walk to the beach. In the early mornings, we would meander down to the esplanade and go for a couple-mile jog along the shore before we went to work. Usually, we had the place to ourselves, so it was peaceful and quiet, giving us a chance to talk and get exercise. Every day, I woke up feeling like I was on vacation.

Jason was actively involved in Little League baseball, scouting, and school projects that consumed most of the weekends. We had fun working together preparing for the Cub Scout Pinewood Derby competition and building a model of an old Spanish mission for a grade school project. Being so close to the beach provided us with hours of free entertainment between splashing in the surf and long rides on the bike path.

During the time we lived in Redondo Beach, my ex-wife notified us that she did not want Heidi to return home after her summer visit with us. Playing into Alice's decision was the fact that she was getting prepared for her next divorce, and she was making plans for her own future without Heidi. So, we enrolled Heidi in the local high school where she developed a group of friends from her special education classes. Soon, we were hosting slumber/pizza parties, and all the girls seemed to have a great time. Heidi participated in Special Olympics, and we took her for ice skating lessons on Saturday mornings.

The only thing missing was "a dog."

We all agreed that we should have one. The only problem was what kind of a dog should we get? My first choice was a Labrador Retriever. I had wanted one for years, but we had a small patio and no yard for a big dog. So, the next choice was a Cocker Spaniel, and everyone seemed to like that idea. Yvonne called her mother in Phoenix one evening and mentioned that we were thinking about getting a dog. Shortly thereafter, Yvonne's mother called back to inform us that her friend's dog had given birth to a litter of puppies out behind a barn north of Phoenix. They were not Cocker Spaniels, but she asked if we would consider a Cockapoo? I thought that was pushing it a bit but agreed to drive over and check it out.

Yvonne's mother, Jene, who is very creative, suggested that we stage a "Name the Puppy Contest." While he didn't know it at the time, Jason was the only contestant, so he was certain to win. Together, we thought long and hard for several days, and since the dog was born out behind a barn, we decided it would be appropriate to name the dog "Moonshine." We completed the application and mailed it back to Jene. Low-and-behold, Jason won the contest. So, the next weekend we drove over to Arizona to get the dog.

When we arrived, Jene opened the front door, and this little animal came running out to greet us. When I first saw it, I screamed and jumped back a foot or two. I was in shock. It didn't even resemble a dog. It looked like Yoda from Star Wars. I yelled out loud, "Cockapoo my ass!" This was the damnedest thing I had ever seen. It had two coats of hair — short little fluffy stuff and long strands of wiry hair that randomly protruded from the fluffy stuff in all directions. All I could think of was, "Holy cow, this was not my idea of a family pet, and it certainly was not coming back to California with us."

This dog was such a mutt that it reminded me of the Mr Potato Head game we played when we were kids. You started out with a real potato and a box full of various plastic facial features such as noses, eyes, ears, mouths, etc. to choose from. By sticking the pieces onto the potato, you could create your own character. That was the best way to describe how I viewed the appearance of this dog. I imagined it coming through an assembly line. It passed by a box of tails, so you grab any old one and stick it on. Then come the legs. You need four of them, but they do not necessarily have to match. The same with eyes and ears. By the time the poor hound got to the end of the assembly line, it was clearly a Heinz 57 of uncertain ancestry. Had I known ahead of time I would have named her "Spare Parts" instead of Moonshine.

On Sunday morning, I thanked my mother-in-law for her gallant effort, but kindly told her to return it to the barn from where it came. I piled everyone in the car and headed west toward Los Angeles. But I made a big mistake. Thirty minutes out, I decided to stop for gas. When I got back in the car, everyone was crying, and I knew I was overruled. We drove back, picked up the dog, and once again headed home to California.

Over time Moonshine and I became friends, and I must admit she was the best dog I ever had. She was extremely intelligent, had a great personality, and got cuter as she got older. I think our guests came to see the dog as much as us. Moonshine learned some tricks that were legendary and kept everybody in stitches.

Moonshine lounging

The tricks were normal dog tricks. She would respond to hand gestures or voice commands, but it was the voice commands that made the common come alive. She could easily sit up on her hind legs and beg for food. However, instead of saying, "Beg" or "Sit-up," I would tell her, "Show us your tits." When I gave the command, she would sit down on her hind legs, raise her torso, sit up, spread her front paws, and show us her tits.

I taught her to roll over. The hand gesture was twirling my arm in a circular motion. However, the voice command was, "Shoot a beaver." And that she did. The crowd went wild, and she got a nice treat. She could also "shoot and hold." She would roll over halfway and lay on her back with all four paws extended upward. She would hold that position until I said, "Good girl," and then she would complete the roll. The dog enjoyed the attention, got more treats, and the guests begged for more.

Moonshine lived for 18 years. One day as she got very old, she fell in the pool and could not get out. I fetched her from certain drowning. Another day she fell down the stairs. Then, she squatted to pee and could not get back up. We all realized the day had come for her to leave. The kids were out of the house on their own by this time. Yvonne, Moonshine, and I remained in our family home. The three of us sat down on the living room couch for a final meeting. Yvonne cradled Moonshine in her arms as I sat next to her. She looked at us with those big brown eyes as if to say, "It is time, isn't it?" We put her in the car and took her to the vet. Reluctantly, we did what we had to do. The vet had cared for Moonshine since she was a puppy, and his compassion for us was extraordinary. He walked us through the process while putting the dog on the table and giving her an injection that allowed her to pass without pain into an eternal sleep. He felt her chest and when there was no longer a heartbeat, he said, "It is over." Yvonne and I came unglued as we said good-bye to a loving family member that brought joy into our lives for 18 years. It was so painful that 14 years would pass before we would consider getting another dog.

CHAPTER 50
COMMUNING WITH NATURE

When I adopted Jason, we established Adoption Day and celebrated it each year like a birthday. The first year I bought Jason a baseball, glove, and bat. The second year he got a new bike. Each year, the event got bigger, better, and more creative. One year, I took him and his buddies deep-sea fishing. The next year was a hot-air balloon ride. Another time, we flew back to Indianapolis for the Indy 500. In other years, I would take Jason and a couple of his friends on backpacking trips into the High Sierra mountains of California. Adoption Day has become one of our most memorable occasions each year.

Me and Jason at the Indy 500

One year I invited my buddy, Rob Knaap, and his son, Robby, to join us on a backpacking trip. Our destination was the Golden Trout

Wilderness. We would be hiking up the Sierra-Nevada Mountain Range to the 11,000-foot mark.

Once we arrived at our destination and set up camp, we hit the streams with our fishing gear in hopes of harvesting enough fish to provide a bountiful evening meal. Within an hour, the four of us caught more fish than we could consume. Two of us cleaned the fish while the other two collected firewood to prepare our dinner. The meal was fantastic, and nobody went to bed hungry.

Our trip was so successful, we planned another one for the following year. This time, we were headed to a spot called Onion Meadows. I do not know how it got its name because there were no onions for 100 miles, and there was no meadow to be found. However, there were bears, and lots of them. We set up camp along a mountain stream that meandered through a forest of Ponderosa Pines. It was a beautiful setting. I felt like we had walked into the cover of *Field & Stream* magazine.

Jason and me on a backpacking trip

Other groups of campers were set up nearby on both sides of the stream. From time-to-time, they would yell to us, "Bears headed your way." We thanked them for the warning. With our campsite set up, and dinner completed, we went about "bear proofing" our location for the evening. This entailed bagging up all the food and stringing it high above on a tree branch so that the bears could not get it. Then we tied pots and pans to the bags for an alarm system that warned us when the bears came into our camp.

The boys went into their tent, and Rob and I went into ours. With a hard day of hiking and the lack of oxygen, we crawled into our fartsacks and fell asleep. Soon thereafter, the pots and pans began to bang loudly, and we knew that we had visitors. Rob and I jumped out of bed, put on our boots, grabbed flashlights, and peered into the darkness to see what awaited us. What a sight that must have been — two grown men in nothing but our underwear and hiking boots holding flashlights.

Methodically illuminating our surroundings with the flashlights, we were greeted with the reflection of two metallic green eyes staring back at us. On the hillside above our tent was a 900-pound black bear sitting on his haunches eating a jar of peanut butter. The night was so dark, it made the scene even more frightening. Rob yelled, "Holy fat ass bear," and started picking up rocks and throwing them at the creature. I quickly grabbed his arm and told him to knock it off. Up to that point, the bear only wanted the peanut butter. If Rob pissed it off, it could attack and kill us. I reminded Rob that we had no place to run and no place to hide. I also told him that there was no way we could out-run a bear. Rob looked at me and said, "I am not worried about out-running the bear, I just want to make sure I can out-run you."

The bear finally had his fill and wandered off. We went back to bed. The next morning, we observed the bear's claw marks in a tree trunk and found that one of our fuel canisters had been punctured by the bear's sharp teeth.

Undeterred, the four of us took a day hike to a higher elevation, returning to camp in time for our evening meal. As we ate dinner, we were talking about the bears, and soon, three more came wandering into our camp. There were just too many bears, and we did not want to go through another night like the one before. So, we took a vote and decided to get out of there. We struck camp and headed down the mountain hoping that we could reach the car before it got too dark. We barely made it and started our six-hour drive back to Los Angeles. By the time we got home it was 1 a.m. Jason and I double-locked the doors and went to bed. There would be no bears that night!

Over time, the fear of bears evaporated from our minds. The weather was fantastic, and the mountains beckoned our return. I told Jason to call his buddies, and I would take them into "the wild." I also invited my CPA and friend, Kenny McKiven, to join us. Everyone jumped on the invitation. Our destination was McGee Creek in central California on the east side of the Sierra-Nevada Mountain Range. The elevation at our campsite was 11,500 feet, and my concern was altitude sickness. So, I called the pack station at the trailhead and asked them if they had horses or mules we could hire to take our gear and supplies to the top of the mountain and drop it off at our campsite. If we could lighten the load, we had less chance of getting sick. They said they could accommodate us, so I made the necessary reservations.

On the way up, we stopped in the town of Bishop for dinner. We found a steakhouse that looked inviting, so we pulled in for a hearty meal. With five hungry guys at the table, we ordered T-Bones that were quickly devoured. With full bellies, we proceeded to the trailhead located at 8,700 feet elevation. We parked the car, rolled out sleeping bags on the dirt, and went to bed without bothering to pitch a tent. The night was warm, the sky was clear, and we stared up at a full moon with thousands of stars that stared back at us. Within minutes we were all asleep.

The next morning, we were up bright and early and wandered down to the stables to meet the trail boss about 7 a.m. We loaded our gear onto the horses, and they took off at a much faster pace than we did. I could tell immediately this was going to be a fantastic backpacking trip. The temperature was brisk, the sky was blue, there was no wind, and the trail led us into a beautiful forest of Aspen trees. They were majestic. With their white trunks and silver leaves shimmering in the sunlight, they looked like a brigade of cadets proudly standing at attention on the West Point Military Academy parade ground.

As we continued our ascent, we left the Aspens behind and entered a forest of Ponderosa Pines. This aroused a whole new set of senses. The aroma of evergreen trees has always been one of my favorites, and it would linger in our air space for the rest of our trip. It smelled so fresh and clean, and I think that is what helped me to sleep so soundly at night.

By the time we reached the 10,000-foot mark, we were all getting a bit woozy but kept plugging away at the trail. It was my turn to get the dreaded altitude sickness. My body felt like a stone block, and I could not put one foot in front of the other. I tried to walk but could only make it five feet. I told the others to continue up the trail, and I would eventually catch up to them. Meanwhile, the cowboy with the pack animals was coming back down the mountain. He told me my group was almost at our destination and informed me how much further I had to go to catch up with them. I was in bad shape.

When I reached the top, I realized that it was going to take a while before my body would acclimate to the altitude. I just had to hang in there until everything returned to normal.

The cowboy who delivered our belongings did a great job. He found the perfect campsite, and except for pitching our tents, arranged everything in a practical manner. We had a beautiful setting at the edge of a crystal-clear lake. It was embedded in a pine forest shadowed by a majestic mountain that must have peaked out at about 14,000 feet.

We went fishing that afternoon and brought in 15 rainbow trout. With five mouths to feed, that gave us three fish each. It was a bountiful meal. That night, we sat around the campfire and told ghost stories until it was time to go to bed. There was no sign of bears in the area, so we crawled into our tents with peace of mind and had a sound night of sleep. During the three days we were in the wilderness, we did not see another human being, nor did we run into any animals that would cause us concern for our safety. It was just the five of us and nature.

After several days, it was time to leave. When we got back down to the trailhead, we loaded our car and headed for town. It was Sunday morning. We had been hiking since dawn on an empty stomach, and we were all so hungry we could have eaten the crotch out of a Raggedy Ann doll. Spotting a shabby café at the side of the road, we made a beeline for the front door. Before the waitress could hand us menus, we were placing our order.

We consumed eggs, pancakes, French toast, bacon, and sausage. We ate so much I was afraid to ask for the breakfast bill. Once we were tanked-up, it was time to head back to civilization. We had just completed another wonderful trip that would stay in our memories forever.

CHAPTER 51
THE PRANKS KEPT COMING

Living in Redondo Beach was wonderful. However, we wanted a pool, Moonshine was a young puppy at the time and needed a yard, and Yvonne and I wanted to get away from the hustle and bustle of Los Angeles.

So, we bought a house nestled in the orange groves of a cozy little town called Yorba Linda, located in Orange County. Orange County lies between Los Angeles and San Diego.

The house was just what we were looking for and sat high on a knoll overlooking other Orange County towns. We had an unobstructed view, and from our back yard on a clear day, we could look out over the ocean and see all the way to Catalina Island. In the evenings, we would have dinner on the patio, then enjoy a glass of wine while watching beautiful sunsets. At 9 p.m. in the summer, Disneyland put on their nightly fireworks display, so we would watch that before going to bed. Yorba Linda was a great place to raise a family and one of the smartest moves we ever made.

I continued to be a creative practical joker, and family members had to stay on their toes to keep from falling prey to my antics. By this time in our marriage, Yvonne was always on high alert to avoid becoming the victim of my pranks. So, Jason was the next target for my harassment and entertainment.

Occasionally, he would ask me to give him a ride to school. I drove a red convertible Mercedes 450SL which was a pretty hot ride in the day and a vehicle most boys his age would love to have transport them to school. One day we pulled up to the front of his junior high school with the top down, and I dropped him off. As he climbed the steps to the entrance of his school, I yelled out, "Hey Jason, you forgot to kiss your father good-bye." What adolescent boy wouldn't be embarrassed by that request? Reluctantly, he walked back down the stairs and gave me a peck on the cheek. I was laughing my ass off, but it wasn't so funny in Jason's world.

A couple weeks later he asked me for a ride again. I stopped for a red light a few blocks from his school, and he jumped out of the car saying, "Thanks, Dad. I'll walk the rest of the way."

Yvonne would usually pack Jason's lunch. However, from time-to-time I got in on the action. He would sit in the cafeteria with his buddies, and they would dump the contents of their bags out on the table and either eat what landed on the table or trade items that they didn't find appetizing. In addition to a sandwich, chips, and a drink, Jason would also get a dessert that was usually a stack of cookies wrapped in tin foil. Instead of cookies, I would substitute dog treats like Milk Bones or Pupperoni. When he unwrapped them in front of his friends, everyone except Jason would start laughing. They recognized it as a joke, but Jason got embarrassed and failed to see the humor. He came home from school one day and told Yvonne, "Mom, don't ever let Dad pack my lunch again!"

The time for my redemption had come. After Christmas one year, I took Yvonne, Heidi, and Jason to Tahiti to celebrate New Year's and take a couple weeks of vacation. We flew into Papeete, Tahiti to spend a few days, then flew to the beautiful island of Bora Bora. We were playing on the beach one day, and Heidi picked up a small conch shell out of the water. A baby octopus crawled out and up onto her arm. It was both shocking and exciting. After a few days on Bora Bora, we did our next island hop to Moorea.

We checked into the hotel, and our room was one of those bungalows with a grass roof that sat out over the ocean. That was quite a novelty. Every day we were hit with warm tropical rain showers as we went bike riding or hiking. Almost all our clothing was wet, so one afternoon we strung everything up on clothes lines to dry out. With all the rain, we decided that we would take a nap and ride out the daily storm.

About an hour later, Jason and I woke up. The girls were sawing logs, so we silently slipped out of bed, put on our swimsuits, and headed for the beach. Being French Polynesia, many of the girls on the beach were topless. Quite frankly, I just wasn't thinking that far ahead. However, when my 11-year-old son saw what we had just walked into, he got a shit-eating grin on his face, looked up at me, and said, "You know, Dad, I think you are the best dad in the whole wide world." I was speechless, and all I could say was, "Thanks, son."

Jason, Heidi, Yvonne and me in Tahiti

After island hopping in the Pacific for two weeks, it was time to return to the States and face reality. It was a great vacation, but some of us had to return to work, and some had to return to school. I would like to have been a fly on the wall when Jason told his school buddies about his experiences on the island of Moorea.

Another time, Yvonne and I decided to take my parents on a vacation of their choice. They chose a cruise through the Inside Passage of Alaska, and we had an adventurous trip. This must have left an impression on my mother, because soon thereafter, she organized a family reunion aboard a cruise ship that sailed through the Panama Canal. Of the half-dozen cruises we had been on, this was perhaps the best and offered interesting scenery and an education as we passed through the locks. However, the most excitement took place onboard the ship as a result of another one of my pranks.

All our family's staterooms were on the same level, the Promenade Deck. The Promenade Deck offers an unobstructed path around the entire ship, making it ideal for those that wish to take a walk or go for a jog. In other words, it was the most popular deck for foot traffic. All the staterooms had large view windows. One of my brothers got the stateroom next door to mine. At the beginning of the trip, I knocked on his door. He was not there but my sister-in-law invited me in. I looked out the window and said to her, "Isn't this fantastic? You can look out the window and see all the people walking by, but because it's one-way glass, the people cannot see you. Of course, that was B.S. on my part, but she bought it.

Later that evening, my brother walked into his room. His wife was standing stark-ass naked in front of the window, and on the other side of the glass was a growing crowd of passengers gathering to enjoy the show. My brother yelled at her, "Hey, what in the hell are you doing?"

She replied that she was getting dressed for dinner. He asked why she was standing naked at the window. She replied, "Don't worry about it because it is one-way glass, and nobody can see in."

My brother said, "Are you crazy? If that is one-way glass, why are all those people gathering around to peek in?" At that moment she realized that I had pulled a fast one, and she began fuming. The next day, and for several days thereafter, she would not speak to me. To this day, she is vigilant around me.

CHAPTER 52
FINAL DESTINATION

Although our children are in California, Yvonne and I got tired of fighting the congestion of Southern California and decided to move to Arizona. In 2004, we purchased a home in the beautiful community of Anthem, a suburb north of metro Phoenix. Since then, friends and relatives have come for visits, and several of them moved to Anthem as well. With them, and being surrounded by good neighbors, we decided to make this our permanent home.

For the friends and relatives that have never lived in Arizona, they always ask the question, "How do you handle all that heat?" Granted, it is the desert, and it does get hot. But we kindly remind them that this is the reason why swimming pools and gin and tonics were invented. As for the friends that live in New England or the upper Midwest, I always like to call them in January to remind them that it is 75 degrees in Phoenix, the palm trees are swaying in a gentle breeze, and we never have to shovel sunshine! Phoenix is often referred to as "The Valley of the Sun," but in the summer months, it's more like "The Surface of the Sun." However, as Arizonans like to say, "It's a dry heat."

After living 14 years without a dog, we decided it was time. A five-pound black Labrador Retriever puppy came into our lives — I finally got my dream dog. I wanted to name her "Skidmarks," but Yvonne overruled and named her "Boo Bear." She doesn't show us her tits or shoot a beaver like Moonshine did. She is a bit more refined and prefers chasing tennis balls and swimming in the pool, even on the coldest days.

Boo Bear

Arizona provides enjoyment for every lifestyle. But I think the ones that like to commune with nature reap the greatest benefits. We fall into that group. Yvonne, Boo Bear, and I go hiking every chance we get. When it's too hot in Phoenix, we drive north to the higher elevations. The state offers breathtaking scenery and plenty of trails to choose from.

Life had a setback in December of 2017 when for the second time I went in for a stent due to some blockage in my heart. This time I ended up getting my chest sawed open, but two bypasses and a couple months later, I was back on the walking trail and enjoying life.

For work, Yvonne is the Executive Director for a performing arts group. Local residents love the contribution she and her colleagues have made to our community. As for me, I pretend to work and have become the self-appointed Executive Vice President of Practical Jokes.

Yvonne and I continue to fulfill our dream of exploring the world, and we travel every chance we get. We have visited all 50 states together and 77 different countries or islands. We have so many great memories of raising our kids and shelves full of photo albums documenting their sports, our travels, their major school milestones, and much more. Heidi completed high school and is working in Southern California and living in a group home. Jason got bachelor's and master's degrees in business and has had a long career in the pharmaceutical industry. He got married and brought a beautiful daughter-in-law into our lives. They gave us three wonderful grandchildren and live in Southern California.

Me and Yvonne in Arizona

Heidi on a Caribbean vacation

Front: Our grandson, Brandon
Back (from left to right): our grandson, Thomas; granddaughter, Madison; and daughter-in-law, Cindy

I am so proud and happy to be a part of the Boomer Generation. We had fun. I mean "real fun." I wouldn't trade places with anyone from any other era, past or future. I like to think I got the tail-end of the best that life has to offer, and I hope that those that follow will feel the same way about the gift of life that has been given to them. The GI Generation has all but come and gone, and we, the Boomers, are now on deck. I realize that my days are numbered. But I think I have a few more good years before I start to circle the drain. My plan is to live each day to its fullest and take advantage of all the wonderful things that God has provided for us to enjoy. Then, on my final day, I will take a victory lap and cut out of here like a striped-ass ape.

Wishing you, sunny days, blue skies, and as Roy and Dale would say, "Happy trails to you."

EPILOGUE
WHERE DID THEY ALL GO?

WILLIAM F. DOLBY (MY DAD): My dad spent his final years in Seattle. He moved there from Phoenix and lived with my sister Cindy and her husband for a period of time. His antics (even into his nineties) were too much for them, and they moved him to an assisted living facility where he lived for the remainder of his life. During his final years, I wrote him several letters each week, and he seemed to appreciate the letters and replied regularly. Written correspondence was his preferred form of communication.

One August evening, I returned to my home in Phoenix from a business trip to Northern Arizona. I arrived about 9 p.m., poured a scotch and soda, told Yvonne that I was dog-tired, and just wanted to sit out on a lounge chair in the back yard, stare at the sky, sip my drink, and unwind for a bit. My wish was granted.

Now, I have seen many shooting stars in my lifetime, but they only lasted for a fraction of a second. However, on that evening, a most spectacular event took place. A shooting star came flying by. It came from behind me in the east, crossed over my left shoulder, moving in a westerly direction. Unlike all the other shooting stars I've seen, this one lasted a full two seconds, seeming almost like an eternity.

The contrail lit up the sky with a most beautiful emerald, green color that turned to gold, and finally faded to black. It was one of the most magnificent scenes I had ever witnessed. I thought to myself, "There goes my dad." Other than his advanced age, I have no idea what made me think that at that moment. The next morning, my sister called to tell me my father had passed away. The doctors pronounced him dead at 1 a.m. August 12, 2012. I told her, "No, no, no. The doctors discovered him at 1 a.m. However, he died at 9 p.m. the night before because I watched him go as he did a fly-by over my head on his way out." I am 100 percent positive that was the exact way it went down. He was 95 years old when he took his final breath.

MARTHA DOLBY (MY MOM): One morning I took my mother out to breakfast, just the two of us. She said to me, "You know, I am not going to be around much longer." I asked her why she thought that way.

She said, "Because the angels told me." She was very spiritual in nature, and never missed going to church on Sundays. She had no fear of death, and there was an element of excitement in her voice when she told me she was finally going to get her wings. She realized her work on Earth was finished, and it was time to move on to her next assignment. She could not wait to go to heaven and be with God.

In 2005, as I was approaching my 60th birthday, my mom came to live with Yvonne and me in our new house in Phoenix. We provided her with her own bedroom, bathroom, and TV so she could watch *Lawrence Welk* and *Perry Mason*. She was very content. When guests arrived, she was giddy, almost like a little schoolgirl, wanting to show them her bedroom with a view of the golf course and mountains beyond. By this time, my dad had made the unrealistic decision that he and my mom were going to move to Seattle, and he left to go find their new home.

My mom was happy to have no responsibilities — no demanding husband to wait on, no children to take care of, no meals to cook, no dishes to wash, and no house to clean. When we called her for dinner, she would say, "This is like living in a resort. I don't have to do anything but relax." After being a servant to others for so many years, she enjoyed the attention and receiving the break she so rightly deserved.

During the day she would mostly stay in her room. In the mornings, she would watch reruns on TV. In the afternoons, she would lay in bed and nap, or more likely than not, commune with the angels as they gave her instructions on how to prepare for the next journey she was about to embark on. She was so quiet that when it came time for dinner, Yvonne and I were afraid to call her in fear that she may have already passed away. But then, she would emerge from her little cocoon and wonder what was for dinner. In the evenings, she would like to sit on the back patio and gaze at the stars. We would join her for a pleasant conversation before she went to bed. She would tell us stories about her family and her childhood, and we would tell her how happy we were to have this time with her.

However, time was running out. She was in a lot of pain, and we took her to the hospital. We called family members and told them it was time to fly in to say their good-byes. My brother and sisters all came, but my dad never returned to be at her side. At one point in the hospital, my mom said, "After 62 years of marriage, what a way to end it." My heart broke for her.

When the hospital staff could do no more for my mom, we moved her from the hospital to hospice care. It was a very hot Friday afternoon in September when the ambulance transported her across town. The temperature was 112 degrees, and the traffic was brutal. We were not allowed to ride with her, so we followed her in our car.

Once we got her all bedded down in her new location I asked, "How was the ride over here Mom?"

She rolled her eyes into the back of her head and said, "Oh my God. It was horrible. I thought I was going to die." Then she realized what she just said and started to laugh as she continued, "Boy, was that a stupid thing to say." Collectively, we all started laughing at the irony of it all. She had less than 48 hours to go before it would become a reality. The next day, Saturday, we were visiting, and as we began to leave, she made a strange request. She said, "Don't bother coming tomorrow."

We said, "Okay," but planned to visit any way. As we were leaving the house on Sunday morning, the nurses called to tell us the end was near, and that we should get there right away. We told the staff we were already on the road. When we arrived, she was barely coherent and passed away within the hour. That is when we realized why she didn't want us to come. She knew in advance that her train would be pulling out of the station that morning and she was trying to spare us any grief. I called my sister Cindy and told her mom died at 11:04 that morning. The date was September 4th. Cindy said, "Gosh, that would have been the exact time she would be getting home from church on most Sundays." I then called the rest of my family with the news that Mom was gone. Yvonne and I looked at each other and thought, "Wow, wouldn't it be wonderful to be there when she reached her final destination?" She had always been a saint in our eyes. Can you imagine the reception she must have received upon her arrival? She died of cancer at the age of 87.

My mother had always been available to me every day of my life. Now, she was gone. There was no turning back. There were no instant replays. There was no second chance. She was gone and I had to learn to deal with it. A couple weeks had passed, and I was driving through town when I thought of something that I wanted to tell her about. I grabbed my phone and started to call her. Halfway through the dial, I realized that she was no longer with us, so I hung up the phone. From out of nowhere, my emotions got the best of me. I was stopped at a red light when reality set in, and I started to cry like a baby. A man in the car to my left looked over and saw what I was going through. A woman in a car to my right saw the same thing. They looked at me quizzically and must have wondered what was wrong. I looked back at them as if to say, "My mother just died. Why can't you understand that?" In time I learned to deal with the loss. The passage of time is a great healer, but Yvonne and I still talk about my mom and miss her.

WILLIAM F. DOLBY, JR. (MY OLDER BROTHER): When Bill was in college, he met a girl that immigrated to the United States from Australia. They fell in love and got married. Shortly thereafter, she wanted to move back to Australia. The free spirit that he was, brother Bill agreed, and they set sail for "down under." He got a good job, and they purchased a home in the Blue Mountains just north of Sydney. In 1973, I flew down to pay them a visit, and shortly thereafter, my sister Cindy moved down to live with them for about a year. I'm not sure how long they lived there, but it was probably the better part of ten years. Eventually, they moved back to the States, and Bill got a job with the American Automobile Association in Portland, Oregon. They were a happy family, and it did my heart good every time Yvonne and I paid them a visit.

One evening in 1983, I received a call from my sister Sue announcing that "Bill" had died from a massive heart attack. I immediately thought that she was referring to my dad. She said, "No. It

301

is your brother Bill." I was speechless. He was only 39 years old, and he was my best friend since birth.

My initial reaction was, "This just can't be." He was too young to die. He left behind a loving wife and three beautiful daughters. Eventually, they recovered from their loss and went on to live wonderful, productive lives. Bill would have been proud of them.

CINDY (OLDEST OF MY THREE SISTERS): Cindy is two years younger than me. She got married in 1975 and gave birth to twin girls. The marriage did not work out, so Cindy had to raise the girls as a single parent. A number of years later she married her second husband. He was a very nice, generous, and intelligent man with an entrepreneurial spirit. Together, they acquired properties and built a lucrative portfolio of real estate.

When my father left Arizona and moved to the state of Washington, Cindy and her husband became caregivers to him for the remaining seven years of his life. If you knew my father, you would understand the incredible burden that placed on the two of them.

Eventually, the girls grew up, got married, and moved out on their own. Cindy's second husband became ill and passed away unexpectedly. Cindy makes friends easily and keeps busy with travel and outdoor activities such as hiking, biking, and snow skiing. She spends a lot of time with her two daughters and grandchild. She resides in the Pacific Northwest.

CHRIS (MY YOUNGER BROTHER): My brother Chris turned out to be quite an athlete. He excelled in football during his high school years as well as college. My dad was so proud of him and often drove over 100 miles to see his college games. One evening my mom and dad picked me up, and we drove to Pasadena together to watch him. He played fullback, and based on college standards, was on the smaller side. However, he operated on guts and determination, and when they handed him the ball, he went down the field like a bulldozer determined not to let anyone get in his way. We cheered him on to victory.

Chris married, and he and his wife moved to Oregon and started a farming business growing fruit trees from root stock. When the trees are about a foot tall, they are harvested and sold to nurseries and distributors of agricultural products. The business is extremely successful, and Chris and his wife would like to sell it and retire. However, every time I talk to him on the phone, I find out that he purchased additional property, and the business just keeps growing (literally and figuratively). They have four children that are very accomplished, and three are married and have families of their own.

SUSAN (MY SECOND SISTER): Sue moved from Southern California to Seattle in 1979, shortly after Yvonne and I got married. She lived with us for a short time and got her own place once she was established in her new job. She got married a few years later and has two children. Sue picked a good husband, and he became a great brother-in-law. He is always in a good mood, cracking jokes and laughing his ass off. It is my understanding that he was quite a good golfer in college. When he graduated, he had a successful career as a sales representative for a sporting goods manufacturing company in the golf industry. After several decades of living in the Northwest, Sue and her husband finally retired and moved to Austin, Texas. Together, they golf, spend time at the health club, travel, and join friends around the country attending sporting events.

MARK (MY YOUNGEST BROTHER): Mark was a happy-go-lucky guy and had a lot of friends. By the time I got out of the Army, my family had moved to Santa Barbara, California. I was stationed in Germany at the time, so I'm not sure when the move took place, but it was probably around 1969. Mark went to college there, and after graduation, he worked with a local company that manufactured medical devices. He contracted the HIV virus that developed into AIDS, and he died in 1994. He was 41 years old. Mark was eight years younger than me, so I did not spend a lot of time with him when we were growing up. However, when we found out that he had AIDS, Yvonne and I drove from our house in Yorba Linda to Santa Barbara once a month and spent time with him. We did this for about a year. AIDS was not kind to him. It was a slow and debilitating death, and it was heartbreaking to see him go.

MARY KATHERINE (MY YOUNGEST SISTER): My youngest sister goes by her nickname, Kit. She is 16 years younger than me, and she was born shortly before I moved out of my parents' home. I hardly had a chance to get to know her. However, I do remember that she was always laughing and had a very bubbly personality. As the years went by, and after she completed her education, she joined Continental (now United) Airlines as a flight attendant flying domestic as well as international routes. She married a very nice, but very reserved airline pilot. They lived in a beach community in the panhandle of Florida, purchased a nice boat, and spent their leisure time fishing and camping out on the boat.

Kit is very energetic. In addition to her airline job, she also became a very successful real estate agent and purchased rental property as well. She and her husband built a very nice lifestyle for themselves. However, at some point they grew apart and divorced. They both continued to fly, but in different directions. Kit moved to Tennessee, and then to North Carolina. Along the way, she met another man, and she remarried. I have not met her current husband. However, my siblings that have seem to think he is a very nice guy.

Health issues arose and Kit needed a kidney transplant. Out of the clear blue, a stranger offered to give Kit a kidney. Can you imagine that? This gal is truly a saint. The operation went well, and both donor and recipient are living healthy lives.

PETE JAMES: Pete was the hardest working guy I ever met. Some guys are born with no brains but have incredible ambition. Some are born with incredible brains and no ambition. Pete had both brains and ambition, a perfect combination for success. He enrolled at the University of Nebraska, got married at 18, and was a father at 19. With parental responsibilities and little money, not only did he make it through college, but he also made it through medical school as well. He went on to become a successful OB/GYN. He was married for 25 years and is the father of three sons. For reasons unbeknownst to me, that marriage ended. Several years later, he remarried, this time to a doctor who was also an OB/GYN. I referred to them as Mr and Mrs Muff Mechanics. They had a medical practice in Wisconsin, but after practicing medicine for over 30 years, they decided to retire.

They came to visit us in Anthem, Arizona and fell in love with the place, just as Yvonne and I did the year before. Pete was walking around my house with a mopey attitude. I asked him what was wrong, and he confessed that he wanted to live here, too. So, we encouraged him to buy a place. He retired from his practice and has lived here since. He loves it and is quite dug into the community. When he isn't walking around the house scratching his balls, he is out on the golf course hitting them, and making new friends.

Unfortunately, his wife was diagnosed with cancer shortly after her retirement from medical practice. She passed away in December 2017 during the time I was in the hospital recovering from open heart surgery. He later met and married Robin. They have a lot in common and are enjoying life in Arizona. After 60 years, Pete and I remain good friends.

J.P. KIRKPATRICK: J.P. turned out to be one of my best friends for life. He is one of the funniest guys I have ever met. He decided to go into the seminary and become a priest. However, after giving it his best shot, he decided perhaps that wasn't his calling and returned to California to finish his college education. Like me, he eventually got drafted and spent several years in the Army. He married a beautiful bride, and they have three daughters. They are in good health and reside in Central California. We try to get together as often as possible.

MICK ROSE: Mick turned out to be another one of my best friends, always with a jovial disposition. He went into the Army during the Vietnam conflict and became a Green Beret. Although he was a fun-loving guy, he took his military service very seriously, and I would hate to be a Viet Cong soldier that got in his way. After the military, Mick came down with lymphoma as a result of exposure to Agent Orange while fulfilling his military obligation in Vietnam. Miraculously, he beat the disease, and married his soulmate, a beautiful person that Yvonne and I have gotten to know. They lived in Hawaii twice, but when they retired, they moved to Oregon.

MARK DUFF: Mark, another life-long best friend, has an infectious laugh. Every time he started to laugh, it made everyone around him laugh. Mark married and moved to Oklahoma. His wife had a rather unusual personality, and a temper that went along with it. One day they got into a heated discussion, and she threw the dog out the second story window. They divorced, and he moved back to California. He went to law school and became a prominent attorney. He and his current wife are enjoying their retirement years in California.

PHIL AND KATIE VON REMS: Phil married his college sweetheart and moved to Beverly Hills. He made a career for himself at Yellow Freight Lines. Eventually they retired back in Riverside, California where we all first met decades earlier. Phil became a deacon in the church, and he and Katie are enjoying life as happy grandparents.

CLIFF RIFKIN: I am very grateful to Cliff. Not only did he make life enjoyable for me as my roommate at Arizona State University, but he was also very instrumental in getting me my job at TWA and including me in his business venture in Seattle years later. Cliff married his wife, Sharon. Sharon was in the Miss Arizona Pageant years earlier. She is very talented and attractive as one would expect. Somewhere along the way, they fell off my radar screen, and I have no idea where they ended up. With the way life goes, I am confident that we will cross paths again one day.

JOSH BOUDRON: The day I graduated from Officer Candidate School in Oklahoma, Josh and I said our good-byes and went in different directions. Shortly thereafter, when I was stationed in Germany, a couple Army buddies and I were having breakfast in the mess hall one morning and one of the lieutenants said, "I was reading the *Stars and Stripes* newspaper and noticed that our classmate, Josh, was killed in Vietnam." This was heartbreaking news to learn that my good friend was now a casualty of war. Throughout the years I thought of him often. One day I was on a business trip in Washington D.C. and decided to visit the Vietnam Veterans Memorial. I went to the wall and looked for his name, but it wasn't there. Is this a mistake? Could he possibly still be alive? Many years later, and through the help of the internet, I tracked him down. All I knew was that he was originally from Windsor Locks, Connecticut. I sent out a couple letters of inquiry to people with the last name Boudron. Then one day out of the clear blue, I received a phone call. It was Josh.

He was happier than a pig in shit, and greeted me with, "Hey, it's me, Josh. We are truly brothers." After 50 years we finally made contact. Josh and I speak often on the phone, and Yvonne and I hooked up for dinner with him and his wife during a recent trip to the East Coast.

GARY LEWITTS: Gary was not only a good friend, but he was a father image as well. He and his wife, Rene, took me into their "fold" when I was living in Germany, and I looked forward to spending as much time with them as possible. Gary liked to drink Scotch, and once he finished his third one, he would get very complimentary. He would always say, "Dolb, now this isn't liquor talkin', but I think you are a mighty fine lieutenant." Rene and I would start to laugh because we both knew it was about that time the Scotch kicked in and took over the conversation. They had three daughters of high school age at the time and a son about my age stationed in Vietnam. Gary was from Iowa, and Rene was from Germany. They had married when Gary was on a previous tour of duty in Germany. Gary managed to get himself re-assigned, and they bounced back and forth between Germany and the United States on several occasions during his military career. When he retired, he settled in Georgia and had a second career in real estate until his passing. Rene and their daughters stayed in contact with me through the years. However, one of the daughters notified me in 2019 that Rene had passed away due to complications associated with Alzheimer's disease.

LEWIS GILBERT (CAPTAIN HI-YA-PAL): During his final years, Lewis Gilbert and his wife, Carol, moved to Phoenix, not far from where Yvonne and I live. The four of us would get together socially, but sadly it became apparent that he was not his old self. The effects of Agent Orange from Vietnam and other health complications took their toll. He entered a care facility, and we visited him there. One day I went by myself, and the two of us just sat and talked. When it was time to leave, and I was walking out the door, he hollered out, "I love you, pal."

I hollered back, "I love you, too, pal." Sadly, he passed away very soon thereafter.

Lewis and Carol and their daughter and son lived in Indianapolis for many years, and Yvonne and I visited on occasion. Out in public, it was not unusual for someone to recognize Lewis and thank him for impacting their lives in a positive way. On one occasion, a grateful veteran approached him and said, "You may not remember me, but one time I was stuck behind enemy lines in Vietnam. You showed up in your helicopter and swept me away to safety. You saved my life, and I am forever grateful."

After his tour of duty in Germany, Lewis was transferred to Korea. While stationed there, he and Carol adopted an Asian-American orphan. This young baby would not have had a chance in the Korean culture, but Lewis and Carol brought him back to the States and provided him with an excellent life. He turned out to be an extremely accomplished young man.

Lewis left behind a legacy of love and kindness that would not be forgotten. Our loss is heaven's gain. When he arrived at his final destination, I am sure he was greeted with open arms and a pat on the back for a job well done.

LIEUTENANT LEWEN RENGLE: Lewen left the Army in November 1969 and returned to his hometown of Redding, California. He divorced shortly after leaving the Army, and his ex-wife has remarried six more times in an attempt to find her "perfect soulmate." He and I got together once in 1970 shortly after I completed my military obligation. Although we do not see each other, we keep in touch by phone.

ERIC BOGEL (CAPTAIN TOOTH FAIRY): About the time I was to rotate back to the States and leave the Army in July 1970, Eric was diagnosed with diabetes and received a medical discharge. He returned to his home state of Georgia and bought an existing dental practice. He purchased a 50-acre farm just south of Atlanta, got married, and adopted a little girl. He flew out to visit me when I lived in Connecticut and California. Each trip was a skiing trip that brought back old memories of the fun we had in Germany. When I worked for TWA, I would reciprocate by flying down to see him during my free time. Yvonne and I visited and took vacations with him and his wife over the years. He passed in 2004 due to complications associated with diabetes.

WALLY GARVAS: With Captain Tooth Fairy back in the States, Wally and I became travel buddies. We vacationed throughout Europe and skied every mountain the Alps had to offer. But six months after 2nd Lt. Wally Garvas arrived in Germany, it was time for me to rotate back to the States to resume civilian life. A year later, Wally was transferred back to the States as well. His next duty assignment was to become a member of the coaching staff at West Point for the football team. And a year after that, I was being transferred back to the East Coast to start my new job with TWA. I moved to Brookfield Center, Connecticut which was only 50 miles from West Point. One afternoon I drove over to West Point and found Wally standing on the football field. My arrival was unannounced, so he was quite shocked to see me. Living so close, we palled around together. He married, had two children, got out of the military, and moved to New Jersey. Eventually that marriage ended. Several years later, he got married again, and his new wife gave birth to two daughters. He remained in New Jersey for the remainder of his life. After nearly 50 years of friendship, we had made so many great memories — from travel, to ski trips, to fishing trips. Wally died from cancer in 2018. People came from all over to honor him at his farewell service. He was loved by so many and never knew an enemy.

WOLFGANG WARNER. a.k.a. HAUPTMAN SCHEISKOPF (CAPTAIN SHITHEAD): Wolf and I have been buddies for over 50 years. We started our friendship in 1968 when I first arrived in Germany with the Army. When I joined TWA, I flew in and out of Frankfurt periodically for the next five years. Rather than staying at the crew hotel on my layovers, I would usually stay with Wolfgang and his wife, Renate. He had my flight schedule, so when I landed at the airport, he was there to pick me up and take me to his home. The next day he would return me to the airport. This always made my trips to Germany especially enjoyable. He and Renate eventually divorced. Starting in the early 1980s, Yvonne and I have vacationed in Germany from time-to-time. When we do, we always make it a point to get together with Wolfgang and his wife, Rose. Although he has never been to the States, he calls me once a month to stay in touch. He is a very loyal friend, and we all look forward to our next visit.

CARL ROGERS: Carl would prove to be my first TWA buddy. Not only was he the first TWA employee I met, but we also went through the interviewing process together for the DCS job, and ultimately became roommates when we lived on the East Coast. Then we transferred to Los Angeles and became neighbors in the same apartment complex in Marina del Rey. The years clicked by one at a time as did the places we each moved to. Ironically, after 47 years of moves and adjustments, we are still the best of friends and neighbors living only two miles away from each other in Anthem, Arizona. Carl married Victoria, a TWA flight attendant. When he left the airline industry, he had an extremely successful career in the aviation insurance industry. He is truly a rags-to-riches story that deserves all the credit and recognition in the world. As a couple, he and Victoria remain among our best lifelong friends.

DOUG TREVOR: Prior to my meeting him, Doug was a pilot with TWA flying as a flight engineer on the Boeing 727. Like so many pilots during that era, he was furloughed for a while, and that was when he became my colleague as a DCS. In time, he was called back to the cockpit and resumed his job as a pilot where he finished out his career. Eventually he retired and bought a cattle ranch. Then he sold the ranch, retired again, and bought a home on a golf course in Kansas City. We lost contact with each other for decades but reunited though a recent phone call. We already have plans to meet again in the near future.

BILL GERNAL: Bill and I met in New York as colleagues at TWA in 1972. We went on assignment to Lisbon, Portugal and managed an in-flight market segment that consisted of Lisbon, Madrid, Rome, and Athens. We traveled and worked together. When we weren't working, we were enjoying the sights and sounds of Europe on our days off. Throughout the years, we became the best of friends and kept in contact regardless of what part of the globe we were working in. When I was still living in California, Bill completed a seven-year assignment in Saudi Arabia. Bill met and married his wife, Susan, and they set up housekeeping in Chandler, Arizona, a suburb of Phoenix. At the same time Yvonne and I moved to Anthem, Arizona, they purchased a home in Anthem as well. We became neighbors and continue the friendship that has lasted almost five decades. When Bill retired from TWA, he started a new career as an interpreter. Bill has a talent for languages and speaks a number of them fluently — he could be a tour director at the Tower of Babel.

KENNY McKIVEN: I first met Kenny in 1981 shortly after I moved from Seattle to Los Angeles. At the time, I was looking for a CPA to do my taxes. That encounter turned into a long-time friendship with him and his wife Dee. As couples, we did everything together — sailboat races, trips to Catalina Island and Las Vegas, out to dinners, and even a trip to their ranch in Texas. They were a great couple. Almost 40 years later, Kenny still does my taxes, but sadly, Dee recently passed away.

ROB KNAAP: I met Rob through Wally Garvas in 1984. Rob and Wally were classmates at West Point. Like Wally, Rob is a quality guy. He was a superior athlete and a good businessman. We worked together in the wind industry for several years. Once that project was completed, Rob started his own brokerage firm that specialized in selling government securities. He retired and spends his time traveling with his wife, Mary.

JACK AND JENE: Yvonne's parents, my father and mother-in-law, were a blessing from the very beginning. So often, people complain about the adversarial relationship they have with their in-laws. Not me. I lucked out and got the greatest ones in the world. For decades, we traveled and enjoyed each other's company. Jack and Jene moved to Anthem shortly after we did, and Yvonne's sister, Debbi, came a few years later. Jack passed away in 2014. He was a wonderful soul who didn't have a mean bone in his body. We all miss him. Yvonne, Jene, Debbi, and I continue to spend quality time together.

YVONNE: Yvonne is the love of my life. We got married and enjoy each other's company day-after-day. This has been going on for over 40 years. We travel the world together and give thanks on a daily basis that we found each other. To add additional information about Yvonne would require a whole new book.

Printed in the USA
CPSIA information can be obtained
at www.ICGtesting.com
LVHW071242050923
757281LV00018B/447